PUTTING TRUST IN THE US BUDGET

In the United States many important programs are paid from trust funds. At a time when major social insurance funds are facing insolvency, this book provides the first comprehensive study of this significant yet little-studied feature of the American welfare state. Equally importantly, the author investigates an enduring issue in democratic politics: can current officeholders bind their successors? By law, trust funds, which get most of their money from earmarked taxes, are restricted for specific uses. Patashnik asks why these structures were created, and how they have affected political dynamics. He argues that officeholders have used trust funds primarily to reduce political uncertainty, and bind distant futures. Based on detailed case studies of trust funds in a number of policy sectors, he shows how political commitment is a developmental process, whereby precommitments shape the content of future political conflicts. This book will be of interest to students of public policy, political economy, and American political development.

ERIC PATASHNIK is Assistant Professor in the School of Public Policy and Social Research at the University of California, Los Angeles. He was previously Assistant Professor of Political Science and Lecturer in Law at Yale University. He has also been a Research Fellow at the Brookings Institution.

THEORIES OF INSTITUTIONAL DESIGN

Series Editor
Robert E. Goodin
Research School of Social Sciences
Australian National University

Advisory Editors
Brian Barry, Russell Hardin, Carole Pateman, Barry Weingast,
Stephen Elkin, Claus Offe, Susan Rose-Ackerman

Social scientists have rediscovered institutions. They have been increasingly concerned with the myriad ways in which social and political institutions shape the patterns of individual interactions which produce social phenomena. They are equally concerned with the ways in which those institutions emerge from such interactions.

This series is devoted to the exploration of the more normative aspects of these issues. What makes one set of institutions better than another? How, if at all, might we move from the less desirable set of institutions to a more desirable set? Alongside the questions of what institutions we would design, if we were designing them afresh, are pragmatic questions of how we can best get from here to there: from our present institutions to new revitalised ones.

Theories of institutional design is insistently multidisciplinary and interdisciplinary, both in the institutions on which it focuses, and in the methodologies used to study them. There are interesting sociological questions to be asked about legal institutions, interesting legal questions to be asked about economic institutions, and interesting social, economic and legal questions to be asked about political institutions. By juxtaposing these approaches in print, this series aims to enrich normative discourse surrounding important issues of designing and redesigning, shaping and reshaping the social, political and economic institutions of contemporary society.

Other books in this series
Robert E. Goodin (editor), *The Theory of Institutional Design*
Brent Fisse and John Braithwaite, *Corporations, Crime, and Accountability*
Itai Sened, *The Political Institution of Private Property*
Bo Rothstein, *Just Institutions Matter*
Jon Elster, Claus Offe and Ulrich Preuss, *Institutional Design in Post-Communist Societies: Rebuilding the Ship at Sea*
Mark Bovens, *The Quest for Responsibility*
Geoffrey Brennan and Alan Hamlin, *Democratic Devices and Desires*

PUTTING TRUST IN THE US BUDGET

Federal Trust Funds and the Politics of Commitment

ERIC M. PATASHNIK

CAMBRIDGE
UNIVERSITY PRESS

PUBLISHED BY THE PRESS SYNDICATE OF THE UNIVERSITY OF CAMBRIDGE
The Pitt Building, Trumpington Street, Cambridge, United Kingdom

CAMBRIDGE UNIVERSITY PRESS
The Edinburgh Building, Cambridge, CB2 2RU, UK   www.cup.cam.ac.uk
40 West 20th Street, New York, NY 10011–4211, USA   www.cup.org
10 Stamford Road, Oakleigh, Melbourne 3166, Australia
Ruiz de Alarcón 13, 28014 Madrid, Spain

First published 2000

Printed in the United Kingdom at the University Press, Cambridge

Typeset in Minion 10.5/12pt   [CE]

A catalogue record for this book is available from the British Library

Library of Congress Cataloguing in Publication Data
Patashnik, Eric M.
Putting Trust in the US Budget: Federal Trust Funds and the Politics of Commitment/
Eric M. Patashnik.
    p.   cm. – (Theories of institutional design)
Includes bibliographical references and index.
ISBN 0 521 77174 9 (hbk.) – ISBN 0 521 77748 8 (pbk.)
1. Pension trusts – United States.
2. Social security – United States.
3. Infrastructure (Economics) – United States – Finance.
4. Budget – United States.
I. Title.   II. Series.
HD7105.45U6 P366   2000
336.73–dc21   99–057404

ISBN 0 521 77174 9 hardback
ISBN 0 521 77748 8 paperback

For my parents,
Anne and Bernard Patashnik

Contents

Figures

Tables

Preface

The topic of this book – the role of trust funds in American national budgeting – lies at the intersection of public policy and political science. This is not an accident. My graduate training at Berkeley was in both fields. At Berkeley's Graduate (now Goldman) School of Public Policy, I studied the efficient and equitable design of public policies. After I returned to Berkeley for doctoral studies in political science (having spent two years as a legislative aide in Washington), I became interested in the historical and institutional context in which policymaking unfolds, and in the impact of past choices on present and future options. My interest in federal trust funds was originally stimulated by my inability to make sense of contemporary political debates over Social Security. I noticed that whenever lawmakers discussed the relationship between Social Security and the federal budget, they focused on the spending and income flows of the Social Security Trust Fund. But what was the significance of this arcane fiscal device? If, as I soon discovered, the Social Security Trust Fund was not money under the mattress, what governance roles did the device perform? Answering that question took me rather far afield – back to Social Security's adoption and very early development, and to other policy sectors, such as transportation, where the trust fund mechanism is also employed. The common thread was the attempt by current policy actors to put future budget actors under obligation. A study of the trust fund structures in the federal budget thus offered the chance to explore the US government's performance as promise-keeper.

Of course, promises must be paid for. As I began this project in late 1993, America's social insurance system was coming under scrutiny. If anything, the political debate has only intensified in the ensuing years. As the baby boomers approach retirement, massive governmental bills are coming due. The prospect of trust fund "insolvency" focuses attention on the need for change, yet officeholders are reluctant to break faith with those who have paid into the current system. This book does not evaluate particular reform options, but its detailed case studies of the origins and development of the major trust funds provide essential background for an understanding of today's debates.

One of the most pleasant aspects of completing this book is that I can finally thank in print the many people and organizations that have helped me along the way. It seems fitting to begin by expressing my deep gratitude to Professor Eugene Bardach, whose late-night phone call convinced me to enter Berkeley's graduate program in public policy. Although Gene was not an official member of my dissertation committee, he has been a superb mentor – and treasured friend – ever since. Gene also provided extremely helpful comments on several chapters during my final push to finish this book.

When I migrated across the Berkeley campus from the Goldman School to the Political Science Department, I found an excellent adviser in Bruce Cain. His encouragement, insight, and wit made thesis writing far more enjoyable than it would otherwise have been. I learned a tremendous amount from Bruce about how to make the difficult transition from student to scholar. John W. Ellwood shared with me his extensive knowledge of American national budgeting. His stubborn questions forced me to clarify my arguments; and Henry Brady was a very helpful third-reader. Finally, I would be remiss if I failed to acknowledge the considerable influence on my intellectual development of the late Aaron Wildavsky. By the time I decided to write a dissertation on a budgeting topic – one that Aaron had identified in a brief passage as worthy of scholarly attention – he had passed away. But earlier in my graduate career I did get the chance to take his unforgettable seminar on political culture. I feel privileged to have known him.

The Brookings Institution afforded me a Research Fellowship in the Governmental Studies Program, an ideal setting in which to complete most of the research for this book. Kent Weaver made significant contributions to this study. He took the time to read both my thesis and some early conference papers, and offered extremely helpful, detailed suggestions for strengthening my analysis. I also received valuable advice from Sarah Binder, Allen Schick, Tom Mann, and Joe White. Also I am indebted to my fellow graduate students Gary McKissick, Carolyn Wong, and Julian Zelizer both for their many intellectual contributions to this project and for their companionship.

Over the years, Julian, a policy historian who shares my interest in the politics of funding modern American government, has read and reread countless versions of my work. From my initial efforts to construct an argument to my final revisions, he has improved my thinking with penetrating insights of his own. Without his enormous help, this book would look much different.

Since coming to Yale in 1996, I have found a wonderful home in the Institution for Social and Policy Studies. Donald P. Green, the Institute's Director, created a tremendously stimulating environment that aided my work in significant ways. I would like to thank the Institute's talented staff, especially Pam LaMonaca, for all their support. I also wish to express my appreciation to Anthony Kronman, Dean of the Yale Law School, for providing me research support over several summers. And I am happy to give my special thanks to my Yale colleagues and good buddies Martin Gilens and Alan Gerber, whose friendship and lunch-time conversations have kept me grounded and (reasonably) sane.

Paul Pierson gave me excellent advice at a critical juncture in this project's intellectual development. I also wish to thank the scholars who reviewed this book for Cambridge University Press. Their criticisms and suggestions led to many substantive and stylistic improvements. As it happened, my most meticulous and insightful reader chose not to hide her identity. This gives me the opportunity to express my profound appreciation to Martha Derthick for giving me the benefit of her exceptional knowledge about American national government. Martha's sage advice helped me bring out the potential of this book. None of these scholars should be blamed for the remaining defects or mistakes; I alone am responsible.

I thank the Academy of Political Science for allowing me to use greatly revised material from an essay of mine published in *Political Science Quarterly*, vol. 112, no. 3 (1997). Many others also deserve thanks: Jack Citrin, John Cogan, Cathy Cohen, Tom Cuny, Coco Gordon, Michael Graetz, Colleen Grogan, Robert Katzmann, Al Klevorick, Jessica Korn, Martin Levin, Ted Marmor, Jerry Mashaw, David Mayhew, Mathew McCubbins, Roy Meyers, Pietro Nivola, Nelson Polsby, Robert Reischauer, Susan Rose-Ackerman, Irene Rubin, Mark Schlesinger, Stacey Schoenfeld, Ian Shapiro, Stephen Skowronek, Rogers Smith, Fred Thompson, Dan Tuden, Ben Wildavsky, and Ray Wolfinger. I conducted a number of interviews during the course of my research, and I would like to thank the congressional staff members, lobbyists, and executive officials who took the time to speak with me.

Robert Goodin has been an ideal series editor. He was enthusiastic about the project from the start, offered many useful suggestions for strengthening the manuscript, and was patient with me during the long process of revisions. John Haslam guided the book (and me) through the editing process with a steady hand. And I received outstanding copy-editing, indexing, and production assistance from Anne Rix, Shirley Kessel, and Robert Whitelock.

This book is affectionately dedicated to my parents, Anne and Bernard Patashnik. They have believed in me even when I have doubted myself. I am deeply grateful for their love and support. When authors acknowledge their children in pages such as these, they often note the welcome distractions the kids offered from the hard chore of writing. My sons Michael and Josh provided many pleasant diversions, of course, but they also let me know, in their own way, that they are proud to have a dad who teaches and writes books. For this, and for the many other precious gifts they have given me, my heartfelt thanks.

My largest personal debt is to my wife Debbie Gordon. Since our days as graduate school classmates in Berkeley (thanks for that phone call, Gene!), Debbie has supported me in every way possible. I trust she knows how much our commitment to one another – and our life together – means to me.

1

Introduction: trust funds and the politics of commitment

Promise making is at the heart of democratic politics. Candidates make campaign promises to win elections. Elected officials enter into commitments with one another, and with interest groups, during the process of governing. And committing the government to a particular policy vision is central to both party and regime building. Yet, while promises are rooted in the imperatives of democratic life, they nonetheless pose a serious political dilemma for democracy. Without the ability to endow policies with durability, officeholders cannot shape the future of the polity. If every governmental promise is written in stone, leaders will eventually lose the capacity to control the present. How politicians manage and manipulate this fundamental tension between commitment and flexibility is the subject of this book.

As the empirical material for this investigation, the book explores the origins and evolution of an important yet little-studied institutional arrangement – trust funds in the United States national budget. Major examples include the Social Security Trust Fund, the Medicare Hospital Insurance Trust Fund, and the Highway Trust Fund. In contrast to general revenues, which are available for the general purposes of government, trust funds are "restricted by law to designated programs or uses."[1] The funds obtain most of their revenues from specific earmarked taxes (e.g., payroll taxes and gasoline taxes).[2] Certain trust funds, however, also

[1] Allen Schick, *The Federal Budget: Politics, Policy, Process* (Washington, DC: The Brookings Institution, 1995), 14.
[2] This book focuses on trust funds and earmarked taxes in the US national budget. Many state budgets also contain trust funds, but they are not specifically examined in this book.

receive transfers from within the budget, such as interest payments into the Social Security Trust Fund. By 1995, the more than 150 trust funds in the US budget comprised almost 40 percent of total federal revenues (excluding internal transfers), up from less than 10 percent in 1950.[3]

One might think that federal trust funds are an arcane subject, of interest only to government accounting freaks. Nothing could be more mistaken. Trust funds generally embody long-term political commitments. The trust fund device is meant to provide assurance that policy promises, once made, will be kept. "Federal trust funds," writes the Congressional Research Service, "typically have been established for programs that have very long-term purposes."[4] Many trust funds were founded with an explicit understanding that "in exchange for the public's paying certain taxes or premiums, the government would commit itself to finance some activity."[5] At times, trust funds have been seen as a vehicle for building large reserves in order to "prefund" future government spending. In general, however, federal trust funds have been maintained on a "pay-as-you-go" basis, with current taxes used to support current benefits. The existence of trust fund financing, however, is still meant to make long-term promises stick.

If trust funds work as intended (something that obviously cannot be assumed), they narrow the flexibility of future officeholders to allocate budget resources – that is, to exercise public authority – as they see fit. Whether such efforts by current officeholders to tie the hands of their successors can ever be normatively acceptable, or even successful, in a democratic polity has long been the subject of debate. Many democratic thinkers argue that it is immoral to bind the future. "[E]very age and generation must be as free to act for itself, in all cases, as the ages and

---

[3] Some 179 budget accounts officially designated as trust funds existed on the books of the US Treasury in 1995. This figure exaggerates the true number of significant trust fund programs, however. First, some trust fund programs have multiple accounts. Second, the figure includes more than 35 minuscule trust funds established to carry out a conditional gift or bequest. (Believe it or not, some people actually voluntarily donate money to the US government.) Virtually every executive department has at least one conditional gift trust fund. These funds have little political significance and are not examined in this study. See General Accounting Office, "Budget Account Structure: A Descriptive Overview," GAO/AIMD-95-179 (Washington, DC: Government Printing Office, 1995).

[4] David Koitz, Dawn Nuschler, and Philip Winters, "Federal Trust Funds: How Many, How Big, and What Are They For?" CRS Report for Congress, Updated August 30, 1996 (Washington, DC: Congressional Research Service, 96–686 EPW), 2.

[5] *Ibid.*

generations which preceded it," wrote Thomas Paine.[6] In Paine's view, democracy is meaningless if current leaders are blocked from choosing their own path. Thomas Jefferson largely agreed with this position. While Jefferson endorsed limited constitutional protection of basic rights, he believed that officeholders had no right to legislate for the distant future. Accordingly, he insisted that all laws and institutional arrangements must lapse at set intervals. National plebiscites would then be held to determine the new form of government.[7] The great nineteenth-century British legal scholar Alfred Dicey argued that attempts to bind the future were not so much immoral as futile. "That Parliaments have more than once intended and endeavored to pass Acts which should tie the hands of their successors is certain, but the endeavor has always ended in failure."[8] According to Dicey, a "sovereign power cannot, while retaining its sovereign character, restrict its own powers by any particular enactment."[9]

The creation of trust funds, and the politics surrounding their operation, thus provides an excellent setting in which to explore the limits and possibilities of statutory commitment in democratic politics. Why have politicians created trust funds for some programs but not others, and how has the preexistence of trust funds shaped ensuing policy outcomes? What actors have participated in trust fund decisions and why have some trust fund arrangements proved more stable than others? Can politicians "undo" inherited commitments when they become incompatible with present needs? Finally, what are the normative challenges associated with dedicated funding and how can the future use of the trust fund instrument in public budgeting be improved?

The need for this study

A variety of governmental institutions ranging from civil service to bureaucratic structure can be seen as political commitment devices.[10] Most political scientists have directed their attention to written constitu-

---

[6] Quoted in Stephen Holmes, "Precommitment and the Paradox of Democracy," in Jon Elster and Rune Slagstad, eds., *Constitutionalism and Democracy* (Cambridge: Cambridge University Press, 1988), 200. Holmes provides a provocative normative discussion of the issue.

[7] *Ibid.*, 205.

[8] A.V. Dicey, Introduction to the *Study of the Law of the Constitution*, Tenth Edition (London: MacMillian Press, 1959), 65.

[9] *Ibid.*, 68, fn. 1.

[10] Murray J. Horn, *The Political Economy of Public Administration: Institutional Choice in the Public Sector* (New York: Cambridge University Press, 1995).

tions, which determine the basic sources of authority in a given polity. In general, constitutional provisions are indeed quite resistant to change.[11] Yet the same basic tension between commitment and flexibility also arises in the *statutory* realm. To be sure, the commitments embodied in ordinary statutes are generally much easier to reverse than those written in constitutions. But statutory commitments nonetheless often prove quite durable and long lasting. In an era of big government, the impact of past legislative promises on contemporary dynamics simply cannot be ignored.

Indeed, as the modern welfare-administrative state matures, and the range and sheer number of commitments on the statute books expands, with new programs periodically added to a generally stable base of prior obligations, the very nature of governance changes. Increasingly, office-holders in all the major industrialized democracies find that they are constrained by the legacy of previous administrations. As Richard Rose and Philip Davies pointedly argue,

> The familiar maxim *to govern is to choose* is reductionist in the extreme. It implies that government is carried out by individual decisionmakers who have as much freedom of choice as an individual in a shopping mall trying to decide whether to have a pizza or an ice cream cone. The statutory commitments of a newly installed official are not a menu specifying what an individual might choose but a description of what a policymaker is committed to do. Like it or not, each new arrival in office must recognize that *to govern is to inherit*.[12]

The legacy of prior commitments is evident in every policy domain but perhaps nowhere more so than in US budget politics, where demographic and economic factors combine with unusually intricate patterns of institutional design to severely restrict the formal discretion available to officeholders. Annually appropriated spending financed through general tax revenues – the type of spending most susceptible to the control of incumbent politicians – today comprises one-third of the US budget, down from two-thirds a generation ago.[13] According to one

---

[11] Of course, the practical meaning of constitutional provisions is by no means immune to change. For a provocative argument that "higher lawmaking" can occur even without formal constitutional amendment, see Bruce A. Ackerman, *We the People* (Cambridge, MA: Harvard University Press, 1991).

[12] Richard Rose and Philip L. Davies, *Inheritance in Public Policy: Change without Choice in Britain* (New Haven: Yale University Press, 1994), 1–2.

[13] Robert D. Reischauer, "The Unfulfillable Promise: Cutting Nondefense Discretionary Spending," in Robert D. Reischauer, ed., *Setting National Priorities: Budget Choices for the Next Century* (Washington, DC: Brookings Institution, 1997).

policy expert, if this trend is not halted, Americans will soon face a political future that is little more than the "preprogrammed outcome of promises made by past elected officials."[14]

Of course, *all* budget items involve commitments for the future. But some commitments in the budget are reinforced by mechanisms explicitly designed to narrow future officeholders' freedom of choice. Three such major devices exist in the American national budget, of which the trust fund mechanism is one. The two others are entitlements (provisions of law that mandate certain payments to eligible persons) and indexation (automatic program adjustments for inflation).[15] The three devices sometimes occur in conjunction with one another. For example, many of the big indexed entitlement programs (e.g., Social Security) are paid from trust funds. But trust funds are also used to finance so-called discretionary programs, such as highway building. Each of the devices deserves to be the focus of study in its own right, because each "may tie legislators' hands in different ways."[16] Despite trust funds' massive scope and their important role in financing core US domestic programs, however, no generic study of the trust fund device exists.[17]

Trust funds merit attention on both substantive and theoretical grounds. Programmatically, the durability of government programs often turns on continuity of funding. Indeed, the entitlement status of a number of social programs *without* a dedicated funding source has recently been either seriously challenged (food stamps, Medicaid) or repealed (Aid to Families with Dependent Children). Trust funds themselves have moved to the center of recent debates over U.S. social policy because the Social Security and Medicare trust funds are reportedly heading toward "bankruptcy." How to keep these programs solvent for retiring baby boomers is a hot-button issue. Any contemporary under-

---

[14] Eugene Steuerle, "Discretion to Do the Right Things," *The Washington Post*, May 18, 1998, A17.

[15] Joseph J. Cordes, "How Yesterday's Decisions Affect Today's Budget and Fiscal Options," in C. Eugene Steuerle and Masahiro Kawai, eds., *The New World Fiscal Order: Implications for Industrialized Nations* (Washington, DC: The Urban Institute, 1996), 95–116.

[16] C. Eugene Steuerle and Masahiro Kawai, "The New World Fiscal Order: Introduction," in C. Eugene Steuerle and Masahiro Kawai, eds., *The New World*, 8.

[17] By contrast, policy scholars have carefully analyzed the politics of entitlements and indexation. Kent Weaver has done some of the best work on these topics. See R. Kent Weaver, "Controlling Entitlements," in John E. Chubb and Paul E. Peterson, eds., *The New Direction in American Politics* (Washington, DC: The Brookings Institution, 1985); and R. Kent Weaver, *Automatic Government: The Politics of Indexation* (Washington, DC: The Brookings Institution, 1988).

standing of the American welfare state must pay close attention to trust funds and earmarked taxes.

US budget trust funds are theoretically intriguing because their significance as a commitment device is not obvious. The promises underlying public trust funds are not subject to an external enforcement mechanism. Moreover, *as presently constituted*, federal trust funds do not cumulate real wealth. When a trust fund takes in more than it pays out, the cash goes into the general Treasury, and the trust fund is credited with a non-marketable federal security. These securities are backed by the full faith and credit of the United States,[18] earn interest at competitive rates of return,[19] and are subject to the legal debt ceiling set by Congress.[20] Moreover, the securities add to national savings to the extent trust fund surpluses reduce the level of borrowing the federal government would otherwise incur. But trust fund reserves do not themselves constitute economic wealth. The reserves are "claims *on* the Government, not *for* the Government."[21] When the time comes to make good on trust fund spending promises, the government must do what it ordinarily does to finance programs – raise taxes, reduce other expenditures, or increase public borrowing.

Given all this, many observers assert that the US government's trust funds are "bogus."[22] A former top budget official states, "Remember how

---

[18] General Accounting Office, "Financial Audit: 1997 Consolidated Financial Statements of the United States Government," GAO/AIMD-98-127 (Washington, DC: Government Printing Office, March 1998), 8.

[19] Because of differences in statutory language, the interest rates vary slightly among individual trust funds. See Congressional Budget Office, "Federal Debt and Interest Costs" (Washington, DC: Government Printing Office, May 1993a), pp. 32–3.

[20] One consequence of this arrangement is that there is an incentive for the Treasury Department to delay interest payments to trust funds and/or to "disinvest" trust funds by prematurely redeeming their securities when the government bumps up against the statutory debt ceiling. These moves prevent a government default by creating room under the debt ceiling for additional borrowing from the public. This occurred most recently in the budget showdown of 1995, when Treasury Secretary Robert Rubin disinvested two civil service retirement funds. See Andrew Taylor, "Rubin's Footwork Frustrates GOP," *Congressional Quarterly Weekly Report*, December 16, 1995, 3793. On the legal issues, see Thomas J. Nicola and Morton Rosenberg, "Authority to Tap Trust Funds and Establish Payment Priorities if the Debt Limit is Not Increased," CRS Report for Congress (Washington, DC: Congressional Research Service, November 9, 1995, 95–11109 A).

[21] David Koitz, Dawn Nuschler, and Philip Winters, "Trust Funds and the Federal Deficit," CRS Report for Congress (Washington, DC: Congressional Research Service, February 26, 1990, 90–106 EPW), 4.

[22] "Trust Them," *The Wall Street Journal*, May 14, 1993, A10.

awful it was when you realized there wasn't a Tooth Fairy or a Santa Claus? Well, brace yourself for another rude awakening. After working in the bowels of federal budgeting for two years, I'm here to tell you that there are no . . . trust funds."[23] "The federal budget is full of trust funds that deserve neither half of the name. They contain no funds . . . and because they mainly exist on paper, they don't inspire much trust, either; they shouldn't anyway," editorializes *The Washington Post*.[24] "[I]n any sense that matters, the funds do not exist," echoes *The Economist*.[25]

Two arguments are being made here. The first is manifestly wrong, while the second is largely correct but grossly incomplete. The erroneous claim is that the creation of a federal trust fund has no bearing on the politics of resource allocation. Certainly, clientele groups believe otherwise; and they back their beliefs by devoting resources to lobbying for trust fund status.[26] Why do the forecasts of the Social Security and Medicare Boards of Trustees receive such enormous political attention?[27] Why have trust fund taxes grown so much more rapidly than general fund taxes since the 1950s?[28] The evidence presented in this book suggests that federal trust funds *do* make a difference, just as many political actors think they do. As a former Public Trustee of the Social Security and Medicare Trust Funds argues, "While in recent years there has been considerable criticism of . . . trust funds as being illusory, such allegations are not well informed and ignore both the legal and the administrative realities surrounding [them]."[29]

A more credible, yet still incomplete, argument is that federal trust funds are not what they seem to be – exact replicas of trust funds maintained in the private sector. In the private sector, a trust is a fiduciary relationship in which one person (the trustee) holds property for the

---

[23] Matthew Miller, National Public Radio Commentary, October 16, 1995. I thank Mr. Miller for sending me a transcript of his remarks.

[24] "Trust, but Verify," *The Washington Post*, December 1, 1997, A24.

[25] "Put not your trust in Congress," *The Economist*, November 11, 1989, 56.

[26] On lobbying for trust funds, see Lawrence J. Haas, "Paying As You Go," *National Journal*, October 22, 1988, 2644–8; see also Roy T. Meyers, *Strategic Budgeting* (Ann Arbor: University of Michigan Press, 1994).

[27] On the attention given to projections of the "bankruptcy" of the Medicare Trust Fund, see David Rosenbaum, "Gloomy Forecast Touches Off Feud on Medicare Fund," *The New York Times*, June 6, 1996, A1.

[28] On the tremendous increase in trust fund taxes, see John F. Cogan, "The Dispersion of Spending Authority and Federal Budget Deficits," in John F. Cogan, Timothy J. Muris, and Allen Schick, eds., *The Budget Puzzle* (Palo Alto: Stanford University Press, 1994).

[29] Stanford G. Ross, "Institutional and Administrative Issues," in Eric R. Kingson, and James H. Schultz, eds., *Social Security in the 21st Century* (New York: Oxford University Press, 1997), 231.

benefit of another (the beneficiary). The trustee's obligation under trust law is to manage the assets of the trust property "solely in the interests of the beneficiary."[30] Private trusts originated in the late Middle Ages as a device for transferring wealth within the family. The purposes of trusts have since mushroomed. Trusts are now used in a wide variety of commercial settings. Interestingly, private sector trusts remain a "uniquely Anglo-American institution," having never taken root in Continental legal systems.[31] In both the United States and the United Kingdom, political leaders often appeal to the trust analogy when articulating visions of good government. British civil servants, for example, are said to hold "positions of trust under the Crown."[32] "Public office is a public trust" was used by Grover Cleveland as the motto for his administration. Such language is meant to convey not that those who occupy positions of responsibility hold legal title to their offices, only that officials are properly held to a standard of good faith.

The analogy to private trusts is much closer in the case of trust funds in the American national budget. Until fairly recently official US government documents in fact *defined* trust funds as being "held in a fiduciary capacity," the theory being that the money was not really "owned" by the federal government.[33] Unlike their private sector counterparts, however, the overwhelming majority of federal trust funds are *not* based on a true fiduciary relationship.[34] While the creation of a government trust fund does involve a legal commitment to use the money for specified purposes, Congress has the right to "unilaterally alter" the tax rates and benefit levels of trust fund programs by changing existing law.[35] This applies even to those trust funds that finance entitlement programs like Social

---

[30] George Gleason Bogert and George Taylor Bogert, *Handbook of the Law of Trusts*, fifth edition (St Paul, Minn.: West Publishing, 1973), 2.

[31] John H. Langbein, "The Contractarian Basis of the Law of Trusts," *Yale Law Journal*, 625, 1995, 632–43, at 669.

[32] Although the trust analogy is often invoked in British government, use of tax earmarking is relatively rare. See Barry Bracewell-Milnes, "Earmarking in Britain: Theory and Practice," *The Case for Earmarked Taxes: Government Spending and Public Choice* (London: Institute of Economic Affairs, 1991).

[33] See Tax Foundation, *Federal Trust Funds: Budgetary and Other Implications* (New York: Tax Foundation, 1970), 5.

[34] The federal government does have a fiduciary responsibility for several trust funds, including assets held in trust on behalf of American Indian tribes. In fact, however, Indian tribal funds have a sad history of gross mismanagement by the government. See Rochelle L. Stanfield, "Why Indian Trust Funds are in Disarray," *National Journal*, May 2, 1992, 1062.

[35] General Accounting Office, "Budget Issues: Trust Funds and Their Relationship to the Federal Budget," GAO/AFMD-88–55 (Washington, DC: Government Printing Office, 1988a), 6.

Security and Medicare, in which eligible persons have a legal right to benefit payments.

Viewed in another light, however, private and public trusts do share an essential feature. Both can be seen as a kind of contract – an agreement to do something in the future. To be sure, private trusts have seldom been described as deals. Yet as Yale legal scholar John H. Langbein points out, most private trusts are in fact "functionally indistinguishable from the modern third-party-beneficiary contract."[36] The contract involves an agreement between the person who creates the trust (the settler) and the trustee about how the trust will be managed for the beneficiary. Most private trusts contemplate long duration.[37] Contrary to popular belief, private trusts almost never attempt to anticipate every possible future contingency. Trustees usually possess the discretion to make decisions as circumstances change, subject to a legal duty of good faith.

Many federal trust funds can also be seen as involving a kind of contracting behavior – a commitment from the government to constituency groups that particular governmental activities will be funded in a certain way.[38] Political actors themselves often describe government trust funds in precisely these terms. For example, Bud Shuster (R-PA), the chairman of the House Public Works Committee, has stated that the Highway Trust Fund constitutes "nothing less than a contract between the government and the American traveling public."[39] Some of the very same attributes that make the trust device attractive in private settings also commend it to political actors. An example is the segregation requirement, which mandates that resources of the trust be earmarked. In the private sector, this means the property of the trust must be sharply distinguished from the trustee's own property. In the public sector, it means that trust fund income must be accounted for separately from general tax receipts, thus allowing the program's status to be easily inspected by interested parties.[40] Keeping track of specific, long-term

---

[36] Langbein, "The Contractarian Basis of the Law of Trusts," 627. Langbein excludes from this account both charitable trusts and constructive trusts imposed coercively to prevent unjust enrichment.

[37] *Ibid.*, 654.

[38] For a roughly analogous discussion of the similarities and differences between "social insurance" and "private insurance," see Robert J. Myers, *Social Security* (Bryn Mawr, Pennsylvania: McCahan Foundation, 1975), 13.

[39] On Shuster's conception of the trust funds as contracts, see Kirk Victor, "Trust Me," *National Journal*, March 11, 1995, 607–11.

[40] Note the segregation mandate does not prohibit the government from commingling the actual cash generated by earmarked and general fund taxes. There is no separate drawer in the Treasury labeled the Social Security Trust Fund.

budget promises can be quite difficult when various programs are rolled together into a single agency budget. Separate fund accounting reduces the political transaction costs of monitoring compliance with particular deals.

These common elements notwithstanding, there are major differences between public and private trust funds. As I mentioned, public trust funds generally do *not* involve a contractual relationship from a strictly legal standpoint because their provisions can be changed by Congress. In the case of Social Security, for example, the Supreme Court has ruled that the interest of workers in their pensions "cannot be soundly analogized to that of the holder of an annuity, whose right to benefits are bottomed on his contractual premium payments."[41] Indeed, the two forms of trust funds may lead to *opposite* effects. One key advantage of private trusts, for example, is protection from the risk of insolvency. Even if a private trustee experiences personal financial losses, beneficiaries retain their interest in the trust. Ironically, the situation is just the *reverse* in federal budgeting. It is precisely dedicated funding that makes the threat of insolvency possible. As Martin Feldstein observes, "Social Security is said to be heading toward bankruptcy only because it uses earmarked taxes and has a trust fund. Other federal programs like education and defense have no earmarked taxes and no trust fund and would therefore never be perceived to be bankrupt."[42]

Ultimately, the essential difference between private and public trusts is not that the former are somehow more "real" than the latter. The key distinction is that private trust funds implement private deals, subject to private sector enforcement, whereas public trust funds implement social contracts, which are subject to political enforcement. As Alan Blinder correctly argues, many economists may call federal trust funds "fictions, but they are facts – because they have standing in law."[43] What requires scrutiny is why elected officials create trust funds, the nature of the underlying commitments, and how trust fund structures create political facts and shape beneficiary expectations.

Understanding trust fund commitments

Two social science literatures offer limited insights into these issues. The first is the empirical literature on policy inheritances. This literature

---

[41] *Fleming* v. *Nestor*, 363 US 603, 1960.
[42] Martin Feldstein, "The Case for Privatization," *Foreign Affairs*, July/August 1997, 24–38 at 27.
[43] Alan S. Blinder, "Shrewd Politics, Sound Policy," *The New York Times*, March 3, 1998, A19.

demonstrates that the actions of incumbent administrations are massively constrained by the actions of their predecessors, even though current politicians always retain the formal authority to remake any law they wish.[44] This research tends to examine the impact of policy inheritances on the projects of politicians at particular moments, however. In so doing, it directs attention away from both how specific policy commitments evolve over very long periods of time and how they were crafted in the first place.

Another relevant body of work is the growing game-theoretic literature on "credible commitment." This research basically treats commitment making as an exercise in self-restraint. The central problem is said to be one of "time inconsistency." The problem arises when some move maximizes an actor's utility before the fact, but is incompatible with his incentives afterward. Under such circumstances, any commitment to perform the act is simply not credible. One solution is for the person to manipulate his future self by making reneging very difficult, as in the famous tale of Ulysses lashing himself to the mast to prevent his being fatally attracted to the Sirens' song.

Credible commitment often works through reputation effects. For example, if "a union leader stakes his reputation on his refusal to approve a contract that includes a reduction in wages, he might thereby gain the upper hand in wage negotiations."[45] This reputation for trustworthiness, of course, will greatly redound to the union leader's benefit in subsequent rounds of the game. Does this logic apply to federal trust funds? Political actors certainly do pledge fidelity to trust funds. One common vehicle is through political party platforms. The 1996 Republican platform, for example, included the following language:

> We have a legal and moral responsibility to America's seniors and will continue to do everything in our power to ensure that government honors our commitment to Social Security beneficiaries, now and in the future.

---

[44] See especially the excellent analyses contained in Rose and Davies, *Inheritance in Public Policy*; and Paul Pierson, *Dismantling the Welfare State? Reagan, Thatcher, and the Politics of Retrenchment* (Cambridge: Cambridge University Press, 1994).

[45] Donald C. Hubin, "Of Bindings and By-Products: Elster on Rationality," *Philosophy and Public Affairs*, 15, Winter 1986, 82–95. See as well Jon Elster, *Ulysses and the Sirens: Studies in Rationality and Irrationality* (Cambridge: Cambridge University Press, 1979); Thomas C. Schelling, *The Strategy of Conflict* (Cambridge, MA: Harvard University Press, 1960); and Douglass C. North and Barry R. Weingast, "Constitutions and Commitment: The Evolution of Institutions Governing Public Choice in Seventeenth-Century England," in Lee J. Alston, Thrainn Eggertsson, and Douglass C. North, eds., *Empirical Studies in Institutional Change* (New York: Cambridge University Press, 1996).

We will keep it financially sound and keep politics out of its administration. We will work to ensure the integrity and solvency of the Social Security trust funds.[46]

Although often quite vague and open-ended, the promises contained in party platforms are far from meaningless.[47] Still, it would be a grave mistake to look to party manifestos as a major source of trust fund credibility. In the first place, few trust funds outside of Social Security ever receive a mention in platform planks. Moreover, US political parties are simply too weak to serve as effective guarantors of policy credibility.[48] An even more fundamental problem with this perspective is that very often the actors who made the original trust fund vows are dead (or anyway well out of politics) by the time the promises come due. It is *other* politicians, who come later, whose hands the trust funds are meant to tie. With trust funds, it is thus often more a case of binding distant futures than credible commitments as such.[49]

At the deepest level, the problem with the credible commitments literature is its assumption of a perfect analogy between individual and collective commitment.[50] Many rational-choice scholars argue that a major effect of political institutions – the congressional committee system is a favorite example – is to solve the time-consistency problem by preventing opportunistic actors from reneging on their bargains. This, in turn, expands the set of legislative deals that can be struck, fosters political exchange, and ultimately widens the range of options the government can take in promoting social welfare.[51]

In fact, trust funds *do* perform this role, at times at least. By providing a linkage between specific revenues and outlays, trust funds and earmarked taxes may allow deals to be struck that otherwise could not. This is in fact part of the story. But it is definitely not the whole story. The

---

[46] See http://www.rnc.org/hq/platform96/plat6.html#old
[47] Gerald M. Pomper, *Elections in America: Control and Influence in Democratic Politics*, revised edition (New York: Longman, 1980), 185–7.
[48] On the limited importance of party platforms in the evolution of Social Security, see Martha Derthick, *Policymaking for Social Security* (Washington, DC: Brookings Institution, 1979), 183–93.
[49] I owe this insight to Robert Goodin.
[50] On the disanalogies between individual and collective commitment, see John Elster, "Introduction," in Elster and Slagstad, *Constitutionalism and Democracy*, 8–14; and Stephen Holmes, "Precommitment and the Paradox of Democracy," in *ibid.*, 236–8.
[51] For this side of the theoretical story, see Kenneth A. Shepsle, "Discretion, Institutions, and the Problem of Government Commitment," in Pierre Bourdieu and James S. Coleman, eds., *Social Theory for a Changing Society* (Boulder, CO: Westview Press, 1992), 245–63.

other side is suggested in an important series of essays on political commitment by Terry Moe.[52] According to Moe, political actors craft commitment devices not only to promote voluntary exchange, or to solve collective action problems, but also to serve their long-run interests at the expense of their current and future opponents. Fearing their favored policies will be vulnerable to the interventions of subsequent politicians, actors try to entrench their preferences through structural design. The upshot is that even when precommitments are the product of deliberate planning, and serve the goals of their designers, they do not necessarily promote social welfare.[53]

Any normative appraisal of prior commitment, then, should rest on a realistic understanding of democratic politics. Unfortunately, this is not true of most writing by economists on earmarked taxes and trust funds. The leading opponents of dedicated funding are orthodox public finance scholars, who contend that earmarking introduces "rigidities into budgeting, preventing resources from being allocated into the highest priority uses."[54] To public choice school founder James Buchanan, by contrast, tying the government's hands through earmarking and user charges is potentially a good thing. General fund budgeting amounts to a "tie-in" sale. While citizens may have diverse preferences, they face a single distribution of public services to accept or reject. Earmarking allows citizens to express their opinions on each public good separately, thereby promoting individual welfare.[55] Second-generation public choice scholars, however, have questioned whether earmarking arrangements can actually live up to their theoretical promise, arguing that officeholders will simply hoard dedicated taxes for their own purposes whenever they are short on cash.[56] In short, earmarked funds are too rigid in one model; in the other, not rigid enough.

For all their differences these two political models share certain basic

---

[52] Terry M. Moe, "Political Institutions: The Neglected Side of the Story," *Journal of Law, Economics, and Organization*, 6 Special Issue, 1990a, 213–53; and Terry M. Moe, "The Politics of Structural Choice: Toward a Theory of Public Bureaucracy," in Oliver Williamson, ed., *Organization Theory From Chester Barnard to the Present and Beyond* (New York: Oxford University Press, 1990b), 116–53.

[53] Adam Przewroski and Fernano Limongi, "Political Regimes and Economic Growth," *Journal of Economic Perspectives*, 7, Summer 1993, 51–70, at 67.

[54] Thomas F. Pogue and L. G. Sgontz, *Government and Economic Choice: An Introduction to Public Finance* (Boston: Houghton Mifflin Company, 1978).

[55] James M. Buchanan, "The Economics of Earmarked Taxes," *Journal of Political Economy*, 71, October 1963, 457–69.

[56] See Fred S. McChesney, *Money for Nothing: Politicians, Rent Extraction, and Political Extortion* (Cambridge, MA: Harvard University Press, 1997).

defects. Both make the mistake of assuming that "the impact of a given set of institutions on economic policy can be 'read' directly from the institutional structure itself."[57] In fact, the effects of trust funds in the US budget are subtle and contingent. These effects can only be assessed through a careful examination of the historical and institutional context in which particular funds are situated. Another flaw is that both models rest on questionable assumptions about the dynamics of democratic politics. The traditional normative public finance literature presumes that government is run by a benevolent dictator – not necessarily the best starting point for a pragmatic assessment of institutional design and governance in pluralist democracies. By contrast, many younger public choice scholars posit that political actors care only about extracting "economic rent" for themselves. Undeniably, material incentives influence politics. As I shall demonstrate, however, other factors, including policy inheritances, information, and administrative routines, shape outcomes as well.

Plan of the book

The heart of the book consists of detailed case studies of five trust fund programs: Social Security, Medicare, Highways, Airport and Airways, and Superfund. In addition, the book also examines two cases – Energy Security and Lead Paint Abatement – where new trust funds were proposed but not adopted. The nature of the questions addressed in this study makes a comparative case study approach an appropriate one. The political development of individual trust fund programs must be carefully examined in order to identify the objectives each trust fund was designed to serve, the support it has received from key actors, and the evolution of the trust fund over time. The number of cases included in the study represents an attempt to strike an acceptable compromise between a sample size small enough to permit a reasonably detailed analysis of each trust fund, and large enough to provide a conceptual foundation for generalizations about the role of trust funds in the political process. In some instances, the trade-off between richness of detail and analytic tractability is particularly severe. Indeed, entire books could be written about each of the cases in the sample. The contribution of this study is

---

[57] For a cautionary statement against making just this mistake, see Colleen A. Dunleavy, "Early Railroad Policy," in Sven Steinmo, Kathleen Thelen, and Frank Longstreths, eds., *Structuring Politics: Historical Institutionalism in Comparative Analysis* (Cambridge: Cambridge University Press, 1992), 139.

not to write a definitive history of each policy area but rather to provide the first generic study of the trust fund device.

This book is organized as follows. Chapter 2 presents the conceptual framework that will guide the case study accounts. The framework draws on two distinct yet complementary strands of the "new institutionalism": the transaction cost approach and historical institutionalism.[58] The transaction cost approach highlights the fundamental problem of political commitment. It emphasizes the role of purposive institutional design in shaping political transaction costs – the costs of negotiating, monitoring, and enforcing agreements. The historical-institutional perspective contributes three key insights into a study of trust fund politics. First, it emphasizes that institutional arrangements *mediate* policy outcomes but are never the sole cause of them. Second, it holds that policymaking is essentially a developmental process: new structures are often built on preexisting ones, and governmental commitments may create important feedback effects.[59] Finally, the perspective highlights the role of ideas, not just interests, in policymaking.

Chapter 3 examines the place of trust funds in the larger context of changing federal tax regimes and uses regression analysis to compare the responsiveness of trust funds and general funds to various political and economic factors. Chapters 4 through 9 present the detailed case studies. The final chapter summarizes the main findings, analyzes variations across the case studies, and discusses normative implications.

The argument in brief

The trust funds in the US budget are, virtually without exception, the product of deliberate intervention. They are consciously crafted political mechanisms intended by their designers to bind the government to its promises to the public, its constituents.

The examination of trust fund experiences offered in this book demonstrates that the trust fund device has been a consequential US

---

[58] While these two strands of the new institutionalism have different points of departure, they have been moving closer together. For example, economist Avinash K. Dixit's recent work on political transaction costs emphasizes that commitment is an evolutionary process. See Dixit, *The Making of Economic Policy: A Transaction-Cost Politics Perspective* (Cambridge, MA: MIT Press, 1996). Some leading scholars (e.g., Douglass North) are claimed by both camps as their own.

[59] For an excellent literature review, see Peter A. Hall and Rosemary C. R. Taylor, "Political Science and the Three New Institutionalisms," *Political Studies*, 44, 1996, 936–57.

policy instrument, shaping both aggregate patterns of US taxation and the micro dynamics of particular expenditure programs. At the macro level, trust fund taxes have generally been more stable than general fund taxes over the post-war era. Explicit cuts in social insurance payroll taxes, and other trust fund levies, have rarely been on the agenda and have never been seen as vehicles for counter-cyclical fiscal policymaking. By contrast, there have been numerous legislated reductions in income and corporate taxes not tied to specific programs. A focus on trust funds and earmarked taxes thus offers insight into how the federal government has maintained its revenue base at 18–20 percent of GDP during an era of divided party control and increased mistrust in government.

The trust fund device has been an important mediating factor at the level of individual programs. Trust fund financing clearly does not eliminate the impact of other political forces, such as struggles among contending interest groups. But trust funds *do* influence how these struggles play out by distributing procedural advantages, reinforcing symbols of moral deservedness and blame, and affecting perceptions of political fidelity and defection. A striking finding is just how much attention is paid by politicians and interest groups to trust fund accounting, and how the legislative dynamics of programs like Social Security and Medicare are affected by seemingly "artificial" changes in trust fund forecasts. This finding highlights the importance of even arcane institutions in structuring the politics of a polity. Three other findings may surprise many scholars. First, a number of major trust funds owe their origins as much to fiscal conservatives seeking to safeguard the Treasury as to liberal proponents of big government; second, despite the obvious appeal of trust fund financing to pragmatic politicians, trust funds have not taken over the entire federal budget, indeed they have at times been rejected by Congress to preserve budgetary flexibility; and, third, while trust fund architects generally seek to depoliticize programs, many trust funds have been politically contentious and financially unstable.

Political scientists are increasingly recognizing that institutions are a force not only for political inertia but also for political change. Trust funds are an excellent case in point. While trust funds channel contests over scarce budget resources, they are compatible with program trajectories ranging from rapid growth to retrenchment. When surpluses and deficits in the trust funds have emerged, Congress has often enacted "corrective" legislation designed to restore the funds to balance. The future credibility of preexisting trust fund commitments is not fixed, however. There are ongoing struggles among politicians over the rules and procedures under which particular trust funds will operate. And trust fund promises can be renegotiated. In sum, my analysis suggests that statutory precommitment in a democratic polity must be seen not as a final policy outcome, but rather as an evolutionary process in which prior choices shape but do not eliminate the prospects for change.

It should be recognized at the outset that all trust funds are not the same. While trust funds constitute a class, their variations must be explored. Such variations, I contend, are largely the product of two key dimensions of the underlying political commitments: reciprocity and reliance. The former has to do with the degree to which the government and payers are in a reciprocal exchange relationship and whether payers and beneficiaries significantly overlap with one another. The latter concerns the degree to which promisees make long-term commitments in the expectation of the funds' continuation and hence become vulnerable to the consequences of unreliability by the government. The concluding chapter shows that different combinations of reciprocity and reliance shape the political dynamics, and the normative contexts, of governmental promising and promise keeping.

2

Political transaction costs, feedback effects, and policy credibility

This chapter draws on recent work in transaction cost theory and historical institutionalism to provide a framework for analyzing the causes and consequences of trust fund financing. It first explains the relevance of political transaction costs for an understanding of trust funds in the US budget. Next, it outlines four reasons for the creation of trust funds. It then describes the main effects of the trust fund mechanism on the policymaking process, and how current officeholders can try to increase or decrease the credibility of existing trust fund commitments. Finally, the chapter discusses the case selection.

Political transaction costs, trust funds, and government budgeting

It is helpful to begin a study of trust funds with an examination of the larger budgetary system of which the trust fund instrument is a part. Public budgeting must be understood not merely as a technical exercise in resource allocation, but rather as the setting for some of the most crucial tasks of a democratic polity: mobilizing revenues, delivering benefits to constituencies, safeguarding the public fisc. These tasks inherently require politicians to enter into commitments both with one another and with voters and groups in the larger society. Budgeting can thus be seen as a form of contracting behavior, in which the government pledges – not always credibly – to do certain things rather than others in the future. As the late Aaron Wildavsky observed in his classic book *The Politics of the Budgetary Process*:

Viewed in [this] light, a budget may be regarded as a contract. Congress and the president promise to supply funds under specified conditions, and the agencies agree to spend the money in ways that have been agreed upon . . . Whether or not the contract is enforceable, or whether or not the parties actually agree about what the contract purportedly stipulates, is a matter for inquiry. To the extent that a budget is carried out, however, it imposes a set of mutual obligations and controls upon the contracting parties . . . A budget thus becomes a web of social as well as of legal relationships in which commitments are made by all parties, and where sanctions may be invoked (though not necessarily equally) by all.[1]

As I explained in chapter 1, although budgeting "contracts" are not contracts in a legalistic sense, viewing the budget as a set of implicit social contracts directs attention to a number of important questions that might otherwise not be raised. Are all budgetary transactions (e.g., pensions, routine administrative operations, and so on) fundamentally the same, or do some kinds of commitments entail more difficult governance challenges than others? What institutions and beneficiary expectations do particular contract-like commitments create? Why do different forms of budget structures exist?

Transaction costs in budgeting

Recent work on political transaction costs offers a framework to address these questions. The transaction cost approach was originally developed to study private sector organization: primarily firms, markets, and common law institutions. A key puzzle for economists is why firms, which are islands of planning and managerial control, exist at all, given the obvious advantages of market competition. Oliver Williamson suggests that markets do many things well but also have serious limitations.[2] Specifically, markets are poorly equipped to manage transactions characterized by high uncertainty, specific investments, and "sunkenness." While markets supply high-powered incentives that promote efficiency, these incentives invite opportunistic behavior when contracts require ongoing relationships, yet parties have difficulty monitoring one another. If parties fear being exploited, they may not agree to the deal in the first place. Moving such transactions from the market to other organizational settings may allow the deal to go forward.

[1] Aaron Wildavsky, *The Politics of the Budgetary Process* (Boston: Little Brown, 1964), 3.
[2] Oliver E. Williamson, *The Economic Institutions of Capitalism* (New York: Free Press, 1985).

Scholars have recently begun to apply the transaction cost approach to the study of public administration.[3] This is a potentially productive research move since transaction costs are no less pervasive in politics than in economics, and the level and incidence of transaction costs can have a significant impact on policy outcomes. As Howard Frant cautions, however, we cannot make "full use of these ideas by trying to squeeze the public sector into a framework designed for the private sector."[4] The key to making good use of the transaction cost perspective in the study of government is recognizing the distinctive characteristics of politics. Five factors will be stressed here:

1 *Shaky political "property rights."* In the private sector, property rights are generally secure because they are held by named individuals. Political property rights are far more tenuous because these claims attach to public offices, whose occupants are subject to electoral turnover.

2 *Multiple contractors.* While economic contracts are typically between two clearly identifiable contractors, political contracts often have multiple parties (e.g., voters, lobbyists) on at least one side of the relationship.[5]

3 *Ubiquity of compromise.* As Terry Moe stresses, the decentralization of US formal institutions makes accommodation to political opponents "a virtual necessity" in the institutional design process.[6] As the case study chapters will show, the need to satisfy multiple factions may lead to the creation of trust fund structures with embedded tensions and contradictions.

4 *Endogeneity of political transaction costs.* Political transaction costs are to a significant degree "given" by the characteristics of specific governmental policies. But political transaction costs can also be actively manipulated by officeholders seeking to further their political goals.[7] Both the underlying attributes of budgeting pro-

---

[3] See, for example, Douglass North, "A Transaction Cost Theory of Politics," *Journal of Theoretical Politics*, 2 (4), 1990, 355–67 (1990); Charlotte W. Twight, "Political Transaction Cost Manipulation," *Journal of Theoretical Politics*, 6, 1994, 189–216; Horn, *The Political Economy*; Dixit, *The Making of Economic Policy*; and Howard Frant, "High-Powered and Low-Powered Incentives in the Public Sector," *Journal of Public Administration Research and Theory*, 3 (6), 1996, 365–81.

[4] Frant, "High-Powered and Low-Powered Incentives in the Public Sector," 365.

[5] Dixit, *The Making of Economic Policy*, 48–9.

[6] Terry Moe, "The Politics of Bureaucratic Structure," in John E. Chubb and Paul E. Peterson, eds., *Can the Government Govern?* (Washington, DC: Brookings Institution, 1990c), 327.

[7] See Charlotte Twight, "Political Transaction Cost Manipulation."

mises and the content of politicians' agendas therefore demand attention.

5 *Weak incentives for global efficiency.* Two factors may reduce the global efficiency of political institutions. First, the costs associated with political commitment making, such as narrowed flexibility and discretion, are seldom perfectly internalized to the actors making the deal; instead, they may be borne in large part by opposing coalitions and future generations. Second, institutions may take on a life of their own, making reform difficult even when the institutions no longer fit their environment. To be sure, private transactions can also be subject to increasing returns and "path dependence." However serious these problems are in the private sector, they are far more severe in public settings.[8]

These differences notwithstanding, a focus on the strategic management, and shaping influence, of political transaction costs does offer insights into public administration. What makes application of the transaction cost perspective to the study of *government trust funds* especially appropriate is that the transaction cost model grows out of the same intellectual tradition as the theory of budgetary incrementalism. Both incrementalism and the transaction cost approach rest on the behavioral premise of bounded rationality. Incrementalism holds that elected officials must find ways to cope with the overwhelming complexity of budget decisions. In Wildavsky's classic account, politicians are shown to take last year's budget as given, focusing their attention on changes at the margin.[9] Incrementalism can be seen as an effective method for reducing the search and information costs associated with reaching agreements under conditions of uncertainty.

Missing from traditional incrementalist theory, however, is explicit attention to what happens *after* the initial funding decisions are made. Incrementalism basically focuses on the *ex ante* transaction costs of making budget decisions. But there are also the *ex post* costs of monitoring and enforcing taxing and spending promises *through time*. One reason these costs arise is that, as the transaction cost perspective emphasizes, politicians may behave opportunistically. Political promises

---

[8] As developed by Williamson, transaction cost economics presumes that private sector institutions in advanced capitalist societies are *generally* efficient (else they would not exist). For a powerful argument that public sector institutions should not be presumed efficient because their persistence typically owes a great deal to path dependence and lock-in effects, see Paul Pierson, "Increasing Returns, Path Dependence, and the Study of Politics," revised version of 1996 APSA paper, April 15, 1997.

[9] Wildavsky, *The Politics of the Budgetary Process.*

not compatible with the incentives of current officeholders may be broken. Just as private sector actors may remove from the market transactions in which continuity is important, so politicians may seek to shelter certain budget promises from the normal jockeying for appropriations support – the closest approximation to a competitive resource "market" in American government.[10]

It is reasonable to ask why politicians would ever care about the durability of budget commitments. Rank-and-file legislators are often said to have very short time horizons. But the time horizons of other policymakers may in fact be relatively long. Such actors are probably few and far between in American politics. But they do exist. One thinks of program builders like Franklin Roosevelt and Lyndon Johnson, and institutional "budget guardians," such as long-time Ways and Means Committee chairman Wilbur Mills. Alternatively, policymakers may themselves have relatively short time horizons, yet still push for long-term commitment devices because they wish to curry favor with other political actors who *do* tend to care greatly about policy durability, such as well-organized interest groups.[11] As we will see in the case accounts, both of these dynamics help explain the creation of trust funds.

Rationales for creating trust funds

From the standpoint of orthodox public finance theory, the existence of government trust funds presents a puzzle. Dedicating revenue for specific uses prevents policymakers from maximizing social welfare by directing revenues where they are needed most. As one budget expert puts it, "When you earmark, you are giving up the power of the legislature to manage the fiscal affairs of the state."[12]

---

[10] Given the ubiquity of budgetary incrementalism, it might be assumed that funding outcomes are inherently stable – so there is no need for precommitment devices like trust funds or entitlements. Certainly the vast empirical literature on incrementalism in the US budget demonstrates that cabinet departments and other large governmental organizations experience small funding changes most of the time. But budget outcomes at the micro programmatic level are more vulnerable to significant fluctuations. On the competitiveness of the budgetary process and efforts by spending advocates to craft protective budget structures, see the excellent analysis contained in Meyers, *Strategic Budgeting*. See also Charles Stewart III, *Budget Reform Politics: The Design of the Appropriations Process in the House of Representatives* (New York: Cambridge University Press, 1989).

[11] On political time horizons, see Pierson, "Increasing Returns, Path Dependence, and the Study of Politics."

[12] William T. Pound, executive director of the National Conference of State

This puzzle largely disappears once commitment problems are acknowledged. The question then becomes what makes trust fund financing more or less attractive to different actors in various circumstances? There are four main reasons for creating trust funds: (1) to make users pay; (2) to maximize agency budgets; (3) to reduce uncertainty; and (4) to safeguard the Treasury.

Making users pay ("benefit taxation")

The most common rationale for trust fund financing is to charge users. Economists call this "benefit taxation." In the pure version of the model (which contrasts with taxation based on ability to pay), government services would be financed entirely through user fees that reflect marginal costs. Charging directly for public services may not always be feasible, however. For example, pricing highways according to the wear and tear imposed by any single driver would be an administrative nightmare. Earmarking revenue to a trust fund may offer a "second-best" solution, provided the revenue source is properly designed. By imposing a specific earmarked tax on a product (e.g., gasoline) whose usage is correlated with use of the publicly provided service, the government can distribute costs in proportion to benefits received.

Benefit taxation offers policymakers several advantages. First, it enables them to recover the costs of government services in which it is feasible to exclude non-payers. It also promotes allocational efficiency. Taxpayers will only demand an increase in services if they perceive the benefits of the service increment to exceed the costs. Finally, a user–pay approach promotes equity because those who do not want the service are not forced to pay for it.[13]

Budget maximization

A second rationale for trust fund financing takes off from William Niskanen's famous claim that bureaucrats attempt to maximize their

---

Legislatures, quoted in "The Earmarks of a Solution," *Governing*, March 1991, 48.

[13] Some economists also endorse dedicated funding when the revenue source is a fee or tax imposed to internalize social externalities, such as pollution. But such "green" taxes will not promote economic efficiency unless they (1) bear a direct relation to the social liabilities being redressed and (2) cover prospective damages and thus approximate insurance payments. Appearances notwithstanding, neither of these conditions obtains in the Superfund case (discussed in chapter 8).

agencies' budgets in order to obtain more power, higher salaries, and other good things.[14] Niskanen's original model presumes that the bureau is a monopoly with private information, and that it has a passive legislative sponsor. But bureaus may face intense competition for scarce resources, and appropriations committees may well be active.[15] Under these more realistic conditions, budget-maximizing agencies may find access to a dedicated funding source appealing when it offers protection from rival bureaus and insulation from ordinary mechanisms of fiscal control.

Reduction of political uncertainty

A third reason for trust fund financing – reduction of political uncertainty – flows from the premise that political actors are risk averse.[16] Actors here are less concerned with obtaining the largest possible increases than with funding stability.[17] Uncertainty increases the transaction costs of promise making. Policymakers may use trust funds to manipulate the *ex ante* transaction costs of negotiating an acceptable bargain and/or the *ex post* costs of safeguarding promised benefit flows to constituents through time.

Trust funds can help seal bargains by allowing collective decisions on both sides of the budget equation – expenditures and revenues – to be reached simultaneously. Sometimes the enactment of a program requires its proponents to support a revenue expansion favored by another coalition. Under general-fund financing, however, there is often a time lag between taxing and spending decisions, creating the potential for opportunistic behavior. Lawmakers may vote for the tax only to see their colleagues renege on their end of the deal. What is required to escape this trap is a mechanism for assuring parties that commitments will be

---

[14] William Niskanen, *Bureaucracy and Representative Government* (Chicago: Aldine Atherton, 1971).

[15] Gary J. Miller and Terry M. Moe, "Bureaucrats, Legislators, and the Size of Government," *American Political Science Review*, 77, 1983, 297–323.

[16] On risk aversion, see Daniel Kahneman and Amos Tversky, "Choices, Values and Frames," *American Psychologist*, 39, 1984, 341–50.

[17] Roy Meyers suggests that dedicated funding is usually part of a minimax strategy, designed to avoid the "most distasteful" budget outcome – a large reduction in funding. See Meyers, *Strategic Budgeting*, 138. Some scholars argue that Niskanen's theory of budget maximization should be refined to take into account risk aversion. See, for example, Andre Blais and Stephane Dion, "Are Bureaucrats Budget Maximizers?" *The Budget-Maximizing Bureaucrat: Appraisals and Evidence* (Pittsburgh: University of Pittsburgh Press, 1991).

honored. Dedicated funding, the linkage between specific revenues and expenditures, may enable compromises to be reached.[18]

Policymakers may also use trust funds as a mechanism for assuring implementation of long-term promises. The incentive to create trust funds for this purpose is strongest when the net political benefits of funding continuity are higher (to the relevant political actors if not necessarily to society as a whole) than are the net benefits of preserving budget flexibility. This condition often holds in public budgeting, but not always. Commitment devices like trust funds, entitlements, and indexation tend to weaken the capacity of current officeholders to use the annual budget process as a mechanism to control their bureaucratic agents. Where agency problems loom large because the underlying transaction requires bureaucrats to be granted considerable discretion over resource allocation, as is the case for general administrative spending, these mechanisms may become less appealing, even when politicians are narrowly self-interested.[19]

Safeguarding the treasury

A final plausible reason for trust fund financing is to protect the general Treasury. The goals are to prevent deficit spending and perhaps limit government growth. In the United States, the norm of a balanced federal budget has long carried a symbolic importance far beyond its objective economic meaning, standing for the absence of corruption, social harmony, and the preservation of republic government.[20] Trust fund financing can help protect the Treasury directly by helping to mobilize new revenues. Earmarked taxes are often easier to pass than general fund levies.[21] Because the objective is fiscal restraint and not allocative

---

[18] See Buchanan, "The Economics of Earmarked Taxes," 377–90; and Charles J. Goetz, "Earmarked Taxes and Majority Rule Budgetary Processes," *The American Economic Review*, 58, 1968, 128–36.

[19] Horn, *The Political Economy of Public Administration*, 85.

[20] On the power of the balanced budget norm in American history, see James Savage, *Balanced Budgets and American Politics* (Ithaca: Cornell University Press, 1988).

[21] On the greater acceptance of earmarked taxes in the US budget, see Alice M. Rivlin, "The Continuing Search for a Popular Tax," *American Economic Review*, 79 (2), May 1989, 113–17. The appeal of tax earmarking is also discussed in B. Guy Peters, *The Politics of Taxation: A Comparative Perspective* (Oxford: Blackwell, 1991). For a stimulating theoretical discussion of the issue of quasi-voluntary tax compliance, see Margaret Levi, *Of Rule and Revenue* (Berkeley: University of California Press, 1988). See also Barry R. Weingast, "The Role of Credible Commitments in State Finance," *Public Choice*, 66, 1990, 89–97.

efficiency, a direct economic relationship between the spending program and earmarked tax is not necessary. Any targeted tax will do. Trust fund financing may also serve to protect the Treasury indirectly by forcing policymakers to make their spending plans conform to the revenue flows of a particular tax base. As chapter 4 will show, long-term actuarial forecasts for the Social Security Trust Fund have shaped both the timing and magnitude of benefit expansions.

Participants in trust fund decisions

In theory, each of these reasons can be sharply distinguished from the others. In practice, they tend to overlap. Indeed, the perception that a given trust fund will promote multiple goals makes its adoption more likely. Distinguishing analytically among the four reasons for trust fund financing is nonetheless important because tensions among the effective policy goals (efficiency, spending growth, stability, fiscal restraint) can easily give rise to conflicts during the implementation phase. Moreover, each of the four rationales can be expected to draw upon a somewhat different constellation of political support (table 2.1).

Bureau heads, for example, would be expected to be key players in the budget maximization model. To the extent that promoting efficiency is the dominant rationale for trust fund financing, government economists may be significant actors. In general, institutional "budget guardians," such as members of the House and Senate appropriations and revenues committees, and the Office of Management and Budget and Congressional Budget Office, tend to oppose dedicated funding. As Pete Domenici (R-New Mexico) of the Senate Budget Committee has said, "To the people concerned about budgeting and the economy, earmarking and trust funds percolating up all over the place in government is just not a very good way to run the government."[22] In view of their power, however, it is unlikely there would be many trust funds in the US budget unless budget controllers *sometimes* found dedicated funding compatible with their interests. Budget controllers are most likely to be supportive when trust funds promote fiscal restraint, especially when the underlying spending programs have a built-in potential for rapid growth. The Medicare case study will show that Wilbur Mills supported the creation of the Hospital Insurance Trust Fund and Supplementary Medical Insurance trust funds precisely because he believed these fiscal devices would keep future Medicare spending under control and protect the federal government's capacity to meet its preexisting pension commit-

[22] Quoted in Haas, "Paying As You Go," 2645.

Table 2.1. *Four rationales for trust fund financing*

	Benefit taxation	Budget maximization	Reduction of uncertainty	Guarding the treasury
Effective policy goal	Economic efficiency	Rapid spending growth	Political and budgetary stability	Fiscal restraint
Likely sponsors	Government economists; institutional budget guardians	Bureaucrats; interest groups; legislative program sponsors	Program builders; interest groups	Institutional budget guardians

ments. Budget controllers may be especially supportive of trust fund arrangements that allow them to finance a preexisting government activity from new earmarked taxes, thereby "freeing up" the program's former share of general revenues.

Finally, interest group clienteles should be expected to support the creation of trust funds that promise to increase or stabilize the budgets of the programs they care about. When trust fund proposals promote reciprocal exchange, and involve the imposition of new earmarked taxes on program beneficiaries, clientele groups face implicit cost–benefit tests: is the payment of the additional charges worth the benefits of higher or more certain spending? How the affected groups answer this question is likely to be an important factor in the debate.

Diffusion of trust funds across policy sectors

Whatever the motivations behind them, one thing is clear: trust funds have not entered the budget randomly. Rather, the trust fund device has diffused across policy sectors in several major waves, as table 2.2 shows.[23] Prior to 1920, the only trust funds on the books of the Treasury were Indian tribal funds and various "deposit" funds which "had none of the characteristics" of modern trust fund structures.[24] The first important group of federal trust funds was established for veterans and federal

---

[23] Indexing provisions have also been adopted in waves. See Weaver, *Automatic Government*. Excluded from this table are a number of isolated trust funds that fit into no clear category, such as the (now defunct) General Revenue Sharing Trust Fund, which is discussed in chapters 9 and 10.

[24] Tax Foundation, "Federal Trust Funds."

Table 2.2. *Diffusion of trust funds across policy sectors*

Policy Area	1920s and prior	1930s	1940s	1950s	1960s	1970s	1980s	1990s
Veterans and federal employees	Government Life Insurance Fund (1919) Civil Service Retirement and Disability Fund (1920)		National Service Life Insurance Fund (1940)	Employees Life Insurance Fund (1954) Employees Health Benefits Fund (1959)	Retired Employees Health Benefits Fund (1960)		Military Retirement Fund (1984)	
Social Insurance (income maintenance and health)		Unemployment Trust Fund (1935) Railroad Retirement (1937) Social Security (1939)		Disability Insurance Trust Fund (1956)	Hospital Insurance Trust Fund (1965) Supplementary Medical Insurance Trust Fund (1965)			
Transportation				Highway (1956)		Airport and Airway (1970) Inland Waterway (1978)	Mass Transit Account (1982) Harbor Maintenance (1986)	

Environment	Abandoned Mine Reclamation Fund (1977)	Superfund (1980)	
	Deep Seabed Revenue Sharing (1979)	Leaking Underground Storage Tank (1986)	
		Post-closure Liability (1980)	
		Oil Spill Liability (1989)	Radiation Exposure Compensation (1990)
Health damage compensation	Black Lung Disability (1977)	Vaccine Injury Compensation (1987)	
Nature conservation		Aquatic Resources Trust Fund (1984)	National Recreation Trails Fund (1991)

Sources: Office of Management and Budget, *Budget of the US Government*, various years; Nona A. Noto and Louis Alan Talley, "Excise Tax Financing of Federal Trust Funds," CRS Report for Congress 93-6 E, 1993; Tax Foundation *Federal Trust Funds: Budgetary and Other Implications* (New York: Tax Foundation, 1970).

employee retirement programs.[25] A second big wave came in during the New Deal and Great Society, carrying with it major social insurance trust funds for income maintenance (Unemployment, Railroad Retirement, Social Security) and health (Medicare Hospital Insurance and Supplementary Medical Insurance). A third wave began with the creation of the Highway Trust Fund in 1956, which in turn was followed by the enactment of the Airport and Airway (1970), Inland Waterway (1978), Boat Safety (1980), Mass Transit (1982), and Harbor Maintenance (1986) trust funds, each of which provides infrastructure benefits to transportation users. The most recent wave of trust fund adoptions has featured the creation of trust funds for environmental cleanup (Superfund in 1980 and Leaking Underground Storage Tank in 1986) and health damage compensation (Black Lung Disability in 1977 and Radiation Exposure Compensation in 1990).

This developmental pattern suggests a role for policy feedback in the trust fund design process. The establishment of new trust funds reflects not only the goals of current actors but also the openings created by the previous trust fund adoptions. As we will see in the case accounts, prior decisions channel and constrain the structural innovations made thereafter.

The consequences of trust fund financing

An examination of trust fund financing requires attention not only to when and why politicians create trust funds, but also to how the preexistence of the trust fund device affects policymaking. Trust fund financing, I wish to argue, mediates political outcomes in three (partly overlapping) ways: through *procedures* (by influencing how, and in which institutional venue, budgetary decisions are made); through *information* (by affecting the incidence of perceived costs and benefits); and by way of *ideas* (by shaping policy images, political discourse, and issue framings) (Table 2.3). The importance of procedures and information is often emphasized by public choice and transaction cost scholars. The role of ideas receives greater attention from historical institutionalists.

Procedural effects

Procedural protections from tightfisted fiscal review and macro spending constraints are key to the capacity of trust fund structures to promote the

---

[25] John S. Breach, "Provision for Retirement Employees," *The Congressional Digest*, April 1923, 202–3; see also Stephen Skowronek, *Building A New American State* (Cambridge: Cambridge University Press, 1982), 208.

Table 2.3. *Mediating effects of trust fund financing*

Procedural
Interest earnings
Budgetary status
Spending automaticity
Jurisdictional arrangements

Informational
Annual reports
Extended time-horizons

Ideational
Perception of earned rights and moral deservedness
Insurance imagery
Construction of trust fund "bankruptcy" crises

goals of budget maximization and uncertainty reduction. Net, the procedural advantages of trust fund financing have eroded to some degree over time. But certain advantages played a crucial role in the past while others remain important today. These advantages include interest earnings, off-budget status, committee jurisdictions, and spending automaticity.

1 *Interest earnings.* The authority to earn interest on unspent balances distinguishes most trust funds from nearly all general fund accounts.[26] This authority increases the bargaining leverage of trust fund clienteles. Even if budget controllers manage to restrain trust fund spending temporarily, money continues to build up on the books of the Treasury. In addition, projections of future interest earnings greatly improve the reported actuarial condition of the Social Security and Medicare systems.

2 *Off-budget status.* Prior to fiscal 1969, there was no unified federal budget document. The federal government employed three different budget measures. The main one – the administrative budget – excluded the operations of all trust funds.[27] This meant that the

[26] As chapter 6 shows, the Highway Trust Fund no longer earns interest on its balances. In 1998, highway advocates gave up interest earnings in exchange for the creation of a strong new "firewall" mechanism that protects Highway Trust Fund spending from tradeoffs with other programs.

[27] Trust funds were included in the other two budgets measures (consolidated cash and national income accounts), but these received much less political attention.

massive increases in trust fund spending that took place over the 1950s and 1960s (for Social Security, Medicare, interstate highway building, and other programs) were considered "off-budget." All trust funds with the exception of Social Security are officially on budget today.

3 *Spending automaticity.* Most general fund programs need annual appropriations in order to obtain permission to spend. By contrast, a number of the large trust funds that finance entitlement programs receive permanent appropriations that become available without current action by Congress.[28] As long as these trust funds report a positive balance, the Treasury has the legal authority to cut checks for them.

4 *Committee jurisdictions.* When the congressional tax-writing committees (House Ways and Means and Senate Finance) raise general fund taxes, the money is typically allocated to other committees to spend. But in the case of the major social insurance trust funds (Social Security, Disability Insurance and Medicare Hospital Insurance), the tax-writing panels have jurisdiction over both program revenues and outlays. This jurisdictional arrangement reinforces the procedural integrity of the funds. As John Cogan argues, it has historically created an incentive for the tax writers to keep the major trust funds solvent even at the expense of depressing general revenues.[29] Differences in the pattern of post-war tax legislation for trust funds and general funds are discussed in chapter 3.

In 1967, an important presidential commission concluded that the lack of a unified budget hindered effective fiscal policymaking. Almost immediately thereafter, observers raised concerns that trust fund surpluses were being used to "mask" increasing deficits elsewhere in the budget. See General Accounting Office, "Budget Issues: Trust Funds and Their Relationship to the Federal Budget," Report to the Chairman, Committee of Government Operations, House of Representatives, GAO/AFMD-88–55 (Washington, DC: Government Printing Office, September 1988b).

[28] More than two-thirds of trust fund accounts have access to permanent budget authority, meaning budget resources that can be spent without new legislation for the current year. Less than one-tenth of general fund accounts have such permanent authority. See General Accounting Office, "Budget Account Structure: A Descriptive Overview," GAO/AIMD-95–179 (Washington, DC: Government Printing Office, September 1995), Appendix II, 34–5.

[29] See Cogan, "The Dispersion of Spending Authority." Cogan notes that deficits in the general fund were chronic between the 1960s and 1990s; by contrast, the major trusts (with the exception of the Railroad Retirement Fund) avoided running persistent deficits.

Informational effects

Allen Schick persuasively argues that "Budgeting is a process of information exchanges."[30] How information is packaged and presented shapes the articulation of budget demands, perceptions of budgetary "fair shares," and clientele expectations. When trust funds are created, the law typically requires an accounting of their resource flows to be published annually. These annual reports are designed to reduce the transaction costs to affected parties of monitoring implementation of trust fund agreements. The Department of Treasury publishes annual reports for most of the trust funds. In the case of the Social Security and Medicare funds, annual reports are released under the aegis of special Boards of Trustees. These Boards are comprised of the secretaries of Treasury, Labor, and Health and Human Services, the Commissioner of Social Security, and two members of the public appointed by the president and confirmed by the Senate. One of the public trustees must be from each of the political parties.[31] As a policymaking body, the Boards have little independent decisionmaking authority. They rely heavily on the actuarial information provided by the Social Security Administration and the Health Care Financing Administration; nonetheless, the trustees matter. Their annual reports receive considerable media attention and have a great deal of credibility with officeholders.

The information contained in the trustees' reports lengthens the time horizons of policymakers. The official Social Security reports provide projections of income and revenues for the next 75-year period. The purpose of the 75-year estimate is to cover "the entire horizon" of a worker's involvement with the program.[32] No other industrialized democracy uses such long-term forecasts in social policymaking. One of the original aims of these reports was to give workers confidence that the programs were soundly financed for the long run, thereby encouraging promisee reliance. Ironically, the reports have in recent years probably *undermined* public confidence in the programs because of projections of impending insolvency.

It must be emphasized that the information contained in trust fund reports is not neutral. It reflects whatever accounting conventions Congress chooses. Trust fund reports do not necessarily provide an objective analysis of the total costs and benefits of programs, the equity of

---

[30] Allen Schick, *The Capacity to Budget* (Washington, DC: The Urban Institute, 1990), 31.
[31] Ross, "Institutional and Administrative Issues," 233.
[32] *Ibid.*

cost-sharing arrangements, or the existence of "unfunded" liabilities. The reports thus may distort the policy debate. While the policy information generated by trust fund financing does make it easier for groups to see if the government is living up to its past promises, it does not necessarily reveal whether the promises were well-crafted in the first place. This is another example of how trust fund financing does not reduce the transaction costs of budgeting to society so much as to change their political incidence.

Ideational effects

The most slippery effects of trust funds are "ideational."[33] The ideational effects of trust fund financing are important because they shape political understandings, policy images, and norms of rightful action. They are slippery because the role of ideas in politics is hard to quantify; and because, as Douglass North suggests, the "mental models" of individuals and groups may be "continually redefined with new experiences, including contact with others' ideas."[34]

Several ideational effects of trust funds require attention. First is the tendency for trust funds to encourage perceptions of "earned rights," especially when the underlying relationship between promisees and the government is based on reciprocal exchange. When clienteles believe they have an earned right to their benefits, they tend to regard themselves as more worthy and morally deserving than the beneficiaries of other government programs.[35] A closely related ideational effect is the construction of favorable policy images.[36] In the case of Social Security, for example, the trust fund mechanism has been used by program executives

---

[33] On the importance of ideas in policy design, see Giandomenico Majone, "Public Policy and Administration: Ideas, Interests and Institutions," in Robert E. Goodin and Hans-Dieter Klingermann, eds., *A New Handbook of Political Science* (New York: Oxford University Press, 1996). On the role of ideas in American national budgeting, see my essay "Ideas, Inheritances, and the Dynamics of Budgetary Change," *Governance*, 12 (2), April 1999, 147–74.

[34] Douglass C. North, "Epilogue: Economic Performance Through Time," in Lee J. Alston, Thrainn Eggertsson, and Douglas C. North, eds., *Empirical Studies in Institutional Change* (New York: Cambridge University Press, 1996), 347–8.

[35] Argues the Seniors Coalition: "Today the word 'entitlement' is used to describe any government benefit program that, for one reason or another, is a sacred cow and cannot be violated. But the concept is even stronger in the case of Social Security because people have actually paid for their benefits; those benefits aren't just a gift from Uncle Sam." The Seniors Coalition, *What Everyone Should Know About Social Security* (McLean, VA: The Seniors Coalition, 1992), 51–2.

[36] On policy images, see Frank R. Baumgartner and Bryan D. Jones, *Agendas and Instability in American Politics* (Chicago: University of Chicago Press, 1993).

in their public relations efforts to make a compelling (if technically suspect) analogy to private insurance.[37] This reinforces the view that the government has a moral obligation to make good on benefit promises, and that recipients are to be treated as valued policyholders rather than undeserving supplicants.

Finally, trust fund financing may lead to the construction of "bankruptcy" crises when self-financed trust funds face the risk of depletion.[38] Cross-national research on welfare state politics suggests that the United States is unique in the degree to which social insurance financing problems are defined in terms of trust fund solvency crises.[39] From an economic perspective, the notion of a government trust fund going bankrupt is quite dubious. While projections of trust fund insolvency may highlight a gap between what programs cost and what taxpayers are willing to pay, the federal government is not in any danger of literally "going out of business." Policymakers are always free to stave off the bankruptcy of any given trust fund simply by injecting unlimited general revenues into it. Trust fund bankruptcy crises in the United States are thus political constructs, an institutionalized example of what John Kingdon calls "focusing events."[40]

It might seem that the image of trust fund bankruptcy directly *undermines* policy credibility, since the threat of insolvency may open the door to program cutbacks. This argument – often made by liberal defenders of social provision – would be correct if the sole purpose of trust funds were to enhance the well-being of current beneficiaries. As will be seen in the case accounts, however, federal trust funds also exist to enforce long-term commitments to cost recovery and spending restraint. Seen in this light, trust fund solvency crises can potentially help *perpetuate* the goals of fiscally conservative program architects. It is nonetheless true that bankruptcy crisis may also create an opportunity for hard-core opponents of social insurance arrangements to push for far-reaching reforms that might not get a serious hearing otherwise.[41] Ideas and policy images can

---

[37] Derthick, *Policymaking for Social Security*, 198–9.

[38] Virginia P. Reno and Robert B. Friedland, "Strong Support but Low Confidence," in Eric R. Kingson and James H. Schultz, eds., *Social Security in the 21st Century* (New York: Oxford University Press, 1997).

[39] See Pierson, *Dismantling the Welfare State?*; see also Jill Quadagno, "Social Security and the Myth of the Entitlement 'Crisis,'" *Gerontoligist*, 36, June 1996, 391–9.

[40] John Kingdon, *Agendas, Alternatives, and Public Policies* (Boston: Little Brown, 1984).

[41] See chapter 4 on Social Security.

be powerful forces in politics, but their ultimate effects are often difficult to fully predict or control.

Continuing struggles over trust fund credibility

The above discussion of trust fund effects is actually too simple because it presents a static picture. In fact, political commitment is an *evolutionary* process. Governmental commitments, once made, create feedback effects that may have a powerful influence on the political environment in which future actors operate. In his compelling historical–institutional analysis of retrenchment efforts under Reagan and Thatcher, Paul Pierson shows how the "lock-in" effects created by the pay-as-you-go financing of the US Social Security program greatly narrowed the scope for major cutbacks.[42] Millions of American workers have made personal commitments in the expectation that Social Security will be there for them. An examination of the effects of trust fund financing thus requires attention not only to the manifest ways in which the trust fund device shapes political debates over programs, but also to the more hidden ways that trust funds affect administrative routines, policy agendas, and promisee expectations.

While officeholders inherit a political landscape fundamentally shaped by their predecessors, they are not always powerless to change it. Politicians can and do seek to increase or decrease the future credibility of preexisting trust fund commitments. There are a number of strategies available to politicians; none, however, is without limitations (table 2.4).[43] To increase credibility, actors can seek to enact program expansions. Actors can also try to increase the political and fiscal autonomy of a preexisting trust fund by crafting added institutional safeguards. Finally, proponents of existing trust fund commitments can try to increase the pressure on future politicians to make good on prior promises by fostering beneficiary expectations. While this can be a powerful mechanism for strengthening the credibility of a trust fund, the impact may be long delayed.

There are also strategies available to actors who wish to decrease the credibility of a trust fund already in existence. The boldest strategy would be to attempt to dismantle a trust fund entirely. But terminating public policies is generally a difficult thing in American politics, and the

---

[42] Pierson, *Dismantling the Welfare State?*
[43] For other discussions of strategies, see Pierson, *Dismantling the Welfare State?*, especially pp. 19–26. See also Meyers, *Strategic Budgeting*, chapters 5 and 6.

Table 2.4. *Strategies for shaping the future credibility of already established trust funds*

Strategy	Major limitations
Strategy for increasing credibility	
1 Legislating program expansions	Cost
2 Increasing budgetary autonomy	Reversible
3 Fostering beneficiary expectations	Delayed impact
Strategies for decreasing credibility	
1 Dismantling; cutting earmarked taxes; diverting revenues	Opposition of promisees
2 Decreasing budgetary autonomy	May require major budget reforms
3 Allowing earmarked taxes or trust fund structures to expire or a fund to become insolvent	Restricted scope of application; narrow window of opportunity
4 Dampening beneficiary expectations by highlighting uncertainties	Indirect; delayed impact

symbolic and procedural advantages of trust fund financing only makes it harder.[44]

Another strategy would be to freeze or lower the trust fund's earmarked taxes, thereby decreasing the pot of money on which proponents can make future spending demands. Or opponents may seek to divert trust fund revenues to other uses.[45] Since no trust fund structure gives every politically relevant clientele access to dedicated revenues, there is always a potential constituency for diversion efforts. But diverting revenues to new uses generally requires an explicit change in the enabling statute. Moreover, the beneficiaries of the original commitment are likely to oppose diversion attempts vehemently, arguing that it constitutes trust fund "thievery." Indeed, the seemingly technical term "diversion" is anything but neutral. It is packed with political symbolism, implying that

---

[44] On policy termination, see Eugene Bardach, "Policy Termination as a Political Process," *Policy Sciences*, 7, 1976, 123–31; see also Herbert Kaufman, *Are Government Organizations Immortal?* (Washington, DC: The Brookings Institution, 1976); and Bran W. Hogwood and B. Guy Peters, *Policy Dynamics* (New York: St. Martins Press, 1983).

[45] By diversion of revenues, I mean here an explicit change in the permissible uses of trust fund receipts, not the use of trust fund surpluses as an indirect source of general fund financing.

promisees have a preexisting "right" to their budgetary allotment; this is yet another ideational advantage of trust fund status.

Another strategy can be tried when (as is generally the case for trust funds whose spending is considered discretionary) earmarked taxes and/ or trust fund structures are not permanently authorized but must be renewed periodically by Congress. Actors who wish to weaken a particular trust fund may seek to block reauthorization legislation. The advantage is that this works with, rather than against, the natural bias against legislative action. The limitation of the strategy is that it can only be employed when a trust fund structure or its taxes face expiration.

Finally, trust fund opponents may seek to undermine trust funds by arguing that trust fund promises from the government are inherently *untrustworthy*. This is an indirect strategy for dismantling trust funds. It works not by abolishing institutions but rather by reducing beneficiary reliance. As we will see, the credibility of a trust fund promise depends, not only on the rules and procedures that directly protect it, but also on the expectations it creates. As chapter 4 will show, one of the main strategies of conservative opponents of Social Security since the 1930s has been to attack the credibility of trust fund financing itself. They have argued that workers will have to pay twice for their benefits, that the government cannot be trusted to save trust fund surpluses, and that the trust fund is "empty" and on the verge of bankruptcy.

A brief guide to the cases

Chapters 4 through 8 provide detailed case studies of five trust fund programs: Social Security, Medicare, Highways, Airport and Airway, and Superfund. There is a historical logic to the order of the case presentations. For example, I discuss the Medicare case after the Social Security case, not merely because the Social Security Trust Fund was adopted first, but because, as I will show, the precommitments built into the Social Security system affected how the Medicare trust funds were crafted.

The detailed case studies do not cover a random sample of the trust fund universe. The major trust funds are overrepresented. In choosing the cases to study in detail, I sought to focus on the trust funds that have received the most attention in recent political debates while ensuring representation of trust funds across different policy sectors. The case studies thus include trust funds that finance both discretionary (e.g., Highways, Airport and Airways, Superfund) and mandatory (Social Security and Hospital Insurance and Supplementary Medical Insurance) programs. They also include trust fund activities financed almost entirely from specific earmarked taxes (Social Security, Hospital Insurance, and

Highways) and trust fund activities subsidized (directly or indirectly) by large amounts of general revenues (Supplementary Medical Insurance and Airport and Airways). Finally, they include trust funds created during periods of both unified (Social Security, Superfund, and the two Medicare trust funds) and divided (Highways, Airport and Airways) government.

Each chapter examines why the trust fund was adopted, how trust fund financing has affected the program's budgetary claims, and the results of efforts to revise the political terms under which the trust fund operates. Any examination of the politics of trust funds must also investigate the nature of the underlying political commitments (which is both signaled and reinforced by the trust fund device). Do the payers and beneficiaries of a given trust fund significantly overlap with one another? Or is one group taxed to benefit another? Are trust fund payers perceived by relevant actors (including themselves) to be carrying their fair share? What is the magnitude of the promised benefits? How long is the commitment intended to last? Are individual beneficiaries encouraged to make major lifeplans in the expectation of the program's continuation? In sum, is the trust fund commitment based on the perception and reality of reciprocal exchange and does it induce beneficiaries to become reliant on the government?

The next chapter lays the groundwork for the detailed case studies by exploring the overall growth of trust fund revenues in the US budget and by comparing the responsiveness of trust funds taxes and general fund taxes to various political factors. The analysis provides some preliminary evidence that trust fund financing matters.

3

Trust fund taxes vs. general fund taxes

Taxation is inherently political but all taxes do not generate the same political dynamics. An important distinction can be drawn between federal taxes precommitted for specific trust fund activities, on the one hand (mainly payroll taxes), and federal taxes which are considered general revenues (virtually all income taxes, corporate taxes, and certain excise taxes), on the other. This chapter compares the political economies of trust funds and general funds. While a deep understanding of trust fund politics requires a close analysis of actual cases, this approach can produce some insights into overall patterns of resource mobilization in American national government. The chapter begins with a brief look at the place of trust funds within the larger context of changing US tax regimes. The chapter then explores the responsiveness of trust funds and general funds to partisan shifts and other political factors using regression analysis. The results provide support for the claim that trust fund financing has been an important mediating factor in the politics of federal taxation.

Trust funds in the larger context of changing federal tax regimes

Taxation has never been popular in America. As C. Eugene Steurele argues in a penetrating historical essay, however, the United States nonetheless experienced an era of "Easy Financing" between the mid 1940s and the mid to late 1970s.[1] Over this period, the federal govern-

---

[1] Eugene Steuerle, "Financing the American State at the Turn of the Century," in

ment was able to massively expand domestic expenditures while simultaneously cutting general fund taxes and keeping total federal revenues constant at 18–19 percent of gross domestic product (GDP). Steurele argues that there were four main means, beyond economic growth, by which various Congresses and presidents were able to pull off this feat. The first was cuts in the size of the defense budget. The second was inflation-produced "bracket creep," which quietly pushed individual taxpayers into higher tax brackets. The third was the effect of inflation on the value of government bonds. Earmarking taxes for the social insurance trust funds was the fourth major easy financing mechanism – and the only one that involved the explicit passage of peacetime tax increases.

As table 3.1 shows, social insurance taxes were raised in 1950, 1954, 1956, 1961, 1965, and 1971. Between 1950 and 1980, the combined employer–employee payroll tax rate increased from 3.0 percent to 12.23 percent. Trust fund taxes were increased through Republican and Democratic administrations alike. As Congress and the president were increasing payroll taxes, individual income tax rates were regularly being cut and corporate taxes were being allowed to decline as a share of GDP. Major reductions in tax liabilities were enacted in 1948, 1964, 1969, 1975, 1978, and 1981, with smaller cuts in 1954, 1962, 1966, 1971, and 1977 (table 3.1).[2] Some of these tax cuts, most notably the 1962 and 1964 reductions, were explicitly justified by Keynesian fiscal activism.

The House Ways and Means Committee was the key institutional manager of this post war tax regime, and the trust fund device channeled its policy decisions. Faced with the choice of depositing revenue in the general fund or earmarking it to a trust fund, the tax-writing panels much preferred to do the latter. As John Cogan points out, the benefits of trust fund expenditures "could be specifically identified and were directly tied to the revenues raised, but general expenditures were more diffuse." Not only were the benefits of trust fund taxes more visible, but the tax-writing committees possessed jurisdiction over much of the related spending. By contrast, allocating the proceeds of taxes flowing into the general fund "would be determined by at least a dozen other committees" in Congress.[3]

Elliot Brownlee, eds., *Funding the Modern American State, 1941–1995: The Rise and Fall of Easy Finance*, (Cambridge and Washington, DC: Cambridge University Press and Woodrow Wilson Center Press and Cambridge University Press, 1996), 420–1.

[2] Pechman, *Federal Tax Policy*, table 3.1, 40.

[3] Cogan, The Dispersion of Spending Authority, 39–40. Cogan's analysis focuses on six major earmarked trust funds: Social Security, Railroad Retirement, Disability Insurance, Highway Trust Fund, Hospital Insurance, and Airport and Airways. These trust funds account for almost all trust fund receipts from the public.

Table 3.1. *Significant federal tax legislation: Truman to Reagan administrations*

Tax cuts are boxed

Administration	General Fund Taxes	Trust Fund Taxes
Truman	Revenue Act of 1948	Social Security Act of 1950
	Revenue Act of 1950 (Korean war)	
	Excess Profits Tax Act (Korean War)	
	Revenue Act of 1951 (Korean war)	
Eisenhower I	Internal Revenue Code of 1954	Social Security Act of 1954
	Excise Tax Reduction Act of 1954	Disability Insurance Act of 1956
Eisenhower II		Federal Highway Act of 1956
		Social Security Act of 1958
		Penny increase in gas tax for highways (1959)
Kennedy-Johnson	Revenue Act of 1962	Social Security Amendments of 1961
	Revenue Act of 1964	
Johnson	Excise Tax Reduction Act of 1965	Medicare Act of 1965
	Revenue and Expenditure Control Act of 1968 (Vietnam war)	
Nixon	Tax Reform Act of 1969	Airport and Airway Trust Fund (1970)
	Revenue Act of 1971	Social Security Amendments of 1972
Nixon-Ford	Tax Reduction Act of 1975	
	Tax Reform Act of 1976	
Carter	Tax Reduction and Simplification Act 1977	Black Lung Disability Trust Fund (1977)
		Social Security Amendments of 1977
	Revenue Act of 1978	Inland Waterway Trust Fund (1978)
	Crude Oil Windfall Profits Tax (1980)	Superfund Act (1980)
Reagan I	Economic Recovery Tax Act of 1981	Highway Revenue Act of 1982
	Tax Equity and Fiscal Responsibility Act (1982)	Social Security Rescue (1983)
		Railroad Retirement Revenue Act (1983)
	Deficit Reduction Act of 1984	Aquatic Resources Trust Fund (1984)
Reagan II	Omnibus Reconciliation Act of 1985	Major Superfund expansion (1986)
	Tax Reform Act of 1986 (immediate tax hike, but revenue neutral over 5 years)	Leaking Underground Storage Tank Trust Fund (1986)
		Harbor Maintenance Trust Fund (1986)
	Omnibus Reconciliation Act of 1987	Vaccine Injury Trust Fund (1987)
		Airport and Airway expansion (1987)
		Medicare Catastrophic Coverage Act of 1988 (repealed in 1989)

Sources: Joseph A. Pechman, *Federal Tax Policy*, Fourth Edition (Washington, DC: The Brookings Institution, 1983), table 3.1, 40; and David R. Mayhew, *Divided We Govern* (New Haven: Yale University Press, 1990), table 4.1, 52–73.

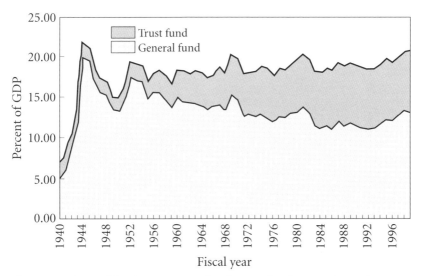

Figure 3.1 General fund versus trust fund taxes, fiscal years 1940–1999
Sources: David S. Koitz, Gene Falk, and Philip Winters, "Trust Funds and Federal Deficit," CRS Report for Congress (Washington, DC: Congressional Research Service, February 26, 1999), table A-1; Office of Management and Budget, *Budget of the United States Government, Fiscal Year 1999 – Historical Tables* (Washington, DC: Government Printing Office, 1998), table 1.3 and unpublished Office of Management and Budget data on file with author.

As a result of these tax-writing dynamics, total trust fund receipts increased from less than 2 percent of GDP in the early 1950s to 6 percent in the late 1970s, while the share of taxes flowing into the general fund declined by roughly three percentage points of GDP over this same period (figure 3.1). Again, most of the increase in trust fund taxes was due to payroll tax expansions. But trust funds also became an important repository of federal *excise* (selective sales) taxes. The total level of federal excise tax receipts declined by about 2 percent of GDP between 1950 and 1975. However, most of this decline reflected a drop-off in general fund excise tax revenues; overall trust fund excise receipts, by contrast, have remained quite steady since 1956, when the Highway Trust Fund was enacted (figure 3.2). In addition to highway construction, federal excise tax revenues have also been earmarked for the Airport and Airway Trust Fund, the Black Lung Disability Trust Fund, the Superfund, and several other trust funds.

In the mid 1980s, the Easy Financing era came to an end with falling inflation rates, the elimination of bracket creep by the indexing of

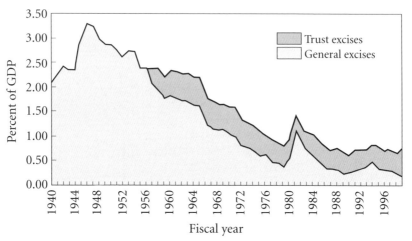

Figure 3.2 General fund versus trust fund excise taxes, fiscal years, 1940–1999
Sources: Office of Management and Budget, *Budget of the United States Government, Fiscal Year 1999 – Historical Tables* (Washington, DC: Government Printing Office, 1998), tables 1.3 and 2.4.

individual income taxes, the Reagan defense buildup, and the increase of the budget deficit. In the tight budget climate of the 1980s and 1990s – which Steurele calls the Fiscal Straitjacket Era – general fund taxes could no longer be cut without putting the budget further in the red. The trust fund side of the budget was also experiencing change. By the 1990s, the payroll tax was the largest tax most American families paid, and the spending precommitments built into the Social Security and Medicare systems had become massive. As the next chapter shows, payroll taxes had to be raised in both 1977 and 1983 merely to maintain trust fund solvency.

To sum up, the two big stories in federal taxation between the mid 1950s and mid 1990s are these: first, the overall stability in federal receipts as a percent GDP, and second the displacement of general fund taxes by trust fund taxes, especially social insurance receipts. These patterns were due to political decisions, not happenstance.[4] In the Easy Financing era, Congress and the president explicitly cut general fund taxes while pumping more money into trust fund activities. After the mid 1980s, further increases in trust fund taxes became less acceptable to taxpayers, but trust funds retained their share of total federal receipts because the government could no longer afford to enact large general tax cuts.

[4] Schick, *The Federal Budget*, 104.

Whether the recent emergence of unified budget surpluses will usher in a new federal tax regime remains to be seen.[5]

Trust funds vs. general funds: statistical analysis

In the remainder of this chapter, I present a statistical analysis of trust fund taxes and general fund taxes, focusing on the responsiveness of the two fund groups to key political variables. Details on data and methods are presented in the appendix.

Two objections might be raised to this exercise. First, trust fund revenues overwhelmingly finance social insurance *entitlements*, whereas most general fund taxes pay for *discretionary* programs. It might be argued that any observed differences between trust funds and general funds have nothing to do with the trust fund device *per se*. The entitlement status of the programs could be "doing all the work." But this objection is hard to sustain. The term "entitlement" actually first came into official usage in modern federal budgeting to refer precisely to those programs in which eligible persons gained an "earned right" to benefits because of their prior work and payroll tax "contributions."[6] Only much later did the term entitlement come to be applied more broadly. Historically, it was trust fund financing and earmarked taxes that carved out special fiscal treatment for federal programs.

A second possible objection to the comparison between trust funds and general funds is that the two revenue pools are supported by very different *types* of taxes. As I mentioned above, most income and corporate taxes flow into the general fund, but more than 95 percent of trust fund revenue comes from payroll taxes.

A straightforward way to respond to both of these methodological concerns simultaneously is to compare separately the performance of trust fund and general fund *excise taxes*.[7] This holds the nature of the tax

---

[5] The above analysis suggests that trust fund taxes should be stickier downward than general fund taxes, since trust fund receipts have been precommitted for future benefit promises. Indeed, if trust funds taxes are cut, it should occur in the context of reforms of the underlying social contracts between beneficiaries and the government (e.g., partial Social Security privatization). About $2 trillion of the $3 trillion ten-year unified budget surplus projected by the Congressional Budget Office in July 1999 comes from the surplus generated by the Social Security Trust Fund.

[6] John H. Makin and Norman J. Ornstein, *Debt and Taxes* (Washington, DC: The American Enterprise Institute, 1994), 223.

[7] Examples of general fund excises include taxes on cigarettes, beer, and telephone services. Trust fund excises include taxes on gasoline, airplane tickets, and domestically mined coal.

Table 3.2. *Growth rates and stability of selected categories of federal tax revenue, fiscal years 1948–1997*

Revenue stream	Mean annual growth rate (%)	Standard deviation	Fiscal years
Total federal taxes	1.3	2.9	1948–97
General fund	1.0	3.3	1948–97
(*Excise taxes only*)	(−0.7)	(7.5)	(1957–97)
Trust fund	2.6	2.7	1948–97
(*Excise Taxes only*)	(1.3)	(5.5)	(1957–97)

Note: Based on author's calculations.
Sources: Office of Management and Budget, *Budget of the United States Government, FY 1999 – Historical Tables* (Washington: Government Printing Office, 1998), Tables 1.2, 2.1, 2.4, and 2.5, and unpublished OMB data. Figures are based on receipts on the public. They exclude intrabudgetary transfers (such as interest earnings on trust fund investments) and offsetting receipts.

approximately constant. In addition, it controls for the legal status of the related budget outlays, because the affected spending programs are all considered discretionary, and not mandatory entitlements. If differences are found to exist in both sets of comparisons – between total trust fund receipts and total general fund receipts, and between trust fund excise tax revenues and general fund excise tax revenues – we can have more confidence that the trust fund structure is playing a role.

Examination of descriptive statistics provides a good starting place for these comparisons (see also table 3.2). Between fiscal years 1948 and 1997 total federal taxes (measured in constant 1992 dollars) grew on average by 1.3 percent per year in real terms, with a standard deviation of 2.9 percent.[8] But total trust fund taxes increased by an average annual rate of 2.6 percent in real terms over this period while total general fund taxes increased by only 1.0 percent annually. Overall, trust receipts were also slightly more stable than general receipts, as evidenced by their smaller standard deviation. These patterns hold when just the excise tax portions of the two revenue streams are examined. While trust fund excises increased on average by 1.3 percent per year, general fund excise taxes

---

[8] Percentage change calculations are based on log (Receipts$_t$ /Receipts$_{t-1}$) in order to provide a symmetric distribution.

declined on average by -0.7 percent. Trust fund taxes excise taxes were also the more stable of the two, with a standard deviation of 5.5 percent compared to 7.5 percent for general fund excise taxes.

Political variables in regression models

A considerable political science literature exists on the politics of taxation. Among the variables hypothesized to influence tax policy outcomes are presidential party, partisan configurations (unified vs. divided government), and lawmakers' preferences. The regressions presented below explore the impact of each of these factors.

1 Presidential party. Many scholars argue that partisan politics has a significant influence on fiscal policy.[9] The claim is that the two parties have different distributional and macroeconomic goals and that party leaders have the capacity to push outcomes in their preferred direction. Scholars often focus on *presidential* party since the historical record indicates that the tax bills enacted by Congress usually hew closely to the revenue targets proposed in the executive budget.[10] Dennis Quinn and Robert Shapiro, for example, demonstrate that taxes on business firms and their owners are higher under Democratic presidents than under Republican ones.[11] Presidential party has also been shown to affect certain spending outcomes. According to one study, Democratic presidents operate at a higher level of non-defense regular appropriations than Republican presidents.[12]

2 Partisan regime. Scholars have also examined the influence of partisan regime (unified vs. divided government) on taxation. Some believe that the capacity to mobilize resources is negatively influenced by divided government. The claim is that divided government makes it more difficult for elected officials to reach a consensus on spending priorities, the allocation of the tax burden, or both. While the literature remain thin, some empirical support for this view exists. For example, states with

[9] See, for example, Douglas Hibbs, *The American Political Economy* (Cambridge, MA: Harvard University Press, 1987).

[10] Paul E. Peterson, "The New Politics of Deficits," in John E. Chubb and Paul E. Peterson, eds., *The New Directions in American Politics* (Washington, DC: Brookings Institution, 1985), 381.

[11] Dennis P. Quinn and Robert Y. Shapiro, "Business Political Power: The Case of Taxation," *American Political Science Review*, 85(3), September 1991, 851–74.

[12] Christopher Wlezien, "The President, Congress and Appropriations, 1951–1985," *American Politics Quarterly*, 24(1), January 1996, 43–67.

divided governments have been shown to produce lower levels of revenue than states with unified governments, controlling for a range of economic and political factors.[13] Divided government states (especially states with divided legislatures) have also been found to be slower in reacting to unanticipated "revenue shocks" that lead to budget deficits.[14]

The impact of divided government on federal taxation has been studied by Gary Cox and Mathew McCubbins.[15] They argue that officeholders' are more inclined to raise taxes when their party controls both branches of government, because unified control gives them more say over both the incidence of taxation (who pays) and where the money goes. In contrast, divided regimes strengthen the bargaining position of the out-party, giving their members a greater opportunity to depress real tax levels, either through legislated tax cuts or through bureaucratic actions (e.g., relaxing audit procedures) that offer the equivalent of a tax cut without explicit legislation.

Based on a regression analysis of federal taxes over the 1934–88 period, Cox and McCubbins find evidence that divided government matters. In particular, shifts away from unified Democratic control lead to reductions in the baseline level of revenues. One major limitation of the Cox–McCubbins analysis, however, is that it examines federal taxes at the highest level of aggregation (total federal revenues). Their analysis thus ignores the crucial distinction between general funds and trust funds.

3 Political preferences. One potential motivation for creating trust funds is to insulate programs from shifts in political preferences resulting from electoral swings. Keith Krehbiel in his important book Pivotal Politics demonstrates that preference changes have a major influence on US lawmaking. Krehbiel's central argument is that what Congress does ultimately depends on the preferences of "pivotal" lawmakers – those lawmakers who (given the preferences of the other players) are in a unique position either to break a filibuster in the Senate or to cast the deciding vote to override a presidential veto. These pivotal players may be either close together or quite far apart, depending upon the distribution

[13] W. Mark Crain and Timothy J. Muris, "Legislative Organization of Fiscal Policy," Journal of Law and Economics, October 1995, 311–33.

[14] James E. Alt and Robert C. Lowery, "Divided Government, Fiscal Institutions, and Budget Deficits: Evidence From the States," American Political Science Review, 88(4), December 1994, 811–28.

[15] Gary W. Cox and Mathew McCubbins, "Divided Control of Fiscal Policy," in Gary W. Cox and Samuel Kernell, Eds., The Politics of Divided Government (Boulder, CO: Westview Press, 1991).

of preferences in a given Congress. In particular, the distance between the filibuster and veto pivots defines what Krehbiel calls the "gridlock interval." The width of the gridlock interval in any given Congress can be measured through an "interelection swing method," which uses the size of partisan swings in presidential and midterm elections as proxies of "changing preferences as manifested in the composition of the Congress and the presidency."[16] Krehbiel shows that expansion of the gridlock interval impedes legislative productivity, as measured by the number of important laws enacted. Since taxation is a subset of lawmaking – and certainly a subset of "important" lawmaking – I explore the impact of changes in the gridlock interval on tax policy outcomes.

Theoretical expectations for general revenues

The literature thus generates three main expectations for the influence of key political factors on general tax levels (table 3.3). First, general tax collections should be higher under Democratic administrations. Second, general fund taxes should decline during periods of divided government. Finally, general revenues should increase when the gridlock interval expands. The intuition behind this last expectation requires elaboration.

Whether and how changes in the distribution of preferences affect any given policy outcome depends crucially upon the location of the status quo. In the case of legislative productivity, for example, the "reversion point" is no new legislation. Without positive action, nothing happens. Krehbiel thus hypothesizes (and empirically shows) that an expansion of the gridlock interval – that is, an expansion of the region in which proposed policies can be killed either through a filibuster or a presidential veto – impedes legislative productivity. As Krehbiel observes, however, most taxes, including most income, corporate, and payroll taxes, "do *not* revert to zero in the absence of a new law. Rather, the core features of the tax code remain intact at previously legislated levels."[17] In other words, if Congress does nothing, tax revenues will still rise automatically because of economic growth and (before indexing) bracket creep. Positive action (e.g., legislated tax cuts) is required to counteract these effects. But such

---

[16] Keith Krehbiel, *Pivotal Politics* (Chicago: University of Chicago Press, 1998), 58.

[17] Krehbiel, *Pivotal Politics*, 206, fn. 29. Certain trust fund excise taxes are in fact among the very few exceptions to this rule. Such taxes are typically authorized for two to ten year periods. If the gridlock interval widens at precisely the moment such taxes lapse, reauthorization could be more difficult. Given that the need for reauthorization does not occur annually (unlike, say, ordinary appropriations), it is not obvious how much this should matter. I therefore retain the two basic trust fund hypotheses for the excise tax model.

Table 3.3. *Summary of hypotheses*

Political variable	General funds	Trust funds	
		Hypothesis 1 *Much ado about nothing*	Hypothesis 2 *Political independence*
Democratic president	$B > 0$	$B > 0$	$B = 0$
Transition to Republican administration	$B < 0$	$B < 0$	$B = 0$
Divided government	$B < 0$	$B < 0$	$B = 0$
Expansion of gridlock interval	$B > 0$	$B > 0$	$B = 0$

action becomes more difficult as the gridlock interval widens. Accordingly, the expectation is that the coefficient on the gridlock interval variable in the general fund model will be positive.[18]

Theoretical expectations for trust funds

The data can be used to test two alternative hypotheses about the impact of politics on trust fund revenues (table 3.3). I label the first a *Much Ado About Nothing* hypothesis. The claim is that no important differences will be observed in the responsiveness of trust fund and general funds to the political factors under consideration. All the expectations for general funds noted above should hold for trust funds as well. Credible support for this hypothesis would imply that trust funds are merely "general funds with a different label."

An alternative view is that trust funds revenues are totally unaffected by the political variables – what might be called a *Political Independence* hypothesis. The prediction is that the coefficients on each political variable in the trust fund model will be zero. Because the claim being tested here is that the political variables have *no effect*, conventional

---

[18] Of course, expansions of the gridlock interval also inhibit legislated tax *increases*. But peacetime tax increases are seldom popular. So the impact of expansions of the gridlock interval on revenue levels is unlikely to be symmetric.

thresholds of statistical significance (0.05 or even 0.10) are actually not conservative enough. They make it too easy to reject the null hypothesis in favor of the theorized "no impact" relationship.[19] Accordingly, I use a 0.35 level (two-tailed) as a reasonable cut-off for tests of the *Political Independence* hypothesis. Results that are not significant at even this conservative level provide reasonable statistical support for the "no impact" hypothesis. Neither position is strongly supported if results fall within the intermediate zone ($0.10 < p < 0.35$).

Data and model specification

Three sets of models are presented below. The first of the three examines total federal taxes, total general fund taxes, and total trust fund taxes over the fiscal period 1948–1997 (results are reported in table 3.4). The key political variables are (1) partisan regime (divided or unified government); (2) presidential administration (Democratic or Republican); (3) a presidential transition variable to capture the first full-year revenue impact of the transition from an administration of one party to the other; and (4) change in the gridlock interval following the most recent federal election.

Each specification includes a lagged dependent variable, because this year's level of taxation is heavily influenced by last year's level. Although trust funds and general funds may exhibit different political dynamics, it seems unrealistic to model the two revenue streams as completely independent. To do so would be to incorrectly assume, as Joseph White and the late Aaron Wildavsky wrote, that the "right ear pays income taxes and the left foot social security, so the person who pays has no glimmer of the total tax burden."[20] Both the trust fund and general fund models thus include on the right-hand side the lagged level of the other revenue stream to reflect these interdependencies.[21]

The next set of models (results reported in table 3.5) compares the responsiveness of trust fund and general fund *excise taxes*. The time series covers the fiscal period 1957–97, because no excise-tax trust funds existed

---

[19] See George Julnes and Lawrence B. Mohr. 1989. "Analysis of No-Difference Findings in Evaluation Research," *Evaluation Review*, 13, 628–55.

[20] Joseph White and Aaron Wildavsky, *The Deficit and the Public Interest* (Berkeley: University of California Press, 1989), 328.

[21] Significant interdependencies have been found on the spending side of the budget. For example, this year's defense spending is influenced by last year's entitlement spending. See Mark S. Kamlet and David C. Mowery, "Influences on Executive and Congressional Budgetary Priorities, 1955–1983," *American Political Science Review*, 81(1), March 1987, 155–78.

Table 3.4. *Determinants of total, general fund, and trust fund taxes, fiscal years 1948–1997*

	Coefficient		
Variable	*Total receipts*	*General funds*	*Trust funds*
Total receipts $_{t-1}$	0.45***		
	(0.11)		
General receipts $_{t-1}$		0.71***	−0.05
		(0.09)	(0.03)
Trust receipts $_{t-1}$		−1.32***	0.52***
		(0.24)	(0.08)
GDP	0.10***	0.15***	0.05***
	(0.02)	(0.02)	(0.01)
CPI	0.41	−0.85	−0.00
	(1.19)	(0.91)	(0.32)
Korean War	48.78***	70.96***	1.71
	(18.78)	(14.65)	(5.06)
Vietnam War	33.2*	15.73	2.16
	(17.30)	(13.18)	(4.55)
Divided government	−12.86	−13.50*	3.53#
	(9.88)	(7.37)	(2.55)
Gridlock interval	2.09***	1.83***	−0.16#
	(0.61)	(0.46)	(0.16)
Democratic president $_{t-1}$	16.05	7.35	−0.57
	(10.91)	(8.30)	(2.87)
Democratic transition $_{t-1}$	−0.71	−3.35	3.37
	(14.95)	(11.12)	(3.84)
Republican transition $_{t-1}$	−16.20	−23.52*	−5.53#
	(16.51)	(12.51)	(4.32)
Constant	18.82	−122.63***	−47.92***
	(12.33)	(36.20)	(12.51)
Adj. R Square	0.99	0.99	0.99
(*N*)	(50)	(50)	(50)

Notes: Standard errors in parentheses; two-tailed tests.
*** $p < 0.01$; **$0.01 < p < 0.05$; *$p < 0.10$
# $p < 0.35$ (for tests of *Political Independence* hypothesis only)

Table 3.5. *Determinants of general fund and trust fund excise taxes, fiscal years 1957–1997*

	Coefficient	
Variable	General excises	Trust excises
General excises$_{t-1}$	0.71***	0.01
	(0.19)	(0.06)
Trust excises$_{t-1}$	−0.32	0.71***
	(0.34)	(0.11)
GDP $_{t-1}$	0.00	0.00***
	(0.00)	(0.00)
CPI$_{t-1}$	0.26	−0.38***
	(0.37)	(0.13)
Divided government	−6.24***	0.61
	(2.40)	(0.81)
Gridlock interval	0.39**	−0.05
	(0.18)	(0.06)
Democratic president$_{t-1}$	1.52	−0.22
	(2.83)	(0.95)
Democratic transition$_{t-1}$	−6.18*	2.01*
	(3.29)	(1.10)
Republican transition$_{t-1}$	2.35	1.60#
	(3.96)	(1.33)
Constant	17.35	3.25
	(12.04)	(4.05)
Adj. R Square	0.81	0.87
(*N*)	(41)	(41)

Notes: Standard errors in parentheses; two-tailed tests.
*** $p < 0.01$; **$0.01 < p < 0.05$; * $p < 0.10$
# $p < 0.35$ (for tests of *Political Independence* Hypothesis only)

earlier. The political variables are the same as in the aggregate taxation models.

In the final set of regressions (results in table 3.6), the dependent variables are tax *rates* rather than tax dollars. I examine the responsiveness of (1) individual income top bracket rates, (2) current payroll tax rates for Social Security, and (3) "ultimate" Social Security tax rates over the 1947–96 calendar-year period. The current payroll tax rate is the actual combined employee–employer payroll rate in effect during any year. The

Table 3.6. *Determinants of top income, current Social Security, and ultimate Social Security tax rates, 1947–1996*

Variable	Coefficient		
	Top income bracket	Current social security rate	Ultimate social security rate
Income rate$_{t-1}$	0.87***	−0.00	
	(0.06)	(0.01)	
Current Social Security Rate$_{t-1}$	−0.85***	0.74***	
	(0.06)	(0.13)	
Ultimate Social Security Rate$_{t-1}$		0.68***	
		(0.12)	
Trust fund assets		0.40	−0.59**
		(0.46)	(0.28)
Social Insurance Benefits		0.17#	0.16*
		(0.12)	(0.09)
Ratio of workers to beneficiaries		−0.07*	−0.06**
		(0.04)	(0.03)
Gridlock interval	0.02	−0.01#	−0.01#
	(0.11)	(0.01)	(0.01)
Divided government	−1.99	0.24*	−0.01
	(1.69)	(0.14)	(0.10)
Election year	−0.31	−0.078	0.09#
	(1.31)	(0.10)	(0.08)
Democratic president$_{t-1}$	−1.39	0.17#	−0.23**
	(1.63)	(0.13)	(0.10)
Democratic Transition$_{t-1}$	2.38	0.03	−0.03
	(2.86)	(0.21)	(0.16)
Republican Transition$_{t-1}$	−7.24**	−0.21	−0.48**
	(2.92)	(0.25)	(0.21)
Constant	16.89**	1.93	3.07***
	(7.12)	(1.32)	(0.91)
Adj. R Square (N)	0.96	0.98	0.97
	(50)	(50)	(50)

Notes: Standard errors in parentheses; two-tailed tests.
*** $p < 01$; **$0.01 < p < 0.05$; * $p < 0.10$
# $p < 0.35$ (for tests of *Political Independence* Hypothesis only)

ultimate Social Security rate is the final combined payroll tax rate that *would* be in effect if the long-range tax schedule contained in any given Social Security Act were followed. This ultimate tax rate is designed to ensure the system's long-term solvency. The original Social Security Act of 1935 called for an ultimate rate of 6 percent in 1949. The ultimate rate was changed many times by subsequent Congresses and reached 12.4 percent under legislation enacted in 1977. What makes the ultimate tax rates important is not that the schedule contained in any Social Security Act has been followed, but rather that it provides a proxy measure of the scope of the future benefit promises that current officeholders intend for their political successors to inherit.

While the first two sets of models control for GDP and inflation, special economic and demographic control variables are required in the payroll tax rate equations to capture the dynamics of Social Security financing. The first control is the annual level of assets of the Social Security (Old Age Survivors and Disability Insurance) Trust Fund, measured as the fund balance at the beginning of the year as a percent of outlays during the year. The second is the prior moving average of the ratio of covered workers to beneficiaries. The final control is the total benefits paid from the social insurance trust funds in the current year as a percent of personal income. These models also include an election year variable because tax rate changes are often adopted in election years.

Results

The results shown in table 3.4 indicate that the total level of federal tax revenues is significantly influenced by changes in lawmakers' preferences, as captured by shifts in the composition of Congress and the presidency.[22]

---

[22] The core finding of this chapter – that trust funds and general funds respond in markedly different ways to key political factors – appears fairly robust. This basic difference between the responsiveness of trust fund and general fund revenues, for example, holds when the model specification is identical to the one (cited above) used by Cox and McCubbins in their study of divided government and federal taxation. In the Cox–McCubbins set-up, both the dependent variable (tax receipts) and the economic control variables are measured in partial log terms and the only independent political variables are various configurations of divided government (e.g., unified Republican control, Republican control of the presidency, and Democratic control of Congress, etc.). I report these results in Eric M. Patashnik, "Divided Government, Partisan Politics, and Tax Policy Outcomes – Does Structure Matter?" paper presented at the meeting of the Midwest Political Science Association, Chicago, Illinois, April 10–12, 1997. In this conference paper, I also experimented with generalized least square regressions but the major findings did not change. I wish to thank Prof. McCubbins for generously sharing his data set with me.

A one unit increase in the gridlock interval (which would occur if the president's party lost one Senate seat and 4.35 House seats) increases total revenue by 2.1 billion (constant 1992) dollars, everything else being equal. No other political variable is statistically significant in this model at the 0.10 level.

Stronger evidence of political responsiveness is seen in the general fund model. The results are mostly consistent with hypothesized relationships. The gridlock variable has the strongest statistical relationship ($p < 0.01$). A one unit expansion of the gridlock interval increases general taxes by approximately two billion dollars. The divided government variable also is significant and has the expected sign. General taxes are negatively influenced by split partisan control, declining by $13.5 billion on average when government is divided. The party of the president influences general fund taxes, but only during Republican transitions. General revenues drop by $23.5 billion during the first year after Republican presidents replace Democrats. The large negative coefficient of the lagged trust fund revenue variable (significant at $p < 0.01$) indicates that the two revenue streams are indeed interdependent. As trust fund revenues have increased, general tax collections have been squeezed.

The results for the trust fund equation do not support the *Much Ado About Nothing* claim. Indeed, the coefficients on both the gridlock and divided government variables have signs (negative and positive, respectively) *opposite* of those in the general fund specification, although both coefficients are small. Neither variable is significant at the 0.10 level. While the Republican transition variable does have the same sign (negative) as in the general fund equation, it is not significant at the 0.10 level. The *Political Independence* hypothesis is also not well supported. If the deck is properly stacked against finding support for the "no impact" claim by adopting a significance level of $p < 0.35$, then three political variables (gridlock interval, divided government, and Republican transition) do pass this threshold. These intermediate results are strong enough to cast doubt on the claim that trust funds are totally independent of political factors, yet they are still too weak to give us much confidence either that the observed political effects are true or that the actual relationships are strong ones. It should be noted that the divided government variable, which was negative in the general fund specification, has a *positive* coefficient in this model. Both the Democratic presidency and Democratic transition variables are insignificant at even the 0.35 level.

Table 3.5 presents results for the two excise tax models. The results indicate that general fund excise taxes and trust fund excise taxes respond to the same political forces in markedly different ways. Both the gridlock and divided government variables have the expected effects in the general fund model and both are statistically significant at the 0.05 level or better. Excise taxes flowing into the general fund fall by about $400 million when the gridlock interval expands by one unit. They decline by $6 billion when control of government is divided. The only presidential control variable that is statistically significant at the 0.10 level is the Democratic transition variable. Contrary to expectations, however, transitions to Democratic Administrations lead to a $6 billion falloff in general excise tax collections. One possible (*ex post*) explanation is that cigarette and beer taxes – which historically have accounted for a large share of general fund excise tax revenues – are not popular with Democratic constituencies, especially when the proceeds are not targeted for popular programs.

The one political variable that is significant at the 0.10 level in the trust fund excise tax model is the Democratic transition variable. But, while this variable had a negative coefficient in the general fund excise tax model, now it is positive. Transitions to Democratic Administrations increase trust fund excise taxes by about $2 billion. Both the gridlock and divided government variables have signs opposite from those in the general fund excise tax model, although neither coefficient is significant.

The final set of models explore the determinants of income and payroll tax rates (table 3.6). Both the divided government and gridlock variables have the expected signs (negative and positive, respectively) in the income tax rate model, but neither coefficient is significant at the 0.10 level. The negative effect of divided government on general fund receipts (observed in table 3.4) apparently occurs through a mechanism (e.g., corporate tax cuts, loophole expansions, etc.) other than cuts in the top individual income tax brackets. What is clearly associated with reductions in top marginal tax rates is the replacement of Democratic presidents with Republicans. Republican transitions cause top individual rates to decline by about 7 percent. This very large effect cannot be chalked up merely to the 1981 Reagan tax cut. If a dummy variable for the Reagan transition is added to the model, it has a significant coefficient of -4.5, but the Republican transition dummy remains substantively unchanged and significant at the 0.015 level. Finally, the results suggest that there is a clear tradeoff between current Social Security payroll tax rates and income tax rates. A 1 percent increase in payroll taxes leads to a 0.87 percent decrease in top marginal rates, all else being equal.

The results of the model in the middle column of table 3.6 indicate that current Social Security rates rise by about 2 percent during periods of divided control (significant at the 0.10 level). Recall that the divided government dummy was also positive in the aggregate trust fund model (table 3.4). To the extent divided government affects trust fund taxes, then, it *boosts* them. This finding is an important refinement of the argument that divided government is always a force for tax reductions; in fact, divided government can also be a force for tax expansions. The actual effect of divided control on tax policy outcomes is importantly mediated by whether revenues are channeled into trust funds.

Why might divided government have a negative influence on general fund taxes but a positive one on certain trust fund levies? One possible explanation – which these data cannot test directly – is that trust funds reduce conflict over the allocation of revenues. When money flows into the general fund, it can be used for programs that disproportionately benefit constituents of the majority party. This may decrease somewhat the "appetite for taxation" among members of the other party. When funds are precommitted for trust funds, however, there is less uncertainty over how the money will be spent. At the same time, proposing cuts in earmarked taxes may be risky for blame-avoiding politicians. The clienteles who stand to benefit from trust fund spending may well view any proposed tax cut as a blatant attempt to defund their programs. By contrast, the impact of the loss of revenue from a general tax cut is diffused throughout the entire budget. No particular expenditure clientele is targeted so no group has a particular incentive to mobilize.

Two other variables (gridlock interval and Democratic Administration) become significant in the current payroll tax model if a cutoff of 0.35 is used. Taken together, these results cast additional doubt on both of the main hypotheses under consideration. While an expansion of the gridlock interval leads to higher general fund taxes (table 3.4), it *lowers* payroll tax rates. In addition, payroll tax rates are higher under Democratic presidents. The Republican transition variable does have a substantively important negative coefficient, but it does not pass even a 0.35 threshold.

The final equation in table 3.6 examines ultimate Social Security tax rates. Note first that each of the three key control variables (social insurance benefits, worker to beneficiary ratio, trust fund assets) has the expected sign and is statistically significant. Ultimate Social Security tax rates have risen with both increases in social insurance spending and decreases in the ratio of workers to beneficiaries. They have fallen with increases in the size of the trust fund balance. In contrast to the current payroll tax rate model, the coefficient of the divided government variable has a very small negative (insignificant) coefficient. The presidential control variables have complex effects. The results suggest that Democratic administrations lower ultimate Social Security tax rates by 2.3 percent, everything else being equal. The decrease in ultimate Social

Security rates is even larger, however, during Republican transitions. Ultimate payroll tax rates decline by 4.8 percent when Republican presidents replace Democrats. Two other political variables (gridlock interval and election year) become significant if a 0.35 standard is used. As in the current payroll tax equation, the gridlock variable has a small negative coefficient. In addition, the election variable has a positive coefficient. This is not surprising because many of the election-year Social Security benefit increases that Congress enacted between 1950 and 1972 provided for ultimate payroll tax rate increases to maintain the program's actuarial solvency. Overall, the results of the two payroll tax models in table 3.6 undercut the claim that Social Security taxes have been totally independent of political factors such as partisanship and divided government. At the same time, it is important to note that Republican transitions have a stronger impact on ultimate than on current Social Security rates. This suggests that payroll tax politics have consisted, not only of the normal sort of bargaining among current officeholders that taxation always produces, but also of political struggles over distant futures.

Conclusions

Neither the *Much Ado About Nothing* nor the *Political Independence* hypotheses emerge from this chapter with much credibility. Contrary to the *Political Independence* hypothesis, trust funds are responsive to political factors, especially if an appropriately conservative standard is used to evaluate the "no-impact" claim. But – and this is the crucial point – trust fund taxes and general fund taxes have responded to political stimuli in quite different ways.

General fund taxes tend to rise when there are large electoral swings and the size of the gridlock interval expands. Trust funds do not. To the extent that divided government has a negative influence on taxes, it is mainly general funds, and not trust funds, that pay the price. While general fund excise taxes fall after Democratic presidents take over from Republicans, trust fund excise taxes rise. The one political variable that has the most negative influence on federal tax levels is Republican transitions. Trust funds are not completely isolated from this phenomenon, but the negative impact of the Republican transition variable is significant at the 0.10 level in only one trust fund specification. At a minimum, then, trust funds seem to dampen the immediate negative influence of transitions to Republican control.

In sum, the statistical results presented in this chapter indicate that while earmarking through trust funds does not remove taxes from politics, it does mediate policy outcomes. A careful understanding of how trust funds shape the politics of promise-keeping for specific programs requires a detailed analysis of actual cases, the research approach of chapters 4 through 9.

Appendix

This Appendix describes the data and methods used in the statistical analysis presented in this chapter.

First, a word about definitions: Technically, the federal government does not have general revenues. The government classifies its budget accounts into two major fund groups: trust funds and federal funds. The largest component of federal funds is the general fund (about 90 percent of the total). The remaining 10 percent of federal funds include revolving funds, intragovernmental funds, and special funds. Revolving funds (e.g., the Postal Service Fund and the Export Import Bank) generate income through continuing cycles of business-like activity. They are programmatically quite different from most trust funds, as are intragovernmental funds (which exist to facilitate transactions within and between federal agencies).

Special funds (e.g., the National Park Service's Operation and Maintenance of Quarters account) are similar to trust funds in every respect but two: (1) they are not designated as trust funds in law; and (2) most special funds do not earn interest on their balances, whereas most trust funds do. Special funds are not specifically examined in this study because they are economically insignificant (comprising less than 0.5 percent of total revenues), because federal budget documents make it difficult to trace their activities (trust funds are easier for scholars to monitor, not just interest groups!), and because the programs they finance are of little political interest. I treat the entire federal fund group as general funds for purposes of this chapter.

The statistical analysis presented in this chapter examines trust fund taxes rather than spending for several reasons. First, it sidesteps a key methodological problem: accounting for the "intrabudgetary" transfers between the trust fund and general fund groups. Such transfers (e.g., interest earnings on trust fund securities) account for a non-trivial amount of spending out of certain trust funds. Second, the most appropriate measure of current congressional spending policy is not annual outlays but rather annual budget authority. Normally, budget authority is based on the appropriations bills enacted by Congress. In the past, however, the government has often measured the budget authority of certain trust funds as the total income to the fund. As a result, it is difficult to compare budget authority across trust funds and general funds. Finally, trust funds statutes are in fact located in the tax code; that's where they exist in public law. The approach of this chapter thus follows the practices of the Office of Management and Budget, which splits out trust funds on the revenue side of the federal budget.

Data and methods

The dependent variables in the models shown in tables 3.4 and 3.5 are based on tax receipts from the public, or what the Office of Management and Budget (OMB) calls "governmental receipts." Intrabudgetary transfers and offsetting receipts from the public are excluded. In sum, this chapter examines earmarked tax revenues, not all trust fund income sources.

Data on current dollar total federal tax revenues, trust fund excise tax revenues, and general fund excise tax revenues are from the OMB, *Budget of the United States Government – Historical Tables*, Tables 2.1 and 2.4 (Washington, DC), various years. Data on trust funds taxes from 1947 to 1989 are from David S. Koitz, Gene Falk, and Philip Winters, "Trust Funds and Federal Deficit," Congressional Research Service Report for Congress (Washington, DC, February 26, 1999), table A-1. Data for later years are from an unpublished historical series obtained from the Office of Management and Budget, on file with the author. General fund taxes are simply total federal taxes minus trust fund taxes. Nominal tax dollars were converted into real 1992 dollars using the total composite outlay deflator reported by OMB, *Budget of the United States government, Fiscal Year 1999 – Historical Tables*, table 10.1, 169.

Income tax rate data in table 3.6 are from Joseph Pechman, *Federal Tax Policy*, Fourth Edition (Washington, DC: The Brookings Institution, 1983), Table A-1 and from unpublished data obtained from the Tax Foundation. Data on Social Security tax rates in table 3.6 are from Robert J. Myers, *Social Security*, Fourth Edition (Philadelphia: University of Pennsylvania Press, 1993), tables 2.13 and 3.3.

The models in table 3.4 control for real gross domestic product in the current fiscal year and for the percentage change in the Consumer Price Index (CPI-U) during the fiscal year. These economic controls are lagged by one fiscal year to provide a better fit of the excise tax models shown in table 3.5. Nominal GDP figures and GDP deflators are from OMB, *Budget of the US Government, Fiscal Year 1999 – Historical Tables*, table 10.1. CPI figures are from Bureau of Labor Statistics data reported in the *Economic Indicators Handbook* (Detroit: Gale Research, 1992, 228–9) and from the *Economic Report of the President* (Washington, DC: Government Printing Office, various years).

The Korean War variable in table 3.4 takes on a value of 1 in fiscal years 1951 and 1952; 0 otherwise. The Vietnam War takes on a value of 1 in fiscal years 1969 and 1970. The two war variables did not influence the results of the excise tax models and are therefore omitted from table 3.5.

A president's first complete budget submission takes place in the fiscal year two years after the calendar year of his election. So, for example, the fiscal year 1982 budget was Reagan's first. Preliminary runs showed that the presidential control variable provided a better fit when lagged by a year. So, the dummy variable for fiscal years of Democratic administrations takes on a value of 1 in fiscal years 1948–54, 1963–70, 1979–82, and 1995–7; 0 otherwise. The presidential transition variables were also lagged by one year. The Democratic transition variable is thus coded one in fiscal years 1963 (Kennedy), 1979 (Carter), and 1995 (Clinton); the Republican transition variable is coded one in fiscal 1955 (Eisenhower), 1971 (Nixon), and 1983 (Reagan).

The divided government dummy variable is coded one in fiscal years of divided control (fiscal years 1948–9, 54–5, 56–61, 70–7, 82–93, and 96–7).

The gridlock interval data are reported in Krehbiel, *Pivotal Politics*, table 3.3, 59. The same gridlock interval measure is used for both years of the two-year Congress.

The trust fund balance variable in table 3.6 is calculated from the expenditure and asset figures shown in tables 4.A1 and 4.A3 of the Social Security Administration, *Social Security Bulletin, Annual Statistical Supplement, 1997*. The data on the ratio of covered workers to beneficiaries is from the web site of the Office of the Chief Actuary, Social Security Administration: http://www.ssa.gov/OACT/STATS/workerBenies.html.

The data on total social insurance benefits are from table 4.A4, Social Security Administration, *Social Security Bulletin*.

4

Social security

As the largest and most important trust fund program in the US budget, Social Security provides an excellent case for exploring the distinctive strengths and weaknesses of trust fund financing as a precommitment strategy.[1] The main argument of this chapter is that the Social Security Trust Fund has been a highly effective instrument for binding politicians to spending promises based on a reciprocal exchange of tax payments now in return for benefits later. The trust fund structure has strengthened the program's budgetary claims in two closely linked ways.

First, it has promoted Social Security's financial autonomy, insulating program spending from regular processes of fiscal control. In general, Social Security cutbacks have been off limits except in the context of internally defined "solvency" crises. Second, the trust fund mechanism has institutionalized the use of elaborate actuarial and long-range estimation techniques. The overall effect has been to reinforce the future orientation of Social Security policymaking, further isolating the program's taxing and spending from short-term partisan forces and economic conditions. In sum, the trust fund device has greatly enhanced Social Security's political strength, providing program builders with the institutional raw materials they needed to fashion a formidable coalition between current and future beneficiaries and to endow the program's spending commitments with moral potency.

---

[1] Unless otherwise noted I use the term Social Security Trust Fund to refer to the Old-Age and Survivors Insurance Trust Fund. There is another (much smaller) trust fund for Disability Insurance. The financial flows of the two trust funds are sometimes combined in actuarial reports.

But all governance structures have their limitations and the Social Security Trust Fund is no exception. It is one thing for current politicians to establish claims against future budgets; it is quite another thing to actually set aside the money to pay for those claims. While the trust fund has been highly effective as a mechanism for entrenching spending promises, its capacity to advance fund the system's liabilities has historically been very weak. Payroll tax revenues have flowed into the US Treasury and trust fund surpluses have been "invested" in federal securities. But these securities are technically no more than IOUs from the Government. They do not consist of pools of cash that can be directly used to finance benefits payments. By characterizing Social Security reserves as economically meaningless, right-wing critics have sought to erode public faith in the system's future credibility. The trust fund has thus had a huge impact, not merely on the structure of the policy choices elected officials have faced, but on the framing of the broader struggle over the American welfare state.

Origins

The framers of the Social Security Act of 1935 deliberately conditioned eligibility for benefits on workers' contributions in order to distinguish the program from welfare, instill perceptions of earned rights, and make the payroll tax politically acceptable. The 1935 Act did not actually create a formal trust fund structure. The Old-Age Survivors Insurance ("Social Security") Trust Fund was not officially established until the Social Security Act Amendments of 1939. Legal considerations, not indifference, were responsible for the four-year delay.

According to J. Douglas Brown, one of Social Security's original designers, "The planners of the old-age insurance program had always intended that, so far as was possible, the financing of the system should be kept distinct from the general fiscal operations of government."[2] While Social Security's designers meant to insulate the program from the vicissitudes of the general budget, they did not denigrate the value of fiscal restraint. On the contrary, Social Security's drafters viewed non-contributory pension proposals like the Townsend Plan with apprehension and horror. Social Security's planners consciously saw themselves as the architects of a permanent social institution. In their view, the sustainability of this institution depended on both public faith and on explicit "safeguards" against the "opportunistic actions" of short-sighted

---

[2] Brown, *Essays on Social Security*, 42–3.

lawmakers.[3] They believed that control over Social Security outlays should be promoted, not through an external competition with other government programs, but rather by establishing a stable equilibrium between the desire of workers/taxpayers for greater benefits and their reluctance to pay more.[4]

Social Security's planners thus always intended to create something akin to a trust fund mechanism. At the time of the Social Security bill's drafting, however, it was uncertain whether a bill that levied earmarked taxes to pay for a national social insurance program could pass constitutional muster.[5] According to Thomas Eliot, chief draftsman of the 1935 Act:

> There was a great fear, which became more acute a little later, that this didn't have a chance, constitutionally speaking. In 1933, Congress had passed the Agricultural Adjustment Act which levied a processing tax on the processing of agricultural products. It took the proceeds and paid them to farmers who agreed to cooperate to reduce production by leaving acres fallow or by not raising little pigs. The question was whether it was constitutional for Congress to take the proceeds of a particular tax and pay them over in this fashion, even for a purpose that might be said to be for the general welfare. The prediction of some of us that the Triple A – the Agricultural Adjustment Act – would be held unconstitutional was borne out a few months later . . . You can see the parallel with what we were proposing in 1935 in the Social Security Bill. A special tax, in effect, on employers and employees and the payment of benefits to the employees made possible by the proceeds of that tax.[6]

To make it easier for a fence-sitting Justice to distinguish Social Security from the Triple A by arguing (contrary to the whole philosophy of the program) that payroll taxes and benefit payments were unrelated, Eliot placed the tax and benefit provisions in separate titles of the bill. Having drafted the measure in this way, it would have been self-defeating to craft a formal trust fund since this would have only called attention to the

---

3 *Ibid.*, 108.
4 Robert M. Ball with Thomas N. Bethell, "Bridging the Centuries: The Case for Traditional Social Security," in Eric R. Kingson and James H. Schultz, eds., *Social Security in the 21st Century* (New York: Oxford University Press, 1997), 263.
5 The creation of the Unemployment Insurance Trust Fund did not pose the same problem because the federal government would nominally be holding money in trust that belonged to the states. Similarly, the payments of government workers and veterans into various pension and life insurance trust funds were considered premiums, not taxes.
6 Thomas H. Eliot, "The Legal Background of the Social Security Act," Speech delivered at general staff meeting at Social Security Administration Headquarters, Baltimore, Maryland, February 3, 1961.

connection between the taxes and the benefits.[7] Under the 1935 Act, payroll tax revenues would nominally be funneled into the general fund of the Treasury. Congress would subsequently draw appropriations from an "Old-Age Reserve Account," whose actuarial operations would be monitored by the Treasury. It was widely understood that the Old-Age Reserve Account was *implicitly* a trust fund. Indeed, appropriations to the account were tied to the level of estimated payroll tax collections (net of the program's administrative expenses).[8]

Two early financial design questions were (1) whether the system should be completely self-supporting from payroll taxes and (2) whether its liabilities should be substantially prefunded by accumulating a large reserve. The cabinet-level Committee on Economic Security, chaired by Frances Perkins, answered both of these questions negatively.[9] In most European nations, social insurance programs were heavily subsidized by general tax revenues. The CES recommended that the United States follow this European practice, both to limit the regressivity of the program's financing and to avoid the need for a large reserve. Under the CES plan, the government subsidy would not be initiated until around 1965 but would eventually finance about one-third of annual spending. In sum, the CES believed that Social Security could be effectively protected from general budget pressures even if the program obtained part of its income from general tax revenues.

But Roosevelt, with the strong encouragement of Treasury Secretary Henry Morgenthau, Jr., rejected the CES plan. Not only would provision for a government subsidy impose an economic burden on future generations, the president argued, it would weaken the program's political durability. As he said in a famous remark: "We put those payroll contributions there so as to give the contributors a legal, moral, and political right to collect their pensions . . . With those taxes in there no damn politician can ever scrap my social security program."[10] Roosevelt ordered the tax rates reworked to avoid any future government subsidy.

The CES also recommended against building a large reserve. Under its plan, workers would "pay for the support of the people then living who are old."[11] But Morgenthau, a strong fiscal conservative, argued that it

[7] This paragraph benefited from a personal correspondence with Larry DeWitt, Social Security Administration, Historian's Office.
[8] Myers, *Social Security*, 409.
[9] Committee on Economic Security, *The Report of the Committee on Economic Security of 1935*, 50th Anniversary Edition (Washington, DC: National Conference on Social Welfare, 1985).
[10] Quoted in Derthick, *Policymaking for Social Security*, 230.
[11] Committee on Economic Security, *Report*, 32.

was both politically risky and morally wrong to "place all confidence in the taxing power of the future." Morgenthau insisted on building a large reserve in order to put the system "on such sound foundations that it can be continued indefinitely in the future."[12] Under the revised tax schedule endorsed by Morgenthau, and approved by Roosevelt, the reserve would climb to nearly $47 billion by 1980, more than triple the $15 billion projected under the CES plan.

Creation of the trust fund

In 1937, following Roosevelt's effective court-packing threat, the Supreme Court upheld the constitutionality of the old-age insurance program.[13] With legal concerns safely aside, the 1937–8 Advisory Council on Social Security recommended that the Old-Age Reserve Account be "specifically" converted into "a trust fund, with designated trustees acting on the behalf of the prospective beneficiaries of the program."[14] The creation of a formal trust fund, which Congress accomplished in the 1939 Amendments, brought out the full potential of Social Security's payroll–tax financing design.

One of the major symbolic advantages of the payroll tax is that it enabled Social Security executives to compare the program to private insurance and savings plans, which citizens were already familiar with. Before the favorable 1937 Supreme Court ruling, however, Social Security leaders were inhibited from introducing insurance terminology into the program.[15] Passage of the 1939 Amendments gave them an opportunity to "enhance public understanding of the contributory insurance system" by inscribing this imagery in the law. Putting "insurance contributions" (as payroll taxes were officially renamed) in trust would help workers grasp their stake in the program.[16]

---

[12] Quoted in Carolyn Weaver, *The Crisis in Social Security* (Durham, North Carolina: Duke University Press, 1982), 85.

[13] *Helvering* v. *Davis*, 301 US 619.

[14] Advisory Council on Social Security, "Final Report," December 10, 1938, Reprinted in Committee on Economic Security, *The Report of the Committee on Economic Security of 1935*, 200.

[15] Jerry R. Cates, *Insuring Inequality* (Ann Arbor: University of Michigan Press, 1983), 31–3.

[16] Polls taken as late as the 1970s suggested that a majority of Americans believed that their payroll taxes were literally set aside at the Social Security Administration in Baltimore. See Paul Light, *Artful Work: The Politics of Social Security Reform* (New York: Random House, 1985), 62. More recent polls suggest that most Americans do recognize that Social Security is financed on a pay-as-you-go basis, although they continued to believe that Social Security is an earned

The creation of the Social Security Trust Fund greatly increased the program's financial autonomy and spending automaticity. Under the new financing arrangement, payroll tax revenues would be automatically credited to the Old-Age Insurance Trust Fund through permanent appropriation. Social Security managers would thus no longer technically be required to obtain yearly spending permission from the congressional appropriations panels. In addition, authority for monitoring the system's actuarial condition and for making policy recommendations (duties which previously had been lodged exclusively in the Treasury Department) was diffused to a three-member "Board of Trustees" (composed of the Secretary of Treasury, Secretary of Labor, and chairman of the Social Security Board). This was a key move because the Treasury Department's ranks then included actuaries and Keynesian economists who were critical of the social insurance approach to pension financing.[17]

The trust fund's creation in 1939 was in one sense ironic. As both Martha Derthick and Carolyn Weaver have noted, the trust fund was enacted at the precise moment when the implied analogy to private insurance became more strained.[18] For reasons I will explain in more detail below, Congress in the 1939 Amendments weakened the link between individual tax payments and benefits and simultaneously abandoned Morgenthau's plan to accumulate a massive reserve. In sum, the symbolism of self-help and savings accounts was grafted onto what was essentially an intergenerational social contract, enforced through the government's coercive power of taxation.

The technically false imagery of Social Security notwithstanding, it is crucial not to lose sight of the trust fund's basis in reciprocal exchange. While most retirees have historically received back far more than they have paid into the system, virtually every beneficiary has either paid

right and that canceling benefits to any retirees to be tantamount to breaking the promise. See Lawrence R. Jacobs and Robert Y. Shapiro, "Myths and Misunderstandings about Public Opinion toward Social Security: Knowledge, Support, and Reformation," in R. Douglas Arnold, Michael J. Graetz, and Alicia H. Munnell, eds., *Framing the Social Security Debate* (Washington, DC: Brookings Institution, 1998b), 370.

[17] On criticism by Treasury economists, see Arthur Altmeyer, *The Formative Years of Social Security* (Madison: University of Wisconsin Press, 1966), 108–10. Secretary Morgenthau actually endorsed the creation of the Board of Trustees, probably because he had lost out in the larger battle (discussed below) over the reserve buildup. See US Congress, House of Representatives, "Social Security," Hearings Relative to the Social Security Act Amendments of 1939 before the Committee on Ways and Means, 66th Congress, 2nd Session (1939), 2113.

[18] Derthick, *Policymaking for Social Security*, 224–6; Weaver, *The Crisis in Social Security*, 123.

payroll taxes or been dependent on someone who paid them. Contributors generally have expected to benefit from Social Security someday themselves. And the trust fund's earmarked revenues have met the costs of current benefit payments without large general fund subsidies. As we will see in subsequent case accounts, other federal trust fund structures have been built on very different political foundations.

Source of autonomy

Viewed, then, not as a repository of individual savings but rather as a device for insulating public pension spending from general fiscal pressures, the Social Security Trust Fund's performance has been exceptional, not typical. While most US trust funds have achieved only partial detachment from regular budgetary processes, the Social Security Trust Fund has enjoyed a substantial degree of financial autonomy throughout its history.

No trust fund has been more heavily protected through procedural safeguards than Social Security. While Congress has retained the authority to change benefit and tax levels at any time, trust fund spending (which bypasses normal appropriations control) has always been considered mandatory because eligible persons receive their benefit checks as a matter of right. Annual trust fund spending (other than outlays for administrative expenses) has just been the sum of the individual entitlements. And prior to the late 1960s, Social Security was excluded from the administrative budget, the budget document that received the most attention from lawmakers and the media. The largest federal domestic program, Social Security has been almost totally immune both to trade-offs with other spending priorities and to efforts to manipulate its finances for short-term economic advantage. To be sure, the Social Security Trust Fund is not a wholly independent economic entity. As we will see, questions have periodically been raised about the government's handling of the system's reserves. Within the existing limits of the form, however, the trust fund device has vastly increased the power of Social Security's claims on the public fisc.

Insulation from general budgetary pressures

The most direct threat to Social Security's financial autonomy has been from attempts to lower the budget deficit or to restructure social insurance. Such challenges have most often occurred under two conditions: when Republicans have controlled all or part of the government and when the total federal budget situation has been tight. But neither conservative rule nor deficit pressures have provided an adequate basis for significant Social Security cost reductions.

When, for example, the Reagan Administration proposed cuts in early retirement benefits in May 1981 as part of its broader retrenchment project, the Senate voted, 96–0, against any Social Security proposal to reduce benefits any more than "necessary to achieve a financially sound system and the well-being of all retired Americans."[19] A very modest benefit cutback was enacted as part of the July 1981 budget reconciliation measure. But Reagan and the Congress agreed to restore most of the benefits five months later. In 1985, an attempt by Senate Majority Leader Robert Dole and Budget Committee Chairman Pete Domenici to balance the budget partly though the spending reductions from a one-year Social Security COLA freeze failed to win even the support of Reagan. Upon becoming House Speaker in 1995, Newt Gingrich pledged to keep Social Security "off limits" to budget cuts for at least the next two Congresses.[20] In the intense war over the budget deficit that dominated American politics between 1982 and 1998, Social Security emerged practically without a scratch. Indeed, Social Security was generally kept off the negotiating table during the budget summits held between Congress and the executive.[21] In a sign of just how deeply the trust fund and earmarking principle had framed the debate, Social Security cutbacks were widely considered to be of little use in deficit reduction packages because if trust fund spending were cut, payroll tax revenues would have to be reduced too, resulting in no net savings.

The proximate reason why Social Security prospered during a time of general fiscal austerity, of course, was because it enjoyed strong public support. Yet, as Paul Starr rightly argues, it would be myopic to conclude that contemporary public opinion produced Social Security's privileged budget status since such opinion was in part the product of Social Security's inherited financial design.[22] Similarly, politicians' fear of tampering with Social Security benefits during the 1980s and 1990s

---

[19] Quoted in David A. Stockman, *The Triumph of Politics* (New York: Harper & Row, 1986), 192.

[20] "Excerpts From Speaker Gingrich's Opening Remarks," *The Washington Post*, January 5, 1995, A12.

[21] On the isolation of Social Security from general budget pressures during the 1980s and 1990s, see Martha Derthick, "The Evolving Old Politics of Social Security," in Marc Landy, Martin Levin, and Martin Shapiro, eds, *Durability and Change: The New Politics of Public Policy, Vol. II* (Baltimore: Johns Hopkins University Press, forthcoming).

[22] Paul Starr, "Social Security and the American Public Household," in Theodore R. Marmor and Jerry L. Mashaw, eds. *Social Security: Beyond the Rhetoric of Crisis* (Princeton: Princeton University Press, 1988), 120.

reflected not only the contemporary organizational and voting strength of seniors' groups, but also the deep beneficiary reliance on the program that had been actively encouraged through years of strategic management of the trust fund.

In the 1950s, a crucial period in Social Security's development, the trust fund was at the heart of the political campaigns of organized labor, then the program's most important external constituency. A key challenge was to get union members (many of whom would not become Social Security recipients until the 1970s and 1980s) to grasp that they were building up rights to future benefits. In a 1953 brochure entitled "Your Stake in the Social Security Trust Fund" that was distributed to union households, Nelson Cruikshank, the director of social insurance activities for the American Federation of Labor, wrote that the existence of a contributory trust fund was "the only guaranty that workers and their dependents will be paid benefits related to past earnings, as a right, and not as a public charity based on a means test."[23]

In 1953, the Chamber of Commerce, the AFL's ideological nemesis, proposed to combine state welfare programs for the elderly and Social Security into a single universal program. Under the proposal, the $18 billion then in the trust fund would have been exhausted in financing the transition to the new system. The plan had an obvious appeal because it promised to expand program coverage without an increase in payroll tax rates. But Cruikshank vehemently argued that support for the needy aged should "be borne out of general taxes and not charged to the trust fund," which, he said, belonged to the workers who had already paid into it. In sum, labor activists during the 1950s used the trust fund to frame conservative proposals for pension reform, not simply as wrong ideas but as "burglary."[24]

The Keynesian threat

Until the 1970s, Social Security's autonomy from general budget pressures was also challenged by the fiscal activism of Keynesian economists. While most leading Keynesians were liberal supporters of the welfare state, they believed that pensions should be financed from general revenues, rather than earmarked payroll taxes, both to improve the system's progressivity and to avoid depressing consumer demand. Unlike social insurance advocates, the Keynesians saw little value in linking

[23] See Statement of Hon. Samuel W. Yorty, "Your Stake in the Social Security Trust Fund," *Congressional Record*, August 1, 1953, A5020.

[24] *Ibid.*

workers' contributions and benefit payments. In their view, Social Security was an income transfer program, not a sacred trust. It was thus appropriate to integrate its finances into the government's general economic and fiscal planning. Social Security executives, for their part, accepted that the program would serve as an automatic budgetary stabilizer as an incidental byproduct of its income maintenance function. But they were consistently adamant that it should not be used as a vehicle for *discretionary* counter-cyclical fiscal policy. "Social Security is a long-term compact between the contributor and the United States government," stated former program commissioner Robert Ball in 1979. "It is difficult for the public to maintain faith in the system if it appears that the financing plan is subject to change because of short-run budgetary, economic, or fiscal goals."[25]

Arguably, Keynesians achieved their greatest influence over Social Security finance in the controversy over Morgenthau's original plan to accumulate a vast reserve. Keynesians argued that a large reserve would drain money out of the economy, making it harder for the nation to overcome a recession.[26] In passing the 1939 Amendments, Congress responded to this criticism by reducing the size of the projected fund buildup by roughly half. This was accomplished through an expansion of benefit payments and the cancellation of a scheduled payroll tax increase – policy moves that Keynesians strongly approved of. Contrary to the wishes of the Keynesians, however, Congress preserved, indeed enhanced, Social Security's budgetary privileges in 1939 by establishing the formal trust fund arrangement.

Keynesians continued to criticize the trust fund and earmarking principle well into the 1970s. But Social Security finance remained largely isolated from general fiscal planning. Indeed, a 1968 Brookings Institution study concluded that payroll tax increases, which were often scheduled years in advance to preserve the system's soundness, had actually produced "perverse fiscal policies" in several instances by going into effect in the midst of economic slowdowns or recessions.[27] In an obvious

[25] Robert M. Ball, "The 1977 Amendments to the Social Security and Financing Social Security," Testimony before the Subcommittee on Social Security, Senate Finance Committee, April 6, 1978.

[26] Edward D. Berkowitz, "Social Security and the financing of the American State," in W. Elliot Brownlee, ed., *Funding the Modern American State, 1941–1995: The Rise and Fall of the Era of Easy Finance* (Cambridge and Washington, DC: Cambridge University Press and Woodrow Wilson Center, 1996), 157–8.

[27] Joseph A. Pechman, Henry J. Aaron, and Michael K. Taussig, *Social Security: Perspectives for Reform* (Washington, DC: Brookings Institution, 1968), 184.

yet striking contrast, policymakers in 1964 had enacted major reductions in income and corporate taxes to achieve full employment.

By the 1960s – the era of peak Keynesian influence in US fiscal policymaking – Social Security had grown so large that its wider economic impact could hardly be ignored. Yet maintaining the system's internal financial stability remained the priority of the Ways and Means Committee, the trust fund's key institutional guardian. Executive requests to mold Social Security finance to larger fiscal needs were accepted only rarely. In 1961, for example, the Ways and Means Committee rejected a modest request from the Kennedy Administration for a one-year delay in the effective date of an increase in the payroll tax rate to avoid reducing consumer purchasing power during an economic recovery. Influential conservative John W. Byrnes (R-Wisconsin) argued that the proposed delay was "dangerous" because it implied modifying a program "in perpetuity," in response to a "temporary" economic situation.[28]

The Keynesians did win an important procedural victory, however, with the adoption of a unified executive budget in fiscal year 1969. President Johnson, following the advice of a presidential commission that was dominated by Keynesian economists, agreed to collapse the federal government's three existing budget documents into one comprehensive system.[29] The major rationale for this change was to promote more effective fiscal policymaking by giving the president a single measure of the federal government's impact on the macroeconomy. Social Security defenders construed this development as a clear threat to the trust fund's autonomy. "I do not think we should view social security amendments in light of the effect that they might have on the so-called unified budget. I think we must look at the suggested changes in the light of the effect they have on the social security trust fund and on the actuarial soundness of that fund," said Wilbur Mills in 1972.[30] But the shift to a unified budget came relatively late both in Social Security's evolution and in the era of Keynesian dominance. By the mid 1970s, Social Security's internal financing problems ensured that the program would receive scrutiny on

---

[28] US Congress, House of Representatives, "Social Security Amendments of 1961," Executive Hearings Before the Committee on Ways and Means, 87th Congress, 1st Session (1961), 103.

[29] While accepting the practice of "earmarking special revenue sources for well-defined programs of long-run character," the presidential commission stressed that the exclusion of the trust funds from budget totals provided a distorted picture of the federal government's economic impact. See *Report of the President's Commission on Budget Concepts* (Washington, DC: Government Printing Office, October 1967), 27.

[30] *Congressional Record*, March 6, 1972, 6987.

its own terms. Moreover, the Keynesian project of economic "fine-tuning" had all but collapsed because of its inability to cope with stagflation. The unified budget would not become an important factor in Social Security finance until large trust funds surpluses emerged in the mid 1980s.

Liquidity constraint

Although spending out of the trust fund has not been much affected by general fiscal pressures, moderate Social Security cutbacks have occurred in the face of internal solvency crises. Such crises, of course, would not have arisen in the absence of the trust fund and autonomy.

In practice, Social Security short-term liquidity constraint is determined by the Trustees' estimate of the program's "year of exhaustion," meaning the first year the system's reserves and current revenues are expected to be insufficient to cover all promised spending.[31] When the trust fund's projected depletion is imminent, policymakers have always taken steps to stave off "bankruptcy." There is no evidence that the adoption of such "rescue packages" has been motored by changes in public opinion. Indeed, the public has never wavered in its support for Social Security.[32] The timing of these actions has been entirely trust fund driven.[33]

As is well known, Social Security got into financial trouble in the early 1970s. There were two major causes: poor economic growth, which caused the system's revenues to come in slower than expected; and an error in the Social Security COLA mechanism, which overcompensated certain beneficiaries for inflation. In 1977, the Trustees predicted that Social Security would be insolvent by 1983. Congress responded by enacting legislation that corrected the indexing problem and raised payroll taxes by $227 billion over the following decade – at the time the largest peacetime tax hike in American history. But while the 1977 legislation was expected to keep Social Security solvent for at least 50 years, the economic slowdown persisted and trust fund deficits continued.

Congress enacted a second rescue measure in April 1983, when the trust fund was only four months away from exhaustion. The measure was based on a bipartisan compromise plan that had been negotiated behind

---

[31] The Trustees make their forecasts based on low-cost, high-cost, and intermediate-cost assumptions. The intermediate forecast generally receives the most attention from policymakers.

[32] See Jacobs and Shapiro, "Myths and Misunderstandings," 20.

[33] Pierson, *Dismantling the Welfare State?*, 64–9.

closed doors by key members of a presidential commission under the chairmanship of Alan Greenspan.[34] The much-heralded 1983 legislation contained six major features: acceleration of payroll tax increases previously scheduled for the late 1980s; partial taxation of Social Security benefits for wealthy households; an increase in the tax rates of the self-employed to bring them to parity with other workers; a six-month delay of cost-of-living increases; expansion of Social Security coverage; and a gradual increase in the normal retirement age from 65 to 67 in 2027.[35] Both conservative and liberal policymakers alike characterized the enactment of the package as a crowning legislative achievement. "Once we stopped being revolutionaries and started being system conservers," one Reagan aide said, "it was a tremendous accomplishment." "We even cut Social Security," said a Democratic politician. "We just didn't say we're doing it."[36] In sum, when Social Security threatened to become "bankrupt" during the Carter and Reagan Administrations, the response of elected officials was urgent, anguished and (in the end) prideful.

Loosening the liquidity constraint

The trust fund's liquidity constraint, which has had a decisive impact on the timing of policy changes by creating the possibility of insolvency crises, can be loosened in three main ways. Ranked in ascending order of their importance, and descending order of their actual use up to 1998, they are (1) reallocation of social insurance tax rates; (2) interfund borrowing; and (3) general fund transfers.

The Social Security, Disability Insurance (DI), and Hospital Insurance (HI) Trust Fund all share the same revenue base – the payroll tax. One way the condition of a social insurance trust fund can be improved without actually cutting spending or raising taxes is by changing its allocation of the tax. Congress has in fact exercised this option on a number of occasions. The 1983 rescue package, for example, dropped the disability insurance tax rate from 1.65 percent to 1.25 percent in order to increase the amount allocated to the Social Security Trust Fund. In 1994, the DI Trust Fund was in financial trouble, and Congress responded by increasing the DI tax rate and decreasing the Social Security tax rate by identical amounts. In a sense, reallocating tax rates does not solve a trust

---

[34] See Light, *Artful Work*.
[35] "Social Security Rescue Plan Swiftly Approved," *Congressional Quarterly Almanac* (1983), pp. 219–26; see also James M. Poterba, "Budget Policy," in Alberto Alesina and Geoffrey Carliner, eds., *American Economic Policy in the 1980s* (Chicago: University of Chicago Press, 1994), 257.
[36] Quoted in White and Wildavsky, *The Deficit*, 322–3.

fund problem – it merely shifts it to whatever fund can best handle it at the moment.

Another way Congress can fudge the commitment to self-support is by giving a financially strapped trust fund authority to "borrow" money from a better-off companion fund. Congress has given Social Security such borrowing authority twice, once in November 1982 and once in December 1982. Social Security borrowed $5.1 billion from the DI Trust Fund and $12.4 billion from the HI Trust Fund. Had these loans not been permitted, Congress's short-term balancing job would have been much tougher. Still, Congress kept meticulous track of these trust fund loans, requiring Social Security to repay the borrowed amounts within a few years, with interest. Barber Conable, the Republican leader on Ways and Means, insisted that Social Security's original borrowing authority expire during the summer of 1983, precisely because he wanted the solvency crisis to occur safely before the 1984 campaign season, thus giving Congress the best possible chance to deal with the solvency crisis in a fiscally responsible way.[37] In sum, Congress used the interfund loan option in the 1982–3 Social Security crisis more to support than to undermine the commitment to self-support.

A greater threat to Social Security's financial autonomy than either of these two techniques would be injecting large amounts of general tax revenue into the system. In most industrialized nations, general government revenues finance a large share of public pension spending.[38] Yet in 1998 general fund transfers comprised only 2 percent of the Social Security Trust Fund's income. Virtually all of this amount was accounted for by the revenue from income taxation of Social Security benefits.[39] As I mentioned earlier, the Committee on Economic Security in 1935 had called for general revenues eventually to finance one-third of the

---

[37] Light, *Artful Work*, 136–7.
[38] Margaret S. Gordon, *Social Security Policies in Industrial Countries: A Comparative Analysis* (Cambridge: Cambridge University Press, 1988), 75.
[39] The remainder came in the form of (1) earnings credits for the military and (2) subsidies for certain persons born before 1920 who were unable to work long enough to establish their eligibility. While the military wage credits constitute a small portion of the trust fund's income, Congress finagled with them in 1983 to help stave off bankruptcy. Before 1983, the Department of Defense had reimbursed the trust funds as benefit checks came due. Other employers, however, paid their payroll taxes as wages were earned. Congress enacted an $18 billion "lump sum military wage credit" to make up for these arrearages, thus giving the trust fund an immediate infusion of cash. See White and Wildavsky, *The Deficit and the Public Interest*, 322; see also Herman Leonard, *Checks Unbalanced: The Quiet Side of Public Spending* (New York: Basic Books, 1986), 65.

program's costs. In the 1940s, politically liberal executive actors like Arthur Altmeyer argued that partial general fund financing of Social Security was "equitable and appropriate" once the contributory system had firmly established itself.[40] In 1944, Congress explicitly authorized general fund appropriations into Social Security when the cost of the program exceeded payroll tax revenues. But Congress, led by Wilbur Mills, eliminated this authorization in 1950.[41]

The issue of general fund transfers into Social Security reemerged during the 1977 solvency crisis. Jimmy Carter had pledged not to increase payroll tax rates in his 1976 campaign. Moreover, his economic advisers, most of them Keynesian in orientation, believed that higher payroll taxes would depress consumer demand. Carter's reform proposal therefore called for (ostensibly temporary) "counter-cyclical" general revenues to be automatically transferred to the trust fund by the Treasury Department whenever the national unemployment rate exceeded 6 percent. The Carter proposal would thus have linked Social Security's financial structure to short-term economic fluctuations and fiscal policy. But Congress remained wary about changing Social Security's inherited financial design and rejected any assignment of general revenues to the system.[42]

Proposals for partial general fund financing of Social Security did not die, however. They could not, given the combination of policymakers' unwillingness to fundamentally renege on the expensive benefit promises of a mature program and (especially after the mid 1980s) their growing resistance to payroll tax rate increases. In 1999, President Clinton suggested transferring general revenues to Social Security as part of his wider proposal for allocating future unified budget surpluses.[43] Under the plan, the transfers would begin in 2011, in an amount equal to the interest

[40] See Arthur J. Altmeyer, "Old-Age, Survivors, and Disability Insurance," *Social Security Bulletin*, April 1949, 13.
[41] See Derthick, *Policymaking for Social Security*, 238–244. See also Julian E. Zelizer, *Taxing America: Wilbur D. Mills, Congress, and the State, 1945–1975* (Cambridge: Cambridge University Press, 1998), chapter 2.
[42] On the 1977 rescue plan, see Derthick, *Policymaking for Social Security*, chapter 19; *Congress and the Nation* (Washington, DC: Congressional Quarterly Press, 1981), 235–8. My understanding of Carter's proposal also benefited from reading an April 29, 1977 decision memorandum prepared for President Carter by Stu Eisenstat and Frank Raines. I thank Prof. Derthick for sharing this document with me.
[43] For an analysis, see Congressional Budget Office, *An Analysis of the President's Budgetary Proposals for Fiscal Year 2000* (Washington, DC: Government Printing Office, April 1999a).

that would be saved by reducing the public debt.[44] Significantly, the proposal was presented to the public not as a major policy innovation but rather as a way to breathe additional years of life into the trust fund. When policymakers have considered Social Security reforms, they have done so under the guise of protecting existing arrangements.

Actuarial forecasting

What has historically distinguished the Social Security Trust Fund from other trust funds in the US budget is not only the exceptional level of spending automaticity it has experienced, but also the technically sophisticated and long-term actuarial estimating techniques that have come with it. The trustees forecast Social Security's outlook over the next 75 years.[45] Most other industrial democracies, in contrast, plan their pension systems on a 25-year basis or less. The rationale for the use of a 75-year "valuation period" in the US Social Security program is that it covers the entire horizon of workers' involvement with the program as contributors and recipients and that workers require assurance that the program will be there for them when they need it.

Such long-term forecasts are inherently sensitive to a variety of economic and demographic assumptions. But elected officials have treated the Trustees' forecasts (which are actually prepared by professionals in the Office of the Actuary of the Social Security Administration) as definitive estimates. As Congressional Research Service analyst David S. Koitz observes, "the limitations implied by the exactness of the resources posted or projected to be posted to the trust funds have both permitted and set the bounds of expansion of the program's benefits, as well as thwarted enactment of measures thought to be fiscally irresponsible."[46] Not only has the apparent precision of the forecasts shaped legislative decisions, but the benefits of more accurate forecasts have historically been emphasized in the presentation of policy options.

---

[44] In his original budget plan announced in January 1999, Clinton called for $1.3 trillion in general fund transfers to Social Security over the 2000 to 2009 period. But Republicans in Congress balked, in part because the plan failed to guarantee that near-term Social Security surpluses would not be used to pay for other things. See Richard W. Stevenson and Adam Clymer, "Clinton to Unveil Plan to Shore Up Social Security," The New York Times, June 29, 1999, A1.

[45] The long-range basis of Social Security financing was changed from perpetuity to a 75-year period following the recommendations of the 1963–4 Advisory Council.

[46] David S. Koitz, "The Social Security Surplus: A Discussion of Some of the Issues," CRS Report for Congress (Washington, DC: Congressional Research Service, November 21, 1988), 88–709 EPE, 22.

During the late 1940s for example, program executives argued that expanding coverage to agricultural workers would eliminate the considerable actuarial uncertainty created by workers who moved "in-and-out" of the industrial labor force.[47]

A major effect of the emphasis on actuarial forecasting has been to reinforce the future orientation of Social Security politics. As Martha Derthick argues in her classic account of Social Security's evolution from 1935 to 1977, "Because so much of the impact of social security lay in the future, policymaking consisted, not just of bargaining among present contestants, but of calculating the burdens of future contestants, anticipating their reactions, and contriving constraints on them."[48] The statistical findings discussed in the previous chapter reinforce this conclusion. As I showed, transitions to Republican government have been associated with reductions in ultimate, but not current, payroll tax rates.

The impact of actuarial forecasts

Assessing the impact of the actuarial forecasts – whether they have had a net expansionary or contractionary effect on policy *outcomes* – is extremely difficult. One reason is because the assumptions used to make these projections have changed. Prior to 1972, for example, Social Security projections were based on the highly unrealistic assumption that real money wages would remain static. Both Robert Myers and Wilbur Mills insisted that this convention provided a desirable margin of safety.[49] The practical effect of this convention, however, was to virtually guarantee that the trust fund would regularly appear "overfunded." Congress – all the while proclaiming its commitment to the system's financial

---

[47] See testimony of Arthur Altmeyer, in US Congress, House of Representatives, "Social Security Act Amendments of 1949," Hearings Before the Committee on Ways and Means, 81st Congress, 1st Session (1949). Agricultural workers had initially been excluded from Social Security coverage in part on actuarial grounds. See Gareth Davies and Martha Derthick, "Race and Social Welfare Policy: The Social Security Act of 1935," *Political Science Quarterly*, 112 (2), Summer 1997, 217–5; for an alternative perspective that emphasizes the importance of racial politics, see Robert C. Lieberman, "Race and the Organization of Welfare Policy," in Paul Peterson, ed., *Classifying By Race* (Princeton: Princeton University Press, 1995).

[48] Derthick, *Policymaking for Social Security*, 244.

[49] On the conventions used for long-term actuarial forecasts, see Robert J. Myers, "Old-Age Survivors, and Disability Insurance: Financing Basis and Policy Under the 1961 Amendments," *Social Security Bulletin*, September, 1961, 12–19. See also Zelizer, *Taxing America*, chapter 2.

soundness – would quickly exploit these artificially pessimistic forecasts by increasing benefits (often in election years), thus postponing the reserve accumulation. New forecasts based on the level-wage assumption would then be made, "unanticipated" surpluses would reappear, and the cycle would start over.[50] Congress switched to a dynamic earnings assumption in 1972, when it indexed benefits for inflation.

A second complication is that Social Security's actuarial forecasts have increased the transparency of the program's costs in certain respects yet reduced it in others. On the one hand, Social Security's actuarial forecasts have provided policymakers with early warning of future difficulties. Tellingly, Social Security's long-range financial problems remained a major political concern during the 1990s *even though the system was in excellent short-run condition*. These distant financing problems have helped keep program liberalizations off the agenda, allowing near-term trust fund surpluses to accumulate. Even when, as in 1977 and 1983, Congress has adopted reforms primarily because of the system's short-range difficulties, it has also endeavored to restore the program to long-range solvency. "Sometimes, Congress is criticized for having only a short-run look, being concerned only about the length of time until the next election. However, in the Social Security field, the Congress . . . [have always] tried to develop a social insurance program that would be viable over the long run," wrote Robert Myers, the program's influential chief actuary from 1947 to 1970.[51]

On the other hand, however, the actuarial methods employed in Social Security have arguably camouflaged the true scope of the long-term promises contained in the program. Traditionally, program actuaries have measured the cost of proposed legislative changes, not in dollars or as share of GDP, but rather as a percent of "taxable payroll." Two rather large effects have flowed from this seemingly minor convention. First, it has created the impression that Social Security has a prior right to future payroll tax revenues. Instead of having to request new revenue sources or general appropriations to finance promises, lawmakers have been in the position of making slight adjustments in the program's existing tax schedule. Second, the focus on taxable payroll made large program changes seem like relatively modest ones, as highlighted in this 1958

---

[50] Derthick, *Policymaking for Social Security*, 48–51. See also Joseph A. Pechman, Henry J. Aaron, and Michael K. Taussig, *Social Security: Perspectives for Reform*, 71.

[51] See Robert J. Myers, "Will Social Security Be There for Me?" in Eric R. Kingson and James H. Schulz, eds., *Social Security in the 21ˢᵗ Century* (New York: Oxford University Press, 1997), 6–7.

exchange between Rep. John W. Byrnes (R-Wisconsin), a leading conservative, and Senator William Proxmire, during a committee hearing on Proxmire's proposal to increase benefits and taxes:

> Mr. Byrnes. What is your dollar cost, Senator?
> Senator Proxmire. My dollar cost? I have had it computed, Congressman Byrnes, on a percentage basis. I do not have the precise dollar cost. It was analyzed by the Administration on that kind of a basis, not on a dollar basis . . . .
> Mr. Byrnes. I may suggest that it is an interesting thing to look at because we are speaking in terms of tax rate on gross income and we very often think of a 1 percent figure or a 2 percent figure as not very significant in the revenue or the cost to the individual. My information from Mr. Myers was that the present intermediate cost estimate is approximately $8 million a year and that your tax increase and the cost of would be $7.2 billion.[52]

Social Security actuaries have traditionally considered the program in "close actuarial balance" if over the 75-year valuation period the revenue from its accumulated balance and projected future income – including interest earnings – is within five percentage points of taxable payroll of its estimated costs. In contrast, private pensions to be considered actuarially sound must, in general, have sufficient funds *on hand* to meet all accrued obligations without assuming the system will remain open to new entrants. During his long tenure as chief actuary, Myers, who enjoyed a reputation for both professional competence and political neutrality, would regularly assure lawmakers that this more stringent concept of actuarial soundness was not appropriate for a compulsory social insurance program that could "be expected to continue indefinitely."[53] In other words, because the government could rely on its coercive power of taxation to meet future needs, Social Security's "unfunded liabilities" did not present the risk of insolvency.

Yet such unfunded liabilities were, and are, hardly unimportant. As Herman Leonard correctly stresses, they are a measure of future spending commitments, no more or less significant than the national debt.[54] According to a 1998 Concord Coalition study, Social Security's "closed-group" liability was $8.9 trillion, more than twice the $3.5 trillion deficit

---

52 US Congress, House of Representatives, "Social Security Legislation," Hearings Before the Committee on Ways and Means, 85th Congress, 2nd Session (1958), 156.
53 See, for example, Robert J. Myers, "Old-Age, Survivors, and Disability Insurance: Financing Basis and Policy Under the 1961 Amendments," *Social Security Bulletin*, September 1981, 12.
54 Leonard, *Checks Unbalanced*, 71.

officially reported by the Trustees.[55] These immense liabilities are the reason why the transition from today's Social Security system to a fully-funded, privatized system of individual accounts would be very expensive. Unless contribution rates were increased dramatically, it would take a full working life to build up enough savings to provide a reasonable pension. The first generation of participants in the new system would therefore have to make "double payments," simultaneously setting aside money for their own personal accounts while paying for the obligations that have been made to older workers and current retirees.

Prefunding and the trust fund's limits

The preceding analysis has emphasized the overall effectiveness of the Social Security Trust Fund as a device for compelling current office-holders to make good on the pension commitments of their predecessors. For all the trust fund's exceptional strengths as a mechanism for locking-in spending promises, however, it is an intrinsically weak instrument for prefunding the system's liabilities. The main reason for this weakness is the lack of a credible mechanism to prevent the trust fund's reserves from becoming a captive market of the Treasury. While the Social Security Trust Fund's revenue flows are monitored and accounted for separately, the Social Security Administration has no independent control over the money. The system's assets have traditionally been invested in Treasury securities to prevent the government from becoming enmeshed in private sector decisions. In theory, this investment approach can be used to promote national savings. In practice, however, there is little to prevent Congress from using trust fund surpluses as an easy source of financing other programs.[56]

The clear incapacities of the Social Security Trust Fund as a prefunding device have created real problems for Social Security defenders. This is not so much because the economic benefits of prefunding are beyond debate, but rather because the *idea* that the federal government sets aside workers' contributions for the future has been at the heart of the program's imagery. In sum, the trust fund's weaknesses as a prefunding instrument pointed to a gap between the symbolism and reality of Social Security financing, a gap that the program's ideological

[55] Concord Coalition, "How To Measure Social Security's Financial Status: Facing Facts Alert," June 15, 1998.
[56] Whether Social Security surpluses are used to retire debt or pay for current government spending has no bearing on the Social Security program's reported actuarial status. By law, the same federal securities are posted to the trust fund in either case.

opponents have long wished to exploit. By arguing that the assets of the Social Security Trust Fund are illusory, mere scraps of paper, conservative critics have sought to undermine the public expectations and promisee reliance upon which the program's sustainability in large measure depends.

Early controversies over prefunding

Historically, these attacks have intensified whenever the system has accumulated a large balance or threatened to do so. Indeed, such attacks were a major reason why Congress jettisoned Morgenthau's original plan to accumulate a massive reserve in 1939. Not only did the prospect of a huge fund buildup spark criticism from Keynesian economists, it also promoted charges of "slippery bookkeeping."[57] Fiscal conservatives like Senator Arthur Vandenberg (R-Michigan) argued that such a large reserve would merely tempt the government into extravagant spending.[58] Social Security defenders hoped that the replacement of the Old-Age Reserve Account with a formal trust fund – along with the reduction in the actual size of the reserve – would assure citizens that the assets were indeed being managed properly. According to Marion Folsom, a business member of the 1937–8 Advisory Council, the trust fund's establishment would create "a better impression on the public than mixing all these funds together."[59]

While the 1939 Amendments made the reserve much smaller than it would have been otherwise, significant annual surpluses continued to accumulate in the trust fund until 1956 because of economic growth and the artifically favorable ratio of workers to beneficiaries typical of a maturing system. These surpluses prompted continuing attacks on the trust fund's credibility. In 1950, the Brookings Institution published a skeptical book on Social Security which flatly stated that "The Trust Fund is thus a fiction – serving only to confuse."[60] Critics insisted that workers would have to pay twice for their pension benefits – once when they contributed to the program, and again when the government raised the money to redeem the bonds. "There are now over thirteen billions in

---

[57] For an effort to defuse these criticisms, see statement of Mr. Buck, "The Social Security Act – Old-Age Reserve Account," *Congressional Record*, April 6, 1939, 3933–9.

[58] Weaver, *The Crisis in Social Security*, 111.

[59] US Congress, House of Representatives, "Social Security," Hearings Relative to the Social Security Act Amendments of 1939, 1151.

[60] Lewis Meriam and Karl Schlotterbeck, *The Cost and Financing of Social Security* (Washington, DC: Brookings Institution, 1950).

IOUs in the social security trust fund of hard-earned dollars collected from employers and employees for old-age security," said one Republican lawmaker in 1951.

> The billions collected for this purpose are spent as received by the Federal Government to meet current expenses and these IOUs put into the Treasury. If a private insurance company did this it would be prosecuted. Eventually when these trust funds are needed additional taxes will have to be levied on the public to meet the payment coming to our retired workers.[61]

With Social Security not yet deeply institutionalized, program advocates felt it crucial to dispel these charges. Long-range forecasts made in the early 1950s showed that payroll tax collections would eventually be inadequate to meet benefit costs; the system would need to draw on the reserve. But the AFL assured its members that "their future benefits were guaranteed by the existence of a trust fund which was held in government securities. The bonds were the instruments indicating the good faith of the government of the United States."[62] The trust fund's defenders received support on this point from some unexpected sources, including from Albert Linton, a private insurance executive who personally opposed a large reserve accumulation. Linton stated that the government bonds held by the Social Security Trust fund were "just as valuable as if they were owned by a private institution."[63] George Humphrey, Secretary of Treasury under Dwight Eisenhower, echoed this point in a 1953 interview on *Meet the Press*. Asked if it were not true that the Treasury had already spent the billions in payroll taxes it had collected, leaving the system with worthless IOUs, Humphrey denied the charge and recounted an earlier conversation of his with the manager of a large private pension fund.

> Now, one day a businessman said to me, 'Isn't that practically thievery; aren't you just reaching in there and stealing that money?' . . .
>
> I said to him, 'What have you got in your pension fund? You have a large amount of pension funds on hand; what are your pension funds invested in?'
>
> He said 'Ours are invested in Government bonds.' I said 'So are ours.'[64]

Program defenders also disputed the claim that workers would have to

---

[61] Statement of Rep. Homer D. Angell, *Congressional Record*, September 19, 1951, A5741.

[62] Nelson H. Cruikshank, "A Philosophy for Social Security," Delivered at the Social Security Administration, Third Robert M. Ball Lecture, Baltimore, Maryland, December 12, 1978.

[63] Quoted in *Congressional Record*, February 22, 1954, 2096.

[64] *Ibid.*, 2097.

pay twice for their benefits. Taxes levied to redeem the bonds held by the trust fund, they said, would "not be levied for the purpose of paying social security benefits. Rather they will be levied for the purpose for which the money was original borrowed, such as the costs arising out of World War II."[65] The media generally sided with the trust fund's defenders during this period. "It is hard to see how a reserve could be made any more real," editorialized the *Boston Herald* in a 1953 article entitled "Social Security Fund Exists."[66] By 1958, one House Democrat could note with satisfaction that the argument that Social Security reserves had been stolen had "been pretty well put to bed."[67]

These early (mainly conservative) efforts to exploit the institutional limits of the trust fund failed for several reasons. First, Social Security benefits grew very rapidly over the 1950s. Most retirees got very high returns on their contributions. Objectively, it was difficult for critics to make the case that people were being cheated. Second, the trust fund's reported long-range fiscal outlook was good. There was little concern yet about the program's future insolvency. Third, alternative strategies for investing trust fund surpluses lacked credibility. The memory of the Great Depression was recent enough that virtually no one was proposing to invest the reserve in private equities. Fourth, trust in government in general was high. Fifth, concerns about the misuse of trust fund assets seemed more hypothetical than real. The operations of the trust fund, both officially and in actual practice, were excluded from the administrative budget, which in any event was generally balanced. Finally, the relative size of the trust fund reserve was growing smaller with every passing year. The reserve declined from 1156 percent of yearly outlays in 1950 to 103 percent in 1965.[68] Between 1956 and 1975 the trust fund was financed on a pay-as-you-go basis (figure 4.1).

The post 1980s trust fund buildup

Beginning in the mid 1980s, however, the trust fund again began producing large annual surpluses. In 1985, Social Security took in eleven billion more than it paid out. In 1990, the annual surplus was $55

[65] "Fifteenth Trustees Report on OASI Trust Fund," *Social Security Bulletin*, May 1955, 26.

[66] Reprinted in *Congressional Record*, February 34, 1953, A840.

[67] See US Congress, House of Representatives, "Social Security Legislation," Hearings Before the Committee on Ways and Means, 26.

[68] For an excellent financial history of Social Security, see Alicia Munnell, "Social Security and National Saving," in John R. Gist, ed., *Social Security and Economic Well-Being Across Generations* (Washington, DC: American Association of Retired Persons Public Policy Institute, 1988).

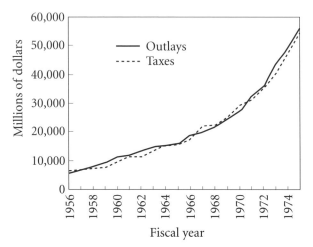

Figure 4.1 Pay-as-you-go financing of Social Security, fiscal years 1956–1975
Source: Office of Management and Budget, *Budget of the United States Government – Historical Tables* (Washington, DC: Government Printing Office, various years).

billion.[69] At the end of 1998, the total balance in the trust fund exceeded $650 billion, or nearly 8 percent of GDP (figure 4.2). In an accounting if not an economic sense, Social Security had shifted from pay-as-you-go toward partial advance funding.[70]

By most accounts, this fundamental change in the trust fund's operations was an indirect consequence of other decisions made by the Greenspan Commission in 1983 rather than a conscious policy choice to build up a huge reserve for the baby boomers.[71] The trust fund's short-term

[69] Office of Management and Budget, "Budget of the United States Government, Historical Tables, Fiscal Year 1995" (Washington, DC, 1994).
[70] The shift toward a funded system was actually set in motion by the tax schedule enacted in the 1977 Amendments, which provided for the accumulation of trust fund reserves around the year 2000. But the 1983 reforms made these reserves larger and much earlier to develop. There was no explicit legislative debate about the desirability of a future reserve buildup in 1977.
[71] See Robert J. Myers, "Will Social Security Be There When the Baby Boomers Retire?" *The 1991 E. J. Faulkner Lecture Series* (College of Business Administration, University of Nebraska, Lincoln, 1991); and Koitz, "Social Security Surplus." For a similar argument that the shift away from pay-as-you-go financing in 1983 was largely unplanned, see Forrest P. Chisman, "Social Security Reserves and the Budget Deficit," in John R. Gist, ed., *Social Security and Economic Well-Being Across Generations* (Washington, DC: American Association of Retired Persons Public Policy Institute, 1988). My interpretation of the

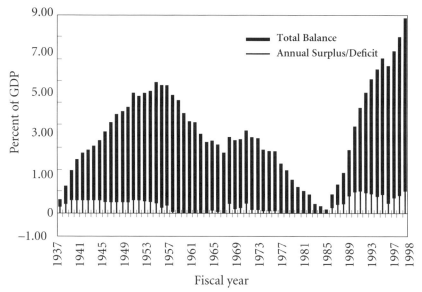

Figure 4.2 Annual surplus or deficit and balance in the Social Security Trust Fund as a percent of GDP, fiscal years 1937–1998
Note: Figures for fiscal years 1937–9 are for the Old-Age Reserve Account
Source: Office of Management and Budget, *Budget of the United States Government – Historical Tables* (Washington, DC: Government Printing Office, various years).

outlook deteriorated rapidly during 1981 and 1982, convincing policy-makers that the 1977 reforms had failed. The first priority of the Greenspan Commission was to assure that Social Security got through the 1980s without another crisis. The commission staff therefore employed extremely pessimistic assumptions in making their short-range forecasts. Members of the Commission were aware that the system also faced a long-range financing problem. When they discussed Social Security's long-range problems, however, they followed the practice of the Trustees and analyzed reform options in terms of their impact on the system's average payroll shortfall over the entire 75-year time horizon, and not on how specific proposals would affect the program's income and outlays

reserve's origins – which is supported by the writings of both Robert M. Ball and Robert J. Myers – is challenged by Daniel Patrick Moynihan. See Daniel Patrick Moynihan, "Conspirators, Trillions, Limos in the Night," *The New York Times*, May 23, 1988, A19.

year by year. Nothing in the record indicates that Congress gave careful attention to the prospect of a major trust fund accumulation during the 1980s and 1990s or to how such an accumulation might be translated into genuine economic savings. In sum, the most important change in Social Security's financial operations in at least a half-century was adopted with virtually no planning. "We should not treat reserve accumulation as the result of a thought-through proposal adopted by the National Commission on Social Security Reform. If that happened, it was when I was out of the room," said Robert Ball.[72]

The effect of the trust fund buildup was to reopen the old debate about the trust fund's limits as a prefunding mechanism, but in a political and institutional context that had changed dramatically since the 1950s.[73] Average rates of return had fallen due to the system's maturing. The system's long-range financial outlook had worsened. The trust fund was included in the unified budget as a legacy of the Keynesian era, and the federal government was running massive peacetime deficits. And trust in American government in general had plummeted. These factors made ordinary citizens receptive to the argument that the trust fund was being abused. According to a 1998 *NBC/Wall Street Journal* poll, 79 percent of Americans believed that the government had used the Social Security Trust Fund for other purposes. More respondents (67 percent) attributed Social Security's financial problems to diversion of trust fund money than to the declining ratio of workers to beneficiaries (59 percent) or to retirees living longer (47 percent).[74]

Ironically, the argument that the government was raiding the trust fund was put into play in the late 1980s by Senator Daniel Patrick Moynihan (D-NY), a strong proponent of social insurance and one of the key architects of the 1983 rescue package.[75] While the trust fund buildup was not the product of extensive planning, once it emerged policy elites were quick to see it as a vehicle for increasing national savings. As a member of

---

[72] Robert M. Ball, "Panel on Formulating a Deficit Reduction Package: What is the Role of Social Security," in Henry J. Aaron, ed., *Social Security and the Budget* (Washington, DC: National Academy of Social Insurance, 1988), 127.

[73] Derthick, "The Evolving Old Politics of Social Security."

[74] See Robert J. Blendon *et al.*, "What Do Americans Know About Entitlements?" *Health Affairs*, September/October 1997, 115. The *NBC/Wall Street Journal* poll cited above was conducted by Hart–Teeter, July 25–7, 1998.

[75] Some argue that Moynihan never saw it as a proposal that could pass, but rather as "a convenient way to dramatize his argument that the regressive Social Security tax is being used unfairly to help finance the federal deficit." David S. Cloud, "Moynihan Tries Again," *Congressional Quarterly Weekly Report*, January 26, 1991, 241.

the National Economic Commission in 1989, Moynihan argued that the accumulation of trust fund reserves presented an opportunity to prepare the economy for the impending retirement of the baby boomers. He warned, however, that a Democratic Congress would not allow the government to repeal progressive taxation by using surplus payroll tax revenues for debt service. "If, in the next five years, no arrangements are made to save the future incomes to the funds, Congress – you may depend on it – will return to "pay-as-you-go" financing," he said.[76]

In early 1990, Moynihan introduced legislation to gradually reduce payroll taxes from 6.2 percent to 5.1 percent in 1996. Moynihan argued that the Social Security surplus was being used to "finance deficits in the operating budget" – a practice he said was tantamount to "thievery."[77] With its promise of a large tax cut, Moynihan's proposal received endorsements from interest groups across the political spectrum.[78] But on Capitol Hill, Moynihan found it impossible to build a winning coalition. The Bush Administration, fearing that passage could add $100 billion annually to the unified budget deficit, strongly opposed the proposal. In the House, Ways and Means chairman Dan Rostenkowski (D-IL) kept the plan from ever coming up for a vote.[79] Senate leaders twice permitted votes, but the measure failed on both occasions. On October 9, 1990, the bill was set aside on the Senate floor by a vote of 54 to 44 over an objection that it would increase the budget deficit.[80] A majority of Democrats (42–13) supported the measure while a majority of Republicans (31–12) opposed it. The measure also produced cleavages along committee lines. Robert Byrd, Jim Sasser, and Lloyd Bentsen, chairmen of three key budget control committees (Appropriations, Budget and Finance, respectively), all voted against it.[81]

[76] "National Economic Commission Report" (Washington, DC: Government Printing Office, 1989), 56–7.
[77] For early reactions, see Susan Dentzer, "Paycheck Politics," *US News and World Report*, January 29, 1990, 16–18; Howard Gleckman, "Social Security's Dirty Little Secret," *Business Week*, January 29, 1990, 66–7; and Robert Kuttner, "Thanks for Tossing that Grenade, Mr. Moynihan," *Business Week*, February 5, 1990, 16.
[78] Many leading budget experts opposed the proposal, however. For a sample of expert opinion, see the contributions by Alice Rivlin, Ralph C. Bryant, Charles Schultze, Joseph White, and Aaron Wildavsky in "Four Reasons Not to Cut Social Security Taxes," *The Brookings Review* , Spring 1990, 3–8.
[79] To protect the surplus, Rostenkowski pushed for a special rule in the 1990 budget agreement requiring Social Security benefits to be cut to pay for any Social Security tax cut. See Cloud, "Moynihan Tries Again," 241.
[80] Sixty votes were needed to waive the budget rules.
[81] "Effort to Shift Social Security Taxes Fails," *Congressional Quarterly Almanac* (1990) (Washington, DC: Congressional Quarterly Press), 170.

As it turned out, 54 votes was the proposal's high watermark. The plan came up again during Senate consideration of the fiscal year 1992 budget resolution, but this time only 38 Senators (including 13 fewer Democrats and three fewer Republicans) voted for it.[82] The Bush Administration waged an aggressive lobbying campaign against the proposal. Senate Minority Leader Dole said it involved "messing" with Social Security.[83] The public never got behind the idea. Asked which tax they would most prefer to see cut – the federal income tax or the Social Security tax – 78 percent of respondents in a 1990 *CBS News/New York Times* Poll said the income tax while only 14 percent said the Social Security tax.[84]

Was the trust fund raided?

Was Moynihan's allegation in fact true? Was Social Security, hugely popular as it was, used by politicians during the 1980s and 1990s to finance other programs? The question is extremely difficult to resolve.[85] It requires precise knowledge of what the government's fiscal policy would have been in the absence of the trust fund buildup. Since the Social Security surpluses could be spent in practice without touching them in principle – or, indeed, on paper – one cannot simply examine whether Congress passed legislation explicitly diverting trust fund money to non-Social Security uses – which it clearly did not.[86] All that is necessary for the charge to have had any empirical basis was for Congress to have taken a more relaxed attitude toward reducing the deficit in the operating budget than it would have otherwise.

Nations that have been successful in translating pension fund accumulations into national savings have generally excluded the systems

---

[82] George Hager, "Domenici vs. Sasser," *Congressional Quarterly Weekly Report*, April 20, 1991, 96.

[83] George Hager, "Senate OKs Fiscal Blueprint, Rejects Payroll Tax Cut," *Congressional Quarterly Weekly Report*, April 27, 1991, 1040–2.

[84] These results are summarized in *The American Enterprise*, March/April 1990, 101.

[85] For discussions of the political and economic significance of large trust fund surpluses, see Carolyn Weaver, ed., *Social Security's Looming Surpluses* (Washington, DC: American Enterprise Institute, 1990); and John Gist, ed., *Social Security and Economic Well-Being Across Generations* (Washington, DC: American Association of Retired Persons Public Policy Institute, 1988).

[86] Herman Leonard, "In God We Trust – The Political Economy of Social Security Reserves," *Social Security's Looming Surpluses* (Washington, DC: American Enterprise Intitute, 1990), 65.

from budget totals and deficit targets.[87] But while Social Security was officially restored to off-budget status beginning in fiscal year 1986, both the CBO and OMB emphasized aggregate budget totals inclusive of Social Security in their reports during the 1980s and 1990s. The main reason is because these agencies continued to believe in the concept of a unified budget. In addition, they feared that excluding Social Security from budget totals might encourage payroll tax cuts or benefit increases, making the overall deficit even higher.[88] Congress and the president encouraged the inclusion of Social Security in the budget totals. In the Gramm-Rudman Hollings Act of 1985, for example, Congress explicitly removed Social Security from the budget for all purposes *except* for calculating deficit-reduction targets. The 1990 Budget Enforcement Act officially removed Social Security from the budget entirely. Yet President Clinton and a Republican Congress in 1998 readily claimed credit for achieving a balanced budget, even though the reported $70 billion surplus would have been a $29 billion deficit without counting Social Security.

Still, this does not prove that the trust fund surpluses were raided. Indeed, despite the inclusion of the Social Security surpluses in budget totals, the deficit in the operating budget declined rapidly after 1992 (table 4.1). The most reasonable explanation for this improvement in the government's fiscal picture is that the American economy performed exceptionally well and Congress adopted budget reforms (caps on discretionary spending and pay-as-you-go rules for entitlements and revenues) that effectively prevented the enactment of expensive new budget promises without offsetting reductions. In sum, the growth of the Social Security surpluses did not erode the commitment to fiscal restraint, at least not during the Clinton Administration.

Social security reserves in an era of budget surpluses

In fiscal 1998 and 1999, the federal government ran its first consecutive unified budget surpluses since 1956–7. As officeholders struggled to control the new fiscal terrain, both political parties sought to cast themselves as the Social Security Trust Fund's most trustworthy defender. Aiming to block Republican demands for across-the-board tax cuts,

[87] Alicia H. Munnell and C. Nicole Ernsberger, "Foreign Experience with Public Pension Surpluses and National Savings," in Carolyn Weaver, ed., *Social Security's Looming Surpluses* (Washington, DC: American Enterprise Intitute, 1990), 85–118.

[88] For this view, see, for example, Congressional Budget Office, "The Economic and Budget Outlook: Fiscal Years 1991–1995" (Washington, DC: Government Printing Office, January 1990), 53.

Table 4.1. *Social Security surpluses and budget deficits, 1985–1998 in billions of dollars*

Fiscal year	Deficit Excluding Social Security	Social Security surplus	Total deficit
1985	222	9	212
1986	238	17	221
1987	169	20	149
1988	194	39	155
1989	205	52	153
1990	278	58	221
1991	322	54	269
1992	341	51	290
1993	300	47	255
1994	259	57	203
1995	226	60	163
1996	174	66	107
1997	103	81	22
1998	29	99	(70)

Source: OMB, Budget of the US Government, various years.

President Clinton in his 1998 state of the union address promised ("save Social Security first") to reserve future budget surpluses for the program. But Republicans countered by pointing out that Clinton's own budget proposals contemplated some use of Social Security surpluses for his new spending initiatives. The president, they declared in a familiar refrain, was "raiding" the trust fund. The GOP then decided to trump Clinton by pledging to devote *all* of the surpluses generated by Social Security to debt reduction. Clinton had little choice but to accept the challenge. In sum, a partisan bidding war ushered in a new standard of fiscal rectitude.[89]

With the aid of some fairly egregious bookkeeping tricks, the two parties managed to balance the fiscal 2000 budget without counting Social Security. Yet the defects of the inherited trust fund structure as a prefunding instrument had not been repaired (by completely removing control of the Social Security surpluses from government hands). Operating budget surpluses over the next decade are likely to be quite modest

---

[89] See Andrew Taylor, "Clinton, GOP Bet the Farms on More and Bigger Surpluses," *Congressional Quarterly Weekly Report*, November 20, 1999, 2767.

if discretionary spending is assumed to grow at the rate of inflation.[90] The question thus remained whether politicians would be able to stay within their new mandate to avoid tapping future Social Security surpluses when strong demands emerged for major new programs or tax cuts.

Conclusions

Social Security presents a leading case of institutional designers thinking about political risks and crafting a structure to promote a program's long-term sustainability.[91] The trust fund has strengthened a social compact based on the explicit exchange of taxes in return for future benefits, encouraging millions of American workers to rely on the government's commitments. The design has worked not so much by overriding elected officials' natural incentives to claim credit and avoid blame as by channeling those incentives toward the system's maintenance. As successful as the design has been, it has nonetheless encountered stress whenever large surpluses have accumulated. Social Security has been most stable when the trust fund has been maintained on a pay-as-you-go basis.

The resilience of the existing system will be tested in the years ahead. The system's long-term deficit will require some adjustments. The fact that this long-term deficit has opened during an era when both the trust fund and the overall budget are in near-term surplus creates reform possibilities, ranging from partial privatization to injecting general revenues into the system, that might well seem too expensive under other conditions. Whether or not Congress enacts major Social Security reforms in the coming decades, the benefit promises to those who have made substantial contributions under the current system will be kept. In a democratic polity, no institutional design eliminates the possibility of future political debates. The great achievement of Social Security's financial architects was to ensure that these inevitable debates would be conducted largely on terms of their own choosing.

[90] See Robert D. Reischauer, "The Dawning of a New Era," in Henry J. Aaron and Robert D. Reischauer, eds., *Getting National Priorities: The 2000 Election and Beyond* (Washington, DC: Brookings Institution, 1999).

[91] For an excellent analysis of Social Security reform and political risks, see Hugh Heclo, "A Political Science Perspective on Social Security Reform," in Graetz Arnold and Alicia H. Munnell, eds., *Framing the Social Security Debate* (Washington, DC: Brookings Institution, 1998), 65–88.

5

Medicare

After Social Security, no trust fund program enjoys greater political support, or induces more citizens to rely more heavily on governmental promises, than Medicare, the federal health insurance program for the aged and the disabled. Created in 1965, Medicare has grown into the second largest domestic program in the US budget. What makes the Medicare case especially intriguing is that the program is actually financed through two distinct trust fund structures.[1] Medicare Part A, which covers hospital stays, is financed by the Hospital Insurance (HI) Trust Fund, which in turn obtains its revenue primarily from a 2.9 percent payroll tax. Medicare Part B, which covers doctor visits and outpatient care, is financed by the Supplementary Medical Insurance (SMI) Trust Fund, which is currently funded three-quarters from general revenues and one-quarter from beneficiary premiums.[2]

What accounts for this dual financing structure? Many health experts argue that the historical division of Medicare financing is no more than an "artifact" of legislative bargaining over the Medicare bill in 1965. "The notion of having separate funding was a historical accident," says former Health Care Financing Administration head Gail Wilensky.[3] But while this design clearly did emerge during eleventh-hour legislative negotia-

---

[1] This chapter draws freely on Eric M. Patashnik and Julilan E. Zelizer, "Paying for Medicare: Benefits, Budgets, and Wilbur Mills's Policy Legacy," paper presented at the Policy History Conference, Clayton, Missouri, May 27–30, 1999. See also Zelizer, *Taxing America*, chapter 7.

[2] Medicare Part B is technically voluntary but about 98 percent of eligible persons enroll because the program is such a good deal.

[3] Quoted in Rebecca Adams, "Lawmakers Envision a Medicare System Greater

tions, it was not random or adventitious. Powerful House Ways and Means Committee chairman Wilbur Mills (D-Arkansas) in fact deliberately created separate Medicare trust funds in a conscious attempt to protect the Treasury and, especially, the government's capacity to make good on its existing Social Security promises. As I explain in more detail below, the technical logic of this institutional design weakened over time because of vast changes in patterns of American health care delivery. But the design persisted through a combination of intention and inertia, shaping the dynamics of American social policy and even thwarting the reform projects of subsequent politicians.

The historical–institutional logic of Medicare's financial design

As has been shown by Theodore Marmor, Martha Derthick, and other scholars, the Medicare Act of 1965 was crafted in the shadow of Social Security.[4] In this section, I do not attempt to provide a comprehensive account of the Medicare bill's genesis but rather focus on the considerations that led to the creation of two distinct trust fund structures.

During the 1960s, Social Security's popularity encouraged liberal advocates of national health insurance to propose a hospital insurance program for the elderly within a contributory trust fund framework. Cecil King (D-CA) and Senator Clinton Anderson (D-NM) joined with the Kennedy Administration to introduce a hospitalization program – which the media dubbed "Medicare" – for persons eligible for Social Security. Benefits would be provided on a universal (not means-tested) basis, and workers' coverage would be paid from an incremental expansion of the Social Security payroll tax and wage base. The proceeds of the revenues would be set aside in a new Hospital Insurance Trust Fund. By financing Medicare *through* Social Security, liberals hoped to avoid the disastrous fate that had met past US health reform efforts, thereby laying the

   Than the Sum of Its Parts," *Congressional Quarterly Weekly Report*, April 27, 1999, 891. Many other similar statements could be cited.
4 On the origins of Medicare, see Theodore R. Marmor, *The Politics of Medicare* (Chicago: Aldine, 1973); Derthick, *Policymaking for Social Security*, chapter 16; Jacobs, *Health of Nations*; Robert M. Ball, "What Medicare's Architects Had in Mind," *Health Affairs*, (4), Winter 1995, 62–72; and Jonathan B. Oberlander, "Medicare and the American State: The Politics of Federal Health Insurance, 1965–1995," Yale University, Doctoral Dissertation, 1995. I also profited from reading draft chapters from Marmor's forthcoming 2nd edition of *The Politics of Medicare*. For a superb technical discussion of Medicare finance, see David Koitz, "Medicare Financing," CRS Report for Congress (Washington, DC: Congressional Research Service, July 1, 1991), 91–517 EPW.

groundwork for future expansions.[5] "What is needed," the Social Security Advisory Council wrote in 1965, "is an arrangement under which working people, together with their employers, can contribute from earnings during their working years and have insurance protection against costs in later years."[6] When, for a brief moment in 1960, there appeared to be an opportunity for passing a bipartisan Medicare plan not based upon the Social Security model, liberals rejected it.[7]

Initially, then, trust fund financing was a politically liberal strategy for easing the Medicare program's adoption and endowing it with durability. As in Social Security, the full costs to workers would be strategically hidden by nominally splitting the payroll tax rate increase between employees and their employers.[8] Physician services (which were considered a less pressing need for the elderly) were purposefully excluded from the bill to narrow the opposition of the American Medical Association (AMA). The trust fund device would strengthen the social compact across generations by creating, in the words of Johnson Administration Budget Director Kermit Gordon, a budget account with "special integrity," enabling payers to "see that their own contributions" were financing the program.[9] By fostering notions of reciprocity and self-support, and drawing on the analogy to private insurance, Medicare would be sewn into the social fabric. Conservative opponents of Medicare understood the design in precisely these terms. Indeed, they feared that the political forces unleashed by it would render the program resilient to attack. Once Medicare was passed, warned a Republican lawmaker in 1963, it "would be exceedingly difficult to discontinue without breaking faith with those who have to pay the tax."[10]

---

[5] The Roosevelt Administration had earlier considered adding health insurance to Social Security legislation, but the opposition of physicians and the AMA convinced the New Dealers that its inclusion would jeopardize passage of the entire bill. President Truman also proposed universal health insurance without success.

[6] "Report of the Advisory Council on Social Security: The Status of the Social Security Program and Recommendations for Its Improvement," *Social Security Bulletin*, March 1965, 24.

[7] On the refusal of Democrats to compromise, see John B. Gilmour, *Strategic Disagreement* (Pittsburgh: University of Pittsburgh Press, 1995), 73–4.

[8] Charlotte Twight, "Medicare's Origins: The Economics and Politics of Dependency," *The Cato Journal*, 16 (3), Winter 1997.

[9] US Congress, House of Representation, "Medical Care for the Aged," Hearing Before the House Committee on Ways and Means, 89th Congress, 1st Session (1965), 803.

[10] Quoted in Twight, "Medicare's Origin."

Medicare as threat to social security finance

Although liberals were mainly concerned about binding future politicians to the government's spending promises, and not about protecting distant budgets, the trust fund strategy guaranteed that that bill would be considered by the Ways and Means Committee and that its fiscally conservative chairman Wilbur Mills (D-AK) would have a decisive influence over its final shape. Significantly, Mills believed that Medicare posed extremely serious risks to Social Security, a program with which, as Martha Derthick has shown, he had come to develop a proprietary relationship.[11] A major concern was that the long-term costs of health service benefits were much more difficult to predict than the cash benefits of old-age insurance. There was no linkage between workers' earnings on the one hand, and benefit payments, on the other. The medical services that workers eventually received would depend entirely on their future health status. Mills feared that hospital prices would explode over time, and that beneficiaries would pressure Congress to liberalize coverage once they discovered that physician services were excluded. This might compel future Congresses either to raise the payroll tax beyond politically acceptable levels or to abandon the doctrine of self-support. Either way, the American social insurance project as Mills knew and supported it would be put at risk.

After the Democratic election landslide of 1964, passage of some form of Medicare bill became inevitable. Still, Mills remained the key legislative gatekeeper. President Johnson instructed his Social Security advisers to work closely with Mills to satisfy his fiscal concerns without destroying the bill. At Mills's direction, Social Security actuary Robert Myers revised the bill to help resolve the budgetary tensions between Medicare and Social Security. To provide a greater margin of safety, Myers assumed that hospital utilization rates would be 20 percent higher than in the original proposal and that hospital prices would increase more rapidly. Additionally, he made his long-term actuarial forecasts on a 25-year basis rather than on the 75-year basis that had traditionally been used for Social Security. The final version of the Medicare bill also constructed symbolic distinctions between Medicare and Social Security. For example, tax withholdings for Social Security and Medicare were required to be displayed by the Internal Revenue Service on separate lines on workers' W-2 forms. These steps were intended by Mills, not to make Medicare a more perfect copy of Social Security, but rather to protect Social Security

[11] Derthick, *Policymaking for Social Security*.

from the economic and political pressures Medicare's enactment would release.

Mills as Medicare's financial architect

As Mills was supervising these design changes, two other health care proposals were being circulated in Washington. The AMA was pushing an "Eldercare" bill that offered voluntary medical insurance for poor seniors. Another voluntary alternative, "Bettercare," was proposed by Representative John Byrnes (R-WI). The plan covered both hospital and doctors' bills and certain patient services. Byrnes believed that payroll taxes gave workers a false impression that they had a legally binding right to their benefits, which in turn made spending harder to control. His plan thus relied on general funds for two-thirds of the program's costs and beneficiary premiums for the remainder. While hardly a liberal, Mills vigorously disagreed with Byrnes about the advantages of payroll tax financing; he believed earmarked taxes usefully distinguished social insurance from welfare. The main reason for Mills's commitment to trust fund financing and earmarked taxes, however, was that he believed they promoted long-term fiscal control. "Haven't we done a better job, actually," he asked, "of financing the cost of the social security program out of a separate fund, paid for by a payroll tax, than we have some other expenditures of Government?" For Mills, the answer was clear:

> [W]henever you have a program financed by a specific tax, the willingness of people to pay that tax, that specific tax, limits the benefits of that specific program . . . if you put a program, then, into the general fund of the Treasury, there is less likelihood that you control the package of benefits initially enacted than there is if you put it in a trust fund . . . I can't help but reach the conclusion that a specific fund, supported by a payroll tax, is a more conservative method of financing something than to do it out of the general fund of Treasury.[12]

So, Mills in 1965 had three options before him: a Medicare program funded through earmarked payroll taxes; a Bettercare means-tested welfare plan funded entirely through general revenues; and an Eldercare plan for voluntary hospital and doctor coverage financed through beneficiary premiums and general fund subsidies. In a move that stunned his Ways and Means colleagues, Mills combined Medicare, Eldercare, and Bettercare into a "three-layer-cake." The liberals' Medicare program thus became Medicare Part A (paid from the HI Trust Fund). Bettercare was

---

[12] US Congress, House of Representatives, "Medical Care for the Aged," Hearing Before the House Committee on Ways and Means, 98.

transformed into Medicare Part B (paid from the SMI Trust Fund), and Eldercare became Medicaid (paid from federal general revenues and matching state funds).

It is this three-part structure that many observers call a "historical accident." Certainly it lacks elegance and was not the result of decades of legislative deliberation. Had there been a different constellation of bargaining forces in 1965, a different form might well have emerged. Yet Mills must be seen as a *purposive* designer here, operating strategically within his constraints. In fact, the design satisfied Mills's political and fiscal concerns well given the constraints he faced. Not only did this move undercut the Republican argument that the Democratic bill was inadequate because it failed to cover physician services, it served to lock-in Mills's long-term policy goals. As I previously noted, Mills believed that if physician services were excluded from the bill, Congress would soon face pressures to cover them under Social Security. Accepting Byrnes's proposal would preempt these pressures. As Theodore R. Marmor puts it in his seminal account of Medicare's enactment, Mills had built a "fence" around the Medicare program.[13]

Part B would be financed through a new SMI Trust Fund. Mills believed that beneficiary cost-sharing would serve two roles. First, it would distinguish the program from welfare. Second, it would contain the program's future growth. The Secretary of Health, Education and Welfare (later Health and Human Services) was required to promulgate a premium rate at regular intervals that would cover one-half of the program's projected annual costs.[14] The other half would be paid out of general tax revenues. Normally, of course, Mills disliked committing general funds to long-term social programs. "I have said repeatedly that we cannot run the risk of bankrupting the Federal Treasury once and for all by putting this entire cost upon the general fund of Treasury."[15] Some use of general revenues in Part B could not be avoided, however, if the program were to be voluntary, as both Mills and the AMA insisted.[16] For

---

[13] Marmor, *The Politics of Medicare*, 69.

[14] Originally, the premium rate was to be set every two years, but this was changed to an annual determination beginning in July 1969. The initial decision to delegate authority over the Part B premium rate to the executive bureaucracy was unusual since Congress usually jealously guarded its authority over Social Security financing. According to Robert Myers, this delegation "seemed necessary and desirable at the start of the program because of the short-range nature of the financing provisions and because of the volatile nature of the benefit costs, which were not at the time reliably predictable over a moderate period of years in the future." Myers, *Social Security*, 293.

[15] *Congressional Record*, 89th Congress, 1st session, April 7, 1965, 7213.

[16] Moreover, without a general fund subsidy, premium rates would have been too

Mills, a fifty–fifty cost-sharing arrangement was a reasonable compromise.

Medicare's political and fiscal dynamics

In 1965, Medicare's two divisions corresponded to the organization of health care delivery and insurance in the private sector. There was a clear division between hospital care and physician services. The two Medicare trust funds followed the insurance structures set by the Blue Cross Association hospital insurance and the Blue Shield Association physicians' care programs. Over time, however, the US health care system became fully integrated. Complex medical procedures that once could only be performed in a hospital setting were increasingly done by physicians in their own offices. Blue Cross and Blue Shield were completely merged by 1982.[17]

Despite this systematic integration, Medicare's separate trust fund structures endured. While budget experts and health economists argued that Medicare's financing needs should be evaluated comprehensively, the Medicare Board of Trustees continued to issue annual reports on the condition of each trust fund separately. Because Part A relied on specific taxes to meet its obligations, it could technically go "bankrupt." By contrast, the SMI Trust Fund could not face insolvency since the law required the Treasury to make up any difference between Part B spending and premium contributions.[18] As a result of this seemingly artificial distinction, the two Parts of Medicare have experienced different legislative and fiscal dynamics.[19]

HI Trust Fund dynamics: self-support and the politics of bankruptcy

The evolution of Medicare Part A has been shaped by the imperative of keeping the trust fund solvent. As it has in Social Security finance, Congress has traditionally adhered to a policy of self-support. The HI Trust Fund has been financed almost entirely from payroll taxes. The main exceptions are interest earnings on the trust fund's securities and (since 1993) revenues from the income taxation of Social Security

---

high for younger and healthier elderly persons. By contrast, if the rates were allowed to vary by age, the premiums would have been prohibitive for persons over age eighty. Ball, "What Medicare's Architects Had in Mind," 69.

[17] Adams, "Lawmakers Envision a Medicare System."

[18] Koitz, "Medicare Financing," 44.

[19] Henry J. Aaron and Robert D. Reischauer, "The Medicare Reform Debate: What is the Next Step?" *Health Affairs*, Winter 1995, 14.

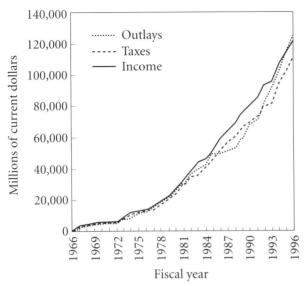

Figure 5.1 Financial history of HI Trust Fund, fiscal years 1966–1996
Note: Income includes interest earnings
Source: *Annual Reports of the Medicare Board of Trustees* (Washington, DC: Government Printing Office, various years).

benefits. As the trends in figure 5.1 show, the trust fund's earmarked revenues have been kept just high enough to cover current payments (and provide for a small contingency reserve). Historically, there has been little discussion of accumulating a large reserve to prefund the system's liabilities. The big concern has been paying current bills.

As I noted above, long-range estimates of Part A's financial status were originally made on a 25-year basis because of the difficulty in forecasting the costs of a service benefit. In the mid 1980s, the time horizon was extended to 75 years in order to highlight the fiscal challenges of the baby boomers' retirement.[20] There are two main elements to these long-range forecasts. First, the Trustees estimate the HI Trust Fund's average surplus or deficit (as a percent of taxable payroll) over the valuation period. While long-term Social Security estimates have sometimes projected large future surpluses, the Trustees' reports have projected long-range deficits for Medicare Part A almost continuously since the early 1970s.[21] While some health experts have argued that the whole enterprise of forecasting

[20] *Ibid.*, 41.
[21] Koitz, "Medicare Financing," 1.

Medicare costs beyond a ten year horizon is "an exercise in comparative fantasy," these projections have had a significant influence on the political debate.[22] Indeed, much of the perception that the United States faces a long-term entitlement crisis has been fueled by the acceptance of the Trustees' convention of looking at Medicare costs 75 years out.

The second and more important number in the Trustees' actuarial forecasts is the estimate of the point at which current revenues plus the accumulated trust fund balance will be unable to fully cover promised benefits. The Trustees have reported that the HI Trust Fund would be exhausted in ten years or less more than a dozen times between 1970 and 1997 (table 5.1). On each such occasion, Congress has taken action to stabilize the trust fund's financial condition. While these steps have tended to improve the system's distant outlook, they have in general not eliminated the system's actuarial imbalances entirely.

The main cause of the trust fund's financial difficulties has of course been the rapid growth of program spending. Throughout much of its history, Medicare spending has climbed at a faster pace than inflation, wages, and GDP. When the original projections of Medicare spending were made in 1965, the trust fund's outlays in 1990 were expected to be $9 billion. The actual figure was $65 billion.[23] Because of the deep reliance of program beneficiaries on Medicare payments (which constitute almost one-fifth of the aged's income on a per capita basis), the accepted belief that enrollees have earned their benefits through taxes and a lifetime of work, and the power and sympathy of the senior lobby, the individual entitlement structure has thus far been preserved.[24] Despite this crucial element of programmatic continuity, however, significant changes have been enacted during moments of trust fund difficulty. As Paul Pierson observes, the political commitment to trust fund solvency has caused Medicare Part A to face "sustained budgetary pressure" despite its entitlement status and middle-class constituency.[25]

Congress initially responded to Part A financing problems by increasing payroll tax rates. The combined HI tax rate climbed from 0.6 percent

[22] Former HCFA Administrator Bruce Vladeck, quoted in Joseph White, "Saving Medicare – From What?" Paper delivered at The Annual Meeting of the American Political Science Association Convention, Boston, Massachusetts, September 3–6, 1996, 4. White provides a sharp liberal critique of the reliance on long-term Medicare estimates.

[23] Some of these differences reflect policy changes and not just forecasting errors, however. See R. J. Myers, "How Bad Were the Original Actuarial Estimates for Medicare's Hospital Insurance Program?" *The Actuary* (February 1994): 6–7.

[24] Koitz, "Medicare Financing," 21.

[25] Pierson, *Dismantling the Welfare State?*, 137–8.

Table 5.1. *Number of years from Medicare Hospital Insurance Part A Trustees' projection until insolvency*

Year of Trustees' report	Years until insolvency under intermediate forecast
1970	2
1971	2
1972	4
1973	None indicated
1974	None indicated
1975	About 20
1976	About 15
1977	About 10
1978	12
1979	13
1980	14
1981	10
1982	5
1983	7
1984	7
1985	13
1986	10
1987	15
1988	17
1989	None indicated
1990	13
1991	14
1992	10
1993	6
1994	7
1995	7
1996	5
1997	4
1998	10
1999	16

Source: Annual Reports of the Medicare Board of Trustees (Washington, DC: Government Printing Office, various years). Based on intermediate projections.

in 1966 to 2.6 percent in 1981, an increase of 333 percent.[26] By the mid 1980s, however, elected officials were no longer willing to raise payroll tax rates further. The last tax rate increase (set in 1977) to 2.9 percent became effective in 1986. Congress managed to pump a bit more money into the HI Trust Fund over the 1980s by periodically raising the maximum level of earnings subject to the Medicare tax. In budget legislation enacted in 1993, Congress eliminated the wage ceiling altogether.[27]

But Congress's main response to the trust fund difficulties has been to reform payments to providers.[28] In 1982, the HI Trust Fund was projected to be exhausted within five years. To keep the system in the black, new limits on provider payments were imposed in the 1982 budget reconciliation bill.[29] Congress also ordered the Health Care Financing Administration, the agency which administers Medicare, to develop a comprehensive plan for controlling Part A spending. The result was a dramatic reform of hospital reimbursement. Previously, the government had reimbursed hospitals for the costs of treatment after services had been rendered. Under the new system, based on a schedule of "diagnosis-related groups" (DRGs) system, the government began paying hospitals *prospectively* for specific diagnoses. The reform received relatively little attention from most voters because it was tucked into the 1983 Social Security rescue legislation.[30] But it had a major policy impact. According to one study, it reduced the "growth rate of real [Part A] spending from 5.4 percent annually between 1980 and 1985 to just 1 percent annually between 1985 and 1990."[31] This extended the HI Trust Fund's projected date of exhaustion from 1991 in the 1981 Trustees report to 2005 in the 1991 report.

The most recent, and politically explosive, Part A solvency crisis began in 1995, when the Trustees warned that the HI Trust Fund might be

---

[26] Myers, *Social Security*, table 7.1, 604.

[27] Marilyn Moon and Janemarie Mulvey, *Entitlements and the Elderly*, (Washington, DC: The Urban Institute, 1996), 73.

[28] Alissa J. Rubin, "Medicare's Woes, While Nothing New, Are Politically Charged This Year," *Congressional Quarterly Weekly Report*, May 6, 1995, 1228–9.

[29] Allen Schick, "Controlling the 'Uncontrollable': Budgeting for Health Care in an Age of Megadeficits," in Jack A. Meyer and Marion Ein Lewin, eds., *Charting the Future of Health Care* (Washington, DC: American Enterprise Press, 1987). See also John L. Palmer and Barbara Boyle Torrey, "Health Care Financing and Pension Programs," in Gregory B. Mills and John L. Palmer, eds., *Federal Budget Policy in the 1980s* (Washington, DC: The Urban Institute Press, 1982).

[30] David G. Smith, *Paying for Medicare: The Politics of Reform* (New York: Aldine, 1992).

[31] Congressional Budget Office, *The Economic and Budget Outlook: Fiscal Years 1993–1997* (Washington, DC: Government Printing Office, January 1992a), 58.

depleted as early as 2002. As other observers have noted, deficit hawks and ideological conservatives tried to exploit this solvency crisis to push through dramatic program cutbacks. The new Republican Congressional majority in 1995 called for $270 billion in Medicare cuts over seven years. By all accounts, Republicans arrived at the $270 billion figure after determining how much they needed to cut Medicare in order to have enough money left over to balance the overall budget by 2002 and still provide a tax cut of $245 billion. Only $90 billion of the Medicare savings would be used to directly stave off insolvency in Part A.[32] In short, conservative Republicans tried to leverage the Part A bankruptcy crisis to pursue a major retrenchment project.

For a time, it appeared that Republicans might win a stunning victory. Early polls revealed broad public acceptance of Medicare cuts if needed to stave off trust fund bankruptcy.[33] But Republican reformers ultimately overreached.[34] In his high-profile budget standoff with Newt Gingrich, President Clinton vetoed the Republican measure, arguing that the proposed cuts were far deeper than necessary to safeguard Medicare's viability. Yet even liberal Democrats were forced to acknowledge that the HI Trust Fund remained in dire shape, and they eventually agreed to substantial Medicare cuts and major program restructurings in the Balanced Budget Act of 1997.[35] At the time, the changes were expected to keep the HI Trust Fund solvent until 2007. Subsequent forecasts were even more favorable. In summary, then, the HI Trust Fund experience has featured a commitment to self-financing, periodic Part A bankruptcy crises, and the enactment of policy changes to extend the trust fund's expected duration.

In his excellent comprehensive study of Medicare policymaking, health

---

[32] See David E. Rosenbaum, "The Medicare Brawl: Finger-Pointing, Hyperbole and the Facts Behind Them," *The New York Times*, October 1, 1985, A18.

[33] See Margaret Weir, *The Social Divide* (Washington, DC: The Brookings Institution, 1998), 523. Weir here refers to evidence summarized in Eric Pianin and Mario Brossard, "Americans Oppose Cutting Entitlements to Fix Budget: Poll Finds Pessimism on Medicare, Social Security," *Washington Post*, March 29, 1997, A4.

[34] See Mark A. Peterson, "The Politics of Health Care Policy: Overreaching in an Age of Polarization," in Margaret Weir, ed., *The Social Divide* (Washington, DC: The Brookings Institution, 1998). Clinton had called for Medicare cuts of roughly $120 billion over seven years.

[35] The 1997 Act created a new Medicare Choice option that opened the program to a variety of new private insurance plans, including medical savings accounts and various managed care plans. For an excellent analysis, see Jonathan B. Oberlander, "Medicare: The End of Consensus," paper delivered at the Annual Meeting of the American Political Science Association Convention, September 3–6, 1998, Boston, Massachusetts.

policy scholar Jonathan B. Oberlander claims that the HI Trust Fund has produced effects precisely opposite from those which were intended.[36] His argument is that the very mechanisms adopted to assure the program's political and financial stability – payroll taxes and a trust fund – have ironically been sources of its *instability*. While the Social Security Trust Fund produced actuarial surpluses during the 1950s and 1960s that could be used to pay for expanded benefits, the HI Trust Fund has constantly been on the brink of exhaustion. The whole atmosphere of the program has been one of fiscal crisis and alarm. It is certainly true that policymaking for Medicare has been more volatile than its legislative architects wished. But this volatility is largely the result of the incessant growth of Medicare spending, which placed enormous strains on the rest of the budget. From a historical perspective, Part A solvency crises – artificial as they may be from an economic standpoint – have arguably served to perpetuate the delicate political balance between secure benefits and fiscal restraint that Wilbur Mills originally sought to engineer. This is not to suggest that the Part A design has been entirely functional, only that the consequences it has produced have not been wholly perverse.

SMI Trust Fund dynamics: increasing government subsidies

However one appraises the performance of the HI Trust Fund, the dynamics of the SMI Trust Fund have been much different. As the fiscally conservative Concord Coalition notes, indeed laments, program solvency has not been an issue with Part B because the SMI Trust Fund "has an open pipeline to the treasury which automatically closes any gap between beneficiary premiums and expenditures."[37]

As we saw, Mills's original plan called for beneficiaries to bear half the program's costs. But this cost-sharing framework did not prove durable. Congress did allow the premium to rise from $3 per month in 1966 to $5.80 six years later, an increase of 93 percent. In 1972, however, a Democratic Congress responded to the unpopularity of rapidly increasing premium rates by enacting a provision that limited future premium increases to the percentage increase in Social Security cash benefits (which would themselves be indexed for inflation beginning in 1975).[38]

The decision to cap Part B premium increases actually represented a compromise between the more extreme positions of congressional liberals

---

[36] Oberlander, "Medicare and the American State," chapter 4.
[37] Concord Coalition, "Issue Brief: The 1999 Report of the Social Security and Medicare Trustees," May 20, 1999.
[38] Myers, *Social Security*, 612.

on the one hand and the Nixon Administration on the other. Senator Frank Church's Special Commission on Aging sought to eliminate the Part B premium altogether.[39] The argument was that high premiums undermined the income protection provided by Social Security.[40] The Nixon Administration agreed with the need to do away with the Part B premium.[41] In sharp contrast to the Church proposal, however, the Administration plan would have had the $1.5 billion then represented by premiums funded out of the payroll tax. But Mills viewed this move as a threat to Social Security's long-range viability. Indexing the premium rate to consumer prices was another strategic accommodation.[42]

As matters turned out, medical inflation increased much faster than general inflation over the 1970s. The share of Part B income accounted for by beneficiary premiums therefore fell from 50 percent to approximately 25 percent by the 1980s, when Congress simply froze it at that level (figure 5.2).[43] Meanwhile, Part B outlays soared, in a number of years exceeding the rate of the growth in Part A.[44] The general fund subsidy climbed from $18 billion in 1986 to $62 billion in 1996.

In theory, Congress might have taken steps to stop this. But without an explicit solvency crisis in the SMI Trust Fund, there was no focusing event for legislative action.[45] "Part B deserves more attention than it

[39] See statement of Frank Church, *Congressional Record*, March 9, 1972, 7789.

[40] *Congressional Record*, April 5, 1972, 11536; see also statement of William D. Hathaway, *Congressional Record*, February 7, 1972, 2984.

[41] At the time, the Nixon Administration was proposing to combine the two Medicare trust funds.

[42] It should be noted that Mills was then a presidential candidate. In the heat of the campaign, he endorsed legislation that in previous years he might well have opposed. On the role of Mills in the larger fight over indexing of Social Security cash benefits, see Derthick, *Policymaking for Social Security*, chapter 17.

[43] During the 1980s, Congress regularly voted to set Part B premiums at 25 percent of program costs. In 1990, however, it set specific dollar figures rather than a percentage. These dollar figures reflected the CBO's estimate of what 25 percent of program costs would be over the next few years. Program costs grew at a slower rate than expected, however, causing the premium level temporarily to reach 31.5 percent of program costs. The Balanced Budget Act of 1997 permanently set the premium equal to 25 percent of program costs. See US Congress, House of Representatives, *1998 Green Book*, Committee on Ways and Means (Washington, DC: Government Printing Office, May 19, 1998), 116–17.

[44] Marilyn Moon, *Medicare Now and in the Future* (Washington, DC: Urban Institute, 1993), 45.

[45] Significantly, Congress did increase beneficiary premiums (which were to be funneled into a new trust fund account) in the ill-fated Medicare Catastrophic Coverage Act of 1988. But the Act was repealed just over a year later after it sparked a backlash from upper-income seniors who believed the new insurance coverage was not worth the increased user charges. The original deal offered less

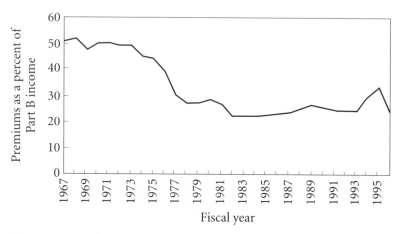

Figure 5.2 Premiums as a percent of Part B income, fiscal years 1967–1996
Source: *Annual Reports of the Medicare Board of Trustees* (Washington, DC: Government Printing Office, various years).

gets," said Richard S. Foster, the chief HCFA actuary. "Under present law, it can't go broke . . . .but it's not good to have outlays growing faster than your financing base."[46] The introduction of the DRG system for hospital insurance in 1983 in response to concerns about the HI Trust Fund's impending bankruptcy may well have increased Part B spending in the mid to late 1980s by creating an incentive for providers to accelerate the shift of procedures from in-patient hospital care to out-patient services, where reimbursement schedules were then more generous.[47] In sum, Medicare's dual financing structure has not only created distinctive political dynamics for the two Parts, but has influenced actual patterns of health care delivery.

Frustrating the reform projects of successor politicians

While the legal and financial barrier between the two Medicare trust funds has been maintained, it has not been impenetrable. Indeed, Congress in the Balanced Budget Act of 1997 deliberately shifted one of

generous net benefits than previous Medicare legislation largely because of deficit constraints. See Julie Rovner, "Congress's 'Catastrophic' Attempt to Fix Medicare," in Thomas E. Mann and Norman J. Ornstein, eds., *Intensive Care: How Congress Shapes Health Policy* (Washington, DC: Brookings Institution, 1995).
[46] Quoted in Adams, "Lawmakers Envision a Medicare System," 891.
[47] Moon and Mulvey, *Entitlements and the Elderly*, 111.

the fastest growing Medicare activities – home health services – from Part A to Part B. This shift did not reduce total Medicare spending, or the federal budget deficit, by a single dime. But it did have the political virtue of painlessly extending the HI Trust Fund's life by six years. To be sure, the accounting change was defended on the grounds that home health services (which are provided in the community) conceptually fit better in Part B. Marilyn Moon, one of the two public Trustees of Medicare, argued that the shift was a legitimate way for Congress to "buy time until a more permanent solution" to the HI Trust Fund's financing problem was found.[48] But President Clinton's transparent motivation for the change was to extend the HI Trust Fund's solvency.

Conservative Republicans (who of course wanted the HI Trust Fund's problems to appear *worse*, not better) initially denounced the proposed shift as an accounting gimmick pure and simple. "It's a sham, a shell game," said Sen. Don Nickles (R-OK).[49] "We need the pressure of having this checkbook of part A, rather than moving some of those expenditures off budget as in part B, which is going to get paid because the government pays its bills," said Charles N. Kahn II, staff director of the Health Subcommittee on Ways and Means.[50] But Republicans ultimately agreed to the transfer in the balanced budget deal.

If the political transaction costs of playing these kinds of accounting games were *de minimis*, the existence of two separate Medicare funds would historically have mattered little. In fact, however, Medicare's inherited financial design has often constituted a formidable barrier to the achievement of the reform projects of successor politicians. In the program's early years, it was mainly liberal program builders who were frustrated by Medicare's design. They saw the dual financing structure as administratively cumbersome, insufficiently redistributive, and incompatible with rapid program expansion. The 1971 Social Security Advisory Council proposed combining the two trust funds, adding some new medical benefits, and financing the whole program two-thirds from payroll taxes and one-third from general revenues. A liberal majority on the 1975 Advisory Council would have gone even further, calling for general tax funds eventually to finance all of Medicare spending. In addition to making Medicare more progressive, this shift would have had

---

[48] Marilyn Moon, "No Medicare 'Gimmick,'" *The Washington Post*, February 10, 1997, A19.

[49] Spencer Rich, "Clinton's Medicare Proposal Draws Bipartisan Criticism At Senate Hearings," *The Washington Post*, January 24, 1997, A16.

[50] Charles Kahn III, "Comment," in Robert D. Reischauer, Stuart Butler, and Judith R. Lave, eds., *Medicare: Preparing for the Challenges of the 21st Century* (Washington, DC: National Academy of Social Insurance, 1998), 53.

the added benefit of freeing up more payroll tax revenues for Social Security, whose own trust fund was then in trouble.

But these liberal proposals for a combined Medicare Trust Fund during the 1970s sparked resistance from fiscal conservatives. Nixon's Secretary of HEW, Caspar Weinberger, claimed that it was "inappropriate" for a program "whose strength" has depended on working people to be financed from general revenues. Weinberger argued that general fund financing would destroy the "earned rights" principle of the HI Trust Fund, transforming Medicare into a welfare program.[51] President Ford took a similar position.[52] Four conservative members of the 1975 Council – Rita Ricardo Campbell of the Hoover Institution, Edwin J. Faulkner of the Woodman Accident and Life Company, John J. Scanlon of AT&T and J. Henry Smith of Equitable Life Insurance Society – argued that general fund financing of Part A would hide the program's costs and "weaken even further the control over it."[53]

By the late 1990s, it was fiscal conservatives' reform projects that were being stymied by Medicare's inherited design. The historic concept of Medicare solvency, argued Senator John Breaux (D-LA) and Representative Bill Thomas (R-CA), chairmen of the 1997–8 Bipartisan Medicare Reform Commission,

> is one that has been partially and inappropriately borrowed from Social Security and has never fully reflected the fiscal integrity, or lack thereof, of the Medicare program. In Medicare, "solvency" has meant only whether the Part A Trust Fund outlays were poised to exceed Part A reserves and collections. That is all. Recently even this partial proof of fiscal integrity has been shattered. The notion of Part A "solvency" or rather 'insolvency' has been used to shift more program costs to the general fund. An act of Congress shifted major home health expenditures from Part A to Part B in 1997, thus extending the fiction of the Part A Trust Fund "solvency" from 2002 through 2008.[54]

[51] US Congress, House of Representatives, "Hearings Before The Subcommittee on Social Security of the Committee on Ways and Means," 94th Congress, 1st Session (1975), 436.

[52] Myers, *Social Security*, 129.

[53] "Reports of the Quadrennial Advisory Council on Social Security," H. Doc 94–75, 94th, congress, 1st Session (Washington, DC: Government Printing Office, 1975), 73.

[54] The Commission disbanded without a formal recommendation. Breaux and Thomas had pushed for a major program restructuring. Under their plan, known as "premium support," retirees would be given a fixed amount of money that they could use to buy either private or public health insurance, with the government's contribution capped at a specific amount. While the Commission did not reach a consensus on the overall direction of Medicare reform, most

Breaux and Thomas called for the creation of a unified Medicare Trust Fund. Under their proposal, the Trustees would be required to notify Congress whenever general revenues were expected to exceed 40 percent of total Medicare costs. Congress would then have the opportunity to debate changes in the program, such as payroll tax or premium hikes, spending cuts, or increased general fund appropriations. In 1999, the Clinton Administration also proposed to erode the financial distinction between the two trust funds by transferring almost $300 billion in general revenues to Part A over the next decade. This would delay the system's insolvency but at the cost of abandoning the longstanding commitment to self-support.

Conclusions

If, as Aaron Wildavksy has observed, the growth of big government causes the "policy space" to become more crowded, it should not be surprising when new instruments of budgetary precommitment are layered atop old ones.[55] Medicare's complex trust fund design is a case in point. As we have seen, the design was meant not only to graft Medicare into the American welfare state (a goal it accomplished in short order), but also to protect the Treasury and respect the fiscal precommitments embodied in the already established Social Security system. Given the political difficulty of keeping all these promises simultaneously, what may be most remarkable is not that Medicare's financial design has experienced policy stress, but that it has worked at all.

Fittingly, Medicare's political dynamics since 1965 have been shaped more by Social Security's internal dynamics than the other way around. Important policy changes have been made to Medicare during those few occasions when Social Security reform was on the agenda. For example, the initial capping of the Part B premium occurred as part of the 1972 Social Security amendments, and the DRG system for hospital reimbursements was enacted as part of the Social Security Amendments of 1983. By contrast, Social Security changes have rarely been on the table when Congress has considered Medicare reform.

Unlike the Social Security case, trust fund financing has clearly not isolated Medicare from general budget pressures. Indeed, Medicare cut-

commission members seem to have accepted the need for a unified financial structure. See National Bipartisan Commission on the Future of Medicare, "Final Breaux-Thomas Medicare Reform Proposal" (Washington, DC: Government Printing Office, March 16, 1999).

[55] Aaron Wildavsky, *Speaking Truth to Power* (New Brunswick, New Jersey: Transaction, 1979), chapter 3.

backs were included in virtually every deficit reduction bill enacted during the 1980s and 1990s. There are several reasons why Medicare's trust fund provided relatively less autonomy. First, the HI Trust Fund has been on the precipice of insolvency nearly continuously while the Social Security system has been in surplus since the mid 1980s. Second, Medicare cutbacks could be targeted against providers rather than beneficiaries. Finally, Medicare has been one of the fastest growing social programs. While Social Security outlays increased modestly from 19.5 percent of the federal budget in 1975 to 21.9 percent in 1995, Medicare's share of federal spending more than doubled from 3.9 percent to 10.5 percent over this same period. Very early on, Medicare's explosive growth stimulated the interest of central budget guardians.[56] Given the integration of US health care delivery, Medicare's split fiscal design no longer makes much sense. The normative challenge for tomorrow's institutional designers is to craft a more technically appropriate structure that will not require politicians to abrogate the social and fiscal promises upon which the Medicare program was founded.

[56] Derthick, *Policymaking for Social Security*, 338.

6

Highways

In a sense, the creation of the Highway Trust Fund in 1956 represented a departure from existing patterns of institutional design. Previously, use of the trust fund device had been restricted almost entirely to public pension and social insurance programs. By their very nature, such programs involve long-term commitments to specific individuals about their personal economic security. By contrast, the Highway Trust Fund finances an infrastructure program providing transportation benefits to a broad-based group (motorists), with spillover benefits to geographic areas (states) and service providers (highway contractors). Yet the Highway Trust Fund, like the social insurance trust funds, was designed to promote policy durability. The trust fund's adoption gave highway interests procedural and symbolic advantages over other lobbies in the yearly scramble for fiscal support. But these advantages have also made the Highway Trust Fund a conspicuous target for highway opponents and institutional budget guardians, forcing the highway lobby to defend the trust fund against wholesale modification.

Rationales for trust fund and earmarked taxes

In mid 1950s America, constructing a transcontinental highway system was a policy idea whose time had come.[1] A "surge of media articles"

---

[1] My discussion of the events leading to the passage of the Federal Highway Act of 1956 draws heavily on the following studies: Gary T. Schwartz. "Urban Freeways and the Interstate System," *Southern California Law Review*, 49 (406), March 1976, 406–513; James A. Dunn, Jr., *Miles to Go: European And American Transportation*

discussed problems in US roadways and the need to improve automotive safety.[2] The main political barrier to the project was money. Congress first authorized construction of a superhighway network in 1944. But interstate construction was vastly more expensive than traditional federal-aid highway projects and Congress offered states no economic incentive to begin the work beyond its normal 50–50 matching grants. Only 1 percent of the planned 40,000 mile interstate system had been completed by the end of 1953.

What may appear surprising from today's perspective is not that Congress ultimately established the Highway Trust Fund in 1956 to pay for the interstate program, but that it did not arrive at this solution more quickly. By the 1950s, earmarking gas tax revenues for highway improvements was a standard practice in many US states.[3] Congress even passed legislation designed to protect the integrity of these state road funds. A 1934 statute provided for a cut in federal highway assistance to states that diverted an "excessive" amount of their gasoline revenues to non-highway uses.[4]

Yet if members of Congress were willing to tie the hands of state legislatures, they were reluctant to bind themselves, especially for a program that, unlike Social Security, did not provide discrete benefits to named individuals. The House in 1954 passed a measure that would have made future federal highway disbursements legally contingent on pre-servation of the existing federal gas tax. But the provision was dropped in conference after House Minority Whip John W. McCormick called it "unusual."[5] It was only after alternative design mechanisms were found wanting that Congress agreed on the trust fund structure.

Policies (Cambridge, MA: MIT Press, 1981); Mark H. Rose, Interstate: Express Highway Politics, 1939–1989 [Revised Edition] (Lawrence: University Press of Kansas, 1990).

[2] Frank R. Baumgartner and Bryan D. Jones, Agendas and Instability in American Politics (Chicago: University of Chicago Press, 1993), 122.

[3] In 1919 Oregon became the first state to levy a gasoline tax. By 1929, every state in the nation had a gas tax. While public support for the gas tax was conditioned on its linkage to road building, the gas tax proved such a lucrative source of revenue that politicians were tempted to divert some of its proceeds to other uses, sparking protests from oil companies, automobile manufacturers, and state highway administrations. See John C. Burnham, "The Gasoline Tax and the Automobile Revolution," The Mississippi Valley Historical Review: A Journal of American History, 98, December 1961, 435–59.

[4] Congress never made good on the threat, however, in part because the definition of "excessive" diversion left states considerable wiggle room.

[5] Congressional Quarterly Almanac (1954), 501.

Alternatives rejected

Congress explicitly considered, and rejected, three alternative designs before adopting the trust fund: general revenues, tolls, and bonds. Tire manufacturers, the American Automobile Association, and the petroleum industry insisted that the interstate system should be paid from general revenues. Their reasoning was that freeways benefited the entire society through economic growth and improved mobility. But Eisenhower demanded a "sound" interstate program, insisting that "highway users" provide "the total dollars necessary for improvements and new construction."[6] In sum, automotive interests may have been at the peak of their power in the 1950s, but they were not formidable enough to win approval of a massive road program unaccompanied by a specific tax increase.[7]

If interest group pressure failed to create a consensus behind general fund financing, economic efficiency proved to be an inadequate rationale for tolls. By the mid 1950s, tolls were a major revenue source for many state highway systems. Eisenhower himself considered toll financing an ideal policy. But the proposal encountered large political and organizational roadblocks.[8] Not only did prior federal law mandate that federal roads be "toll free," but the Bureau of Public Roads deemed toll financing of a transcontinental highway system to be administratively unfeasible. Toll financing was also vehemently opposed by the AAA and many Western state governors.[9]

Of the three revenue options Congress considered and rejected, bond-financing received its most probing scrutiny. In 1955, a special presidential commission headed by General Lucius D. Clay proposed the creation of a new Federal Highway Corporation that would finance interstate construction by issuing 30-year bonds.[10] The bonds would subsequently be retired from the proceeds of existing federal gasoline and tire taxes.[11]

---

[6] Quoted in *Congressional Record*, April 27, 1956, 7213.

[7] For background on early bargaining over the program's financing, see John M. Martin, Jr., "Proposed Federal Highway Legislation in 1955: A Case Study in the Legislative Process," *The Georgetown Law Journal*, 44, 1956, 221–83.

[8] Schwartz, "Urban Freeways," 430–1.

[9] Bert Pierce, "Auto Association Condemns Tolls," *The New York Times*, January 15, 1955b, 9.

[10] "Highway Proposals," *Congressional Quarterly Almanac* (1955), 433.

[11] The federal government had introduced a gas tax of 1 cent per gallon in 1932. Congress subsequently raised the gas tax to 1.5 cents in 1941 and to 2 cents in 1951, with the money retained in the general fund. On the Clay Commission report, see Joseph A. Loftus, "Eisenhower Gets 101 Billion Federal-State Road Plan," *The New York Times*, January 12, 1955, 1; Bert Pierce, "All of US Called a Big Traffic Jam," *The New York Times*, January 14, 1955a, 13.

The Commission argued that public borrowing was appropriate because roads were long-term capital investments.[12] The Eisenhower Administration considered the proposal politically attractive for two reasons. First, no tax increases were required. Second, the federal debt ceiling would not have to be raised because the highway bonds would be on the books of an independent corporation.[13]

Despite the Administration's strong endorsement, however, the Commission's proposal was defeated on partisan votes in both the House and Senate.[14] Both the corporate form and the financing method sparked criticism. Although legislators intended to ensure continuity of program funding, they clearly did not want to sacrifice their ability to claim credit for the distribution of new highway projects. Establishing an independent Federal Highway Corporation would almost certainly have reduced their political control over the program.[15] In addition, legislative budget guardians viewed the bond financing proposal as a threat both to their institutional power and to accepted norms of federal budgeting.[16] Senate Finance Committee chairman Harry F. Byrd (D-Va) complained that the government would have to pay $11 billion in interest charges on the bonds, leaving too little money available for road projects.[17] Byrd further argued that the suggestion to exempt the bonds from the debt ceiling was "legerdemain." Such an accounting move, he said, would weaken "budgetary control," pave the way for "endless outlays for other infrastructure programs," and ultimately destroy congressional power of the purse.[18]

The trust fund solution

What lawmakers like Byrd were grasping for was a fiscal design that would (1) lock-in highway spending promises; (2) avoid debt financing;

[12] Bond financing won the endorsement of many public works experts, including the legendary Robert Moses. See "US Road Program is Backed by Moses," *The New York Times*, May 10, 1955b, 36.
[13] Quoted in Martin, "Proposed Federal Highway Legislation," 227.
[14] In the Senate, the bond proposal was rejected on a 31–60 roll call vote. (R 30–13; D 1–47). The only Democrat to vote for the plan was John F. Kennedy (MA). See *Congressional Record*, May 25, 1955, 6976–7018. In the House, the plan was rejected by a vote 193–221. Republicans voted 186–7 in favor of the plan, Democrats 7–214 against. See *Congressional Record*, July 27, 1955, 11688–718.
[15] See statement of Joseph Campbell, *Congressional Record*, May 25, 1955, 7000.
[16] "Highway Program Attacked by Byrd," *The New York Times*, June 16, 1955a, 56.
[17] "US Highway Plan Assailed By Byrd," *The New York Times*, March 19, 1955, 1. See also Rose, *Interstate*, 78.
[18] See Byrd's statement in *Congressional Record*, May 25, 1955, 6995–6996.

and (3) retain Congress's formal control over the program. Only the trust fund device satisfied all of these concerns. The Highway Trust Fund thus could be considered a political success even before a single interstate mile was built because its creation helped cement a deal, paving the way for overwhelming passage of the Federal Highway Act of 1956 in both chambers.[19] As one highway user group enthusiastically observed in 1958, the trust fund's adoption culminated "efforts of almost two years duration to arrive at an acceptable means of financing an accelerated highway program."[20]

Trust fund financing was meant to strengthen three overlapping policy commitments.[21] The first was a promise from the federal government to state highway officials and private highway contractors that federal highway revenues would be exclusively used for road building. This was a commitment that highway lobbyists had sought for some time. As Ways and Means Committee member Hale Boggs (D-Louisiana) said:

> For a great many years now, highway users have complained, and I think with some justification since the conclusion of World War II and the Korean conflict, that vast revenues were being collected from them but were not being used for purposes of building highways. This bill recognizes that complaint . . . Thus, for the first time, the American motorist will pay the taxes with the assurance that he will be the direct beneficiary of every penny which he pays and he will pay with the knowledge that every cent derived from these taxes will be devoted exclusively to his personal convenience and safety.[22]

A major advantage of trust fund financing, then, is that it would reduce political uncertainty. This assurance of stable funding would in turn allow federal and state highway officials "to plan future budgets" effectively.[23]

The Highway Trust Fund also signaled a political commitment that Congress would forgo the temptation to use highway revenues as a

---

[19] The conference report on the bill was approved by a voice vote in the House and by an 89–1 roll call vote in the Senate. See "13 Year Highway Program," *Congressional Quarterly Almanac* (1956), 398–407. The highway system was dubbed the National System of Interstate and Defense Highways to emphasize the tie-in to military readiness.

[20] National Highway Users Conference, "The Highway Trust Fund: Its Origin and Administration and First Two Years of Operation" November 1958, Washington, DC, 1.

[21] For a parallel analysis, see James A. Dunn, Jr., *Driving Forces: The Automobile, Its Enemies, and the Politics of Mobility* (Washington, DC: Brookings Institution), 32. Although it was sketched before reading Dunn's stimulating book, my analysis of Highway Trust Fund politics is similar to Dunn's in many respects.

[22] *Congressional Record*, April 26, 1956, 7148–51.

[23] *Congressional Record*, April 26, 1956, 7159.

lucrative source of funding other programs. Highway tax rates would be kept no higher than necessary to meet the costs of the highway program. This commitment was crucial to winning the support of motorist groups, oil companies, and the trucking industry.[24]

Finally, the Highway Trust Fund was designed to safeguard the Treasury by avoiding both indebtedness and reliance on general tax revenues. As Wilbur Mills of the Ways and Means Committee stressed, "The committee is, it is true, endeavoring to protect the general fund against the entire road program being charged to existing revenues presently going into the general fund."[25] This last goal was of especial importance to George M. Humphrey, Eisenhower's fiscally conservative Treasury Secretary.[26] Indeed, while proposals for establishing a Highway Trust Fund had circulated among lawmakers for several years, the concept was not incorporated into the main legislative vehicle until Humphrey suggested it to congressional tax writers in 1956 as a device for ensuring the program's self-financing.[27]

Political and institutional protections

Key to the Highway Trust Fund's political durability would be its stimulus of a potent alliance between well-organized producer groups (e.g., truckers and road contractors) and government officials (state highway commissioners) on the one hand, and a broad societal interest (motorists) on the other.[28] The notion that the trust fund rested on a reciprocal exchange of special tax payments for special benefits legitimated the system. As James W. Dunn, the leading scholar of American highway politics, writes, "As long as the trust fund principle was broadly accepted, its client politics operated smoothly and unobtrusively behind the majoritiarian elements, like a road project being built behind a large 'Your Highway Taxes at Work' sign."[29]

These understandings were reinforced through various procedural

---

[24] Dunn, *Driving Forces*, 32.
[25] *Congressional Record*, April 26, 1956, 7156.
[26] *Ibid.*
[27] US Congress, House of Representatives, "Highway Revenue Act of 1956," Hearings Before the Committee on Ways and Means, 84th Congress, 2nd Session, H.R. 9075, (1956), 25. I thank Richard F. Weingroff of the Federal Highway Administration for sending me a copy of this testimony.
[28] For an analysis in these terms, see Theda Skocpol, "The Origins of Social Policy in the United States: A Polity Centered Analysis," in Lawrence C. Dodd and Calvin Jillson, eds., *The Dynamics of Social Policy* (Boulder, CO: Westview Press, 1994).
[29] Dunn, *Driving Forces*, 31.

safeguards. To strengthen the commitment to sound financing, the 1956 Act required the Secretary of the Treasury to issue an annual report of the trust fund's financial condition. This would make it easier "for the Congress, as well as the public, to know exactly how much the program is costing and to determine to what extent the costs are being met on a pay-as-we-build basis."[30] A key amendment sponsored by Senator Byrd ensured that the trust fund's current income and outgo would remain approximately equal. If the Treasury Department determined that the full funding of apportionments would create a trust fund deficit in the near term, state highway grants had to be reduced.[31]

Other mechanisms would provide additional protection from budgetary competition. Under the 1956 Act, trust fund grants would be provided through a special form of budget authority known as "contract authority." This would allow highway officials to enter into binding obligations with highway contractors in advance of appropriations action. Contract authority is technically unfunded, meaning that subsequent appropriations bills are required to "liquidate" the actual obligations. But since the money has already been legally and politically committed, the appropriations committees (absent the adoption of centralizing reforms) would have almost no capacity to determine spending levels. The effect was to shift budgetary power to the public works committees, which historically have been tireless advocates of infrastructure spending. As budget scholar Irene Rubin notes, this meant that highway groups would have "better access" to trust fund money than other clienteles had to grants distributed under normal budgetary procedures.[32]

The Highway Trust Fund would also be excluded from the "administrative budget," the government's main budget document prior to the adoption of a unified budget in 1969. By financing the interstates through a trust fund rather than the operating budget, the federal government was thus able to massively expand the existing federal-aid highway program while recording *reductions* in both gas taxes and highway spending relative to prior levels. Finally, any unspent highway revenues would earn interest for the trust fund.

---

[30] US Congress, House of Representatives, "The Highway Revenue Act of 1956," 45.

[31] The Byrd Amendment was later revised by the Surface Transportation Assistance Act of 1982. The new requirement is that the balance in the highway account plus two years' revenues from future highway user taxes (beyond the current year) be sufficient to pay all outstanding commitments in the current year.

[32] Irene S. Rubin. *The Politics of Public Budgeting* (Chatham, New Jersey: Chatham House Publishers, 1990), 132. Rubin provides an excellent history of the trust fund's early years.

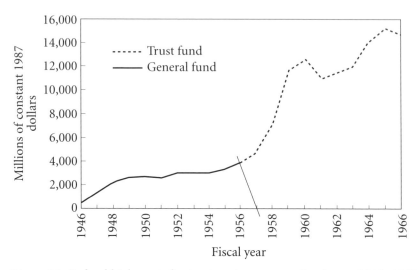

Figure 6.1 Federal highway infrastructure investment, fiscal years 1946–1966
Note: Table 9.6 (highway physical capital investment) and table 10.1 (total composite deflators).
Source: Office of Management and Budget, *Budget of the United States Government, Fiscal Year 2000 – Historical Tables* (Washington, DC: Government Printing Office, 1999).

The creation of the Highway Trust Fund immediately strengthened the highway program's claim on the public fisc. The federal share of interstate costs increased to 90 percent from 50 percent. In constant 1987 dollars, yearly federal highway spending rose from an average of two and half billion dollars during the decade prior to the implementation of the 1956 Act to twelve billion dollars after, a real increase of 380 percent (figure 6.1). The trust fund's spending accelerated very rapidly through fiscal year 1959 after which the rate of increase stabilized. Highway interests during the late 1950s and early 1960s thus enjoyed the benefits of both larger budgets and fiscal predictability.

Contesting the trust fund's integrity

The establishment of the Highway Trust Fund in 1956 seemingly created an autonomous fiscal system in which fuel tax revenues were precommitted for future highway improvements, and each additional highway project stimulated more driving, greater fuel consumption, and the production of additional highway receipts. Indeed, the trust fund has been frequently called a classic example of a self-perpetuating "iron triangle" between the government, road contractors, and consumer motorists.[33]

Yet iron triangles are often more susceptible to attack than they appear. In their excellent book on agenda dynamics in US policymaking, Baumgartner and Jones demonstrate that long periods of agenda stability may be interrupted by bursts of rapid, unpredictable change. Both interests and ideas play key roles in this "punctuated equilibrium" model. Interests excluded from a given policy subsystem constitute "slack resources" that can be mobilized by policy entrepreneurs. New participants are typically attracted to the fray, however, only when issues are redefined.[34] The political evolution of the Highway Trust Fund since 1956 illustrates this dynamic in most (but not all) important respects. Anti-highway forces, often joined by presidents and institutional budget guardians for pragmatic reasons, have attempted to weaken the Highway Trust Fund's political and financial autonomy in two main ways: (1) by diverting trust fund revenues to non-highway uses; and (2) by reducing the trust fund's spending automaticity.

As I explain below, highway opponents have won a few temporary victories, but the basic trust fund structure has endured, outlasting the completion of interstate construction work itself.

Interests, ideas, and policy change

Americans have never fallen out of love with roads and cars. By the mid 1960s, however, some of the spark had clearly gone out of the relationship. An emerging environmental movement was linking interstate construction with the destruction of natural beauty and air pollution.[35] Urban residents were protesting that highway construction displaced homeowners and disturbed businesses and local communities. "Freeway revolts" halted road work in major US cities including Chicago, San Francisco, and Seattle.[36]

By the early 1970s the future of the Highway Trust Fund seemed increasingly uncertain. Advocates for public transportation joined with environmentalists and urban groups in a campaign to open the trust fund

---

[33] For a typical indictment, see A. Q. Mowbray, "Magical Highway Trust Fund," in *Road to Ruin* (Philadelphia and New York: J.B. Lippincott Company, 1969), 18–30.

[34] See the provocative analysis of Baumgartner and Jones, *Agendas and Instability in American Politics.*

[35] Rose, *Interstate*, 101.

[36] See "Movement Began in Late 1960s to Modify Trust Fund," *Congressional Quarterly Weekly Report*, 1975, 736.

to other transportation uses. Senator Gaylord Nelson (D-Wis.) argued that the highway system had "gotten completely out of hand" and that the Highway Trust Fund should be terminated as "soon as possible without breaking legal or clear moral commitments."[37] President Nixon endorsed legislation to give states the flexibility to use a portion of their trust fund allocations for urban mass transportation. In sum, the highway lobby's issue monopoly during the early 1970s was crumbling under the pressure of new ideas and issue coalitions.

Yet the preexisting trust fund mechanism and the user-pay logic continued to structure the debate. In the standard punctuated equilibrium dynamic, previously excluded interests gain influence by shifting the very terms of the political conversation, denying legitimacy to the policy understandings of the previously dominant clientele. But trust funds and user charges make this kind of issue reframing particularly difficult to pull off.[38] While a number of radical environmental groups denied that the Highway Trust Fund implied a moral commitment to motorist groups, most transit advocates felt constrained to acknowledge that it did.[39] Rather than attacking the trust fund and earmarking principle directly, they instead argued that mass transit spending would *benefit* highway users by reducing traffic congestion.[40] By "upgrading mass transit," said Rep. John B. Anderson (R-Ill), "highway users are promoting their own best interest in efficient . . . less hazardous highway travel."[41] Highway lobbyists contended that using gas tax revenues for other purposes would constitute a violation of a sacred trust. House Minority Leader Gerald R. Ford (R-Michigan) argued that channeling gas taxes into transit would destroy the credibility of other federal trust fund promises. "If you start breaking faith with the highway trust fund then

---

[37] "Congress Extends Interstate Highway System, *Congressional Quarterly Almanac* (1970), 793.

[38] On issue reframing, see Gary McKissick, "Issue Manipulation: Interest Group Lobbying and the Framing of Policy Alternatives" (University of Michigan, Ph.D. dissertation, 1997).

[39] For a discussion of how budgetary parasites may try to portray themselves as symbionts, see Roy T. Meyers, "Federal Financing for Medical Research Through Trust Funds and Entitlements," paper presented at the American Association for the Advancement of Science Workshop, "How To Fund Science: The Future of Medical Research," Wye River Conference Centers, Queenstown, Maryland, February 14–16, 1999.

[40] See US Congress, Senate, "Proposed 1972 Highway Legislation," Hearings Before the Subcommittee on Roads, Committee on Public Works, 92nd Congress, 2nd Session, 546–7.

[41] "Rules Committee Helps Defeat Mass Transit Amendment," *Congressional Quarterly Weekly Report*, October 14, 1972, 2688.

pretty soon you are going to find some people who will say, 'Let us divert from the airport trust fund.'"[42]

Policymakers ultimately agreed to a very slight modification in the trust fund's operations. After an intense debate Congress in 1973 narrowly approved a measure permitting cities to use about 10 percent of their highway money for urban buses and rail transit.[43] A number of highway user groups acquiesced in the outcome. Indeed, some even let it be known that they would accept the creation of a separate trust fund for mass transit. Their strategy was to expand the trust fund's base of support in Congress through an explicit logroll between lawmakers from rural and urban districts.[44] In 1982, Congress passed and President Reagan signed a measure to create an earmarked transit account financed by 1 cent from a nickel increase in the gas tax. The other 4 cents were reserved for highways.[45] This gas tax hike permitted a 44 percent increase in nominal highway spending between fiscal years 1983 and 1985 alone. "The highway trust wasn't busted," said one transit advocate. "Instead of bulldozing the house down, we talked to the owners and decided to build on an addition."[46] In sum, the "owners" of the Highway Trust Fund – the road lobby – survived, indeed prospered from, a direct challenge from an interest group competitor by carefully redesigning their institutional inheritance.

Spending controllability and fiscal regimes

Highway interests have long argued that the interstate program could not function effectively without guaranteed funding. "Without the security of known funds, the long-range planning and construction could not have been achieved. This is an attribute of all trust funds and it is the reason that programs financed through trust funds are successful," said the executive vice president of the American Automobile Association in 1972.[47] Yet while funding predictability offers clear advantages, it necessarily hinders the ability of budget guardians to set annual spending

---

[42] *Ibid.*

[43] All the key votes were close, with lines drawn more on urban-rural than on party lines. See "Highway Act: Compromise on Mass Transit Funds," *Congressional Quarterly Almanac* (1973), 435–52.

[44] Michael J. Malbin, "Long Deadlock Ends in Compromise Opening Highway Trust Fund for Mass Transit," *National Journal*, August 11, 1973, 1170.

[45] Stanfield, "Mass Transit Lobby," 227.

[46] Leonard Simon, assistant executive director of the US Conference of Mayors, quoted in *Ibid.*, 227.

[47] Quoted in US Congress, Senate, "Proposed 1972 Highway Legislation," 533.

priorities. As we saw in chapter 4, each Social Security beneficiary is entitled to a specific level of direct governmental benefits. Annual spending from the Social Security Trust Fund is just the sum of the individual entitlements. But there is no individual entitlement to highway benefits. Federal highway funds are allocated to state highway agencies, and the services that motorists actually receive are what can be purchased with the spending. The very nature of the highway program thus makes the application of short-term fiscal control mechanisms administratively (if not necessarily politically) feasible. As Joseph White points out, precisely because spending from non-entitlement trust funds like highways is inherently more controllable, institutional budget guardians tend to regard such trust funds as a more distributing evasion of their authority than trust funds like Social Security.[48]

A continuing theme of Highway Trust Fund politics since 1956 has been the attempt by budget guardians and presidential administrations of both parties to reclaim the flexibility denied them by the trust fund structure.[49] Ironically, even Eisenhower found the rigidity of the Highway Trust Fund an annoyance. When his Administration tried to use a small fraction of gas tax revenues to cover the costs of calculating federally mandated wage rates for the highway program, highway user groups bitterly complained, and Congress halted the practice.[50] Congress fought off similar attempts by the Kennedy and Johnson administrations to finance public land highways from the trust fund and to use gasoline taxes for highway beautification.

When these very modest attempts at executive fiscal control failed, presidents turned to a more aggressive strategy: impoundments. In 1966, the Johnson Administration refused to spend $1.1 billion in previously committed highway funds in an effort to control the inflationary impact of the Vietnam war. Attorney General Ramsey Clark argued that the Highway Trust Fund was identical to an ordinary appropriation, and that presidents thus had the right to impound the money.[51] But Congress rejected this argument. Warren Magnuson (D-Washington), chairman of

[48] Joseph White, "Entitlement Budgeting vs. Bureau Budgeting," *Public Administration Review*, 58 (6), November/December 1998, fn. 14 and *passim*.

[49] Gerald Ford offers a nice illustration of how attitudes toward trust fund financing are shaped by institutional position. As noted above, Ford had been a leading defender of the trust fund's sanctity during his tenure in Congress. As President, however, Ford proposed legislation that would have virtually dismantled the Highway Trust Fund, arguing that it was a "classic example" of a federal program that had outlived its usefulness. See "Highway Act Extension Sent to Congress," *Congressional Quarterly Almanac* (1975), 735.

[50] Cited in Rubin, *The Politics of Public Budgeting*, 135.

[51] *Ibid.*, 135.

the Senate Commerce Committee, stated that Congress intended the Highway Trust Fund to be insulated from presidential control: "These funds were deposited in the Treasury for trust keeping. In a sense they are not Government funds. They are funds of the people."[52]

The impoundment controversy resumed at an even higher pitch during the Nixon Administration. In 1972, Nixon withheld $2.5 billion in highway funds as part of his broader campaign to gain fiscal power from Congress.[53] Outraged by Nixon's actions, a group of Democratic Senators, led by Sam J. Ervin (NC), filed a court suit challenging presidential authority to impound highway funds. In a major victory for Congress, the Eighth US Circuit Court of Appeal in 1973 ruled that the Administration had indeed violated the law.[54] The enactment of the Congressional Budget and Impoundment Control Act in 1974 brought the impoundment era to a close.

Congress's ability to protect the Highway Trust Fund from executive poaching contrasts sharply with the dedicated road fund experience in other advanced democracies. In France, a separate highway fund, le Fonds special d'investissement routier, was established in 1952 to receive a portion of the petrol tax. But the powerful Ministry of Finance quickly began diverting its receipts to other programs.[55] In Britain, Lloyd George established a Road Fund to receive "hypothecated" petrol and motorcar taxes in 1909. But subsequent Treasury ministers repeatedly raided the fund, and chancellor of the exchequer Winston Churchill denounced the idea of a binding agreement between highway users and the government as patently "absurd."[56] While motorist groups and members of Parliament vehemently protested these actions, the Treasury's monopoly of fiscal power precluded it from taking strong action. The British Road Fund was eventually dismantled. In sum, there is nothing at all unusual about executives trying to raid dedicated highway funds and legislatures seeking to defend them. What is distinctive about the US case is that the

---

[52] Quoted in National Highway Users Conference, The Highway Trust Fund, 21.

[53] On the Nixon impoundments, see Allen Schick, Congress and Money (Washington, DC: The Urban Institute, 1980).

[54] The case was State Highway Commission of Missouri v. Volpe. The issue eventually reached the Supreme Court, which ruled in State Highway Commission v. Volpe (1973) that the executive branch did not have the authority to withhold highway aid funds authorized by Congress. See Dunn, Miles to Go, 281; and Congressional Quarterly Almanac (1973), 253.

[55] Pietro S. Nivola and Robert W. Crandall, The Extra Mile: Rethinking Energy Policy for Automotive Transportation (Washington, DC: Brookings Institution, 1995), 69.

[56] Ibid., 70. On the British Road Fund, see Dunn, Miles to Go, 101–4; and Ranjit S. Teja and Barry Bracewell-Milnes, The Case for Earmarked Taxes: Government Spending and Public Choice (London: Institute of Economic Affairs, 1991), 57–61.

legislature has the capacity to defend its structural creations. The US Highway Trust Fund's greater political durability thus reflects in part the institutional endowment of the separation of powers.[57]

Centralization of congressional budgeting

Madison's fragmented constitutional design obviously remains in place. With the enactment of the Congressional Budget Act of 1974, however, Congress's internal budgeting procedures gained a measure of centralization. The preexisting decentralized authorization–appropriations process was not abolished, but a new centralized budget process was layered atop it, creating all sorts of budgetary frictions.[58] For the Highway Trust Fund, the result of this institutional "layering" was a significant erosion of its autonomy. This is particularly ironic since Congress's ire at Nixon's impoundment of highway funds was one of the reasons for the adoption of the Budget Act in the first place.

The legislative history of the 1974 Budget Act provides no evidence that Congress intended to weaken the autonomy of the Highway Trust Fund. Indeed, Congress went out of its way to grandfather the Highway Trust Fund from the Act's new restrictions on use of contract authority. But implementation of the new process inadvertently provided a procedural opening for the appropriations committees to divest the public works committees of their control over trust fund spending levels. Because the highway program continued to rely upon contract authority, appropriators could not directly limit the amount of cash available to state highway officials for reimbursement. Rather, they began controlling trust fund spending indirectly by setting a limitation on the amount of new highway contracts that states could enter into during the next year.

Congress's decision to impose these highway "obligation limits" was initially prompted by the sudden release in 1975 of more than $9 billion in previously impounded highway funds. This was such a large infusion of cash that even federal highway officials recognized the need for fiscal restraint. Congress enacted a $7.2 billion spending limit to its fiscal year 1976 transportation appropriations bill. The spending cap produced a clash between members of the House Budget and Appropriations committees, who argued that the ceiling was needed to make the new budget process work, and members of the House Public Works committee, who

---

[57] Dunn, *Miles to Go*, 104.

[58] For a generic discussion of the frictions created by institutional layering, see Karen Orren and Steven Skowronek, "Beyond the Iconography of Order," in C. Dodd and Calvin Jillson, eds., *The Dynamics of Social Politics* (Boulder, CO: Westview Press, 1994).

insisted that it represented "the beginning of the end of the Highway Trust Fund."[59] An effort to eliminate the cap failed by a vote of 297–95.[60] The battle was replayed the following year with essentially the same outcome. By the late 1970s, the establishment of annual ceilings on highway obligations had become routine.

Deficit reduction pressures

The large budget deficits of the 1980s and 1990s also tested the trust fund's autonomy. Program advocates on the public works committees vigorously argued that the Highway Trust Fund was not part of the budget problem because it "paid its own way." As fiscal pressures intensified, however, budget controllers claimed that the highway program was just another activity competing for scarce federal dollars.[61] Under the Gramm–Rudman–Hollings Act of 1985, highway spending was made subject to budget sequestration. Even more damaging to the trust fund's procedural integrity was the adoption of the Budget Enforcement Act of 1990. The BEA divided the federal budget into two parts: discretionary spending (which was controlled by annual spending caps), and mandatory spending and revenues (controlled by pay-as-you-go rules). The Highway Trust Fund's spending was classified as discretionary and therefore subject to the spending caps. But the trust fund's revenues were controlled by pay-as-you-go (PAYGO) rules. In sum, earmarked gas taxes could no longer directly offset trust fund spending, and highway outlays had to compete with other programs for support.

Reclaiming gas taxes for the general fund

Deficit pressures also increased somewhat the willingness of policymakers to raise gas taxes for purposes other than road building. Between 1957 and 1989, Congress raised gas taxes on only two occasions (table 6.1). Both of these gas tax hikes came after reports of the Highway Trust Fund's deteriorating financial condition. In 1957, Congress passed a penny increase after early program spending exceeded initial projections. The nickel increase enacted in 1982 followed a decade in which the trust fund's revenues had dwindled due to the energy crisis and the introduction of more fuel-efficient automobiles.

[59] *Congressional Record*, November 11, 1975, 35947.
[60] Republicans voted 106–22 in favor of the caps; Democrats voted 191–73 in favor.
[61] Mike Mills, "Trust Fund 'Sanctity' Crumbling Under Pressure From Budget," *Congressional Quarterly Weekly Report*, October 20, 1990, 3503.

Table 6.1. *Federal gas tax increases, 1956–1993*

Year	Amount (cents)	Recipient	President and party	Majority party in Congress
1956	1.0	HTF	Eisenhower (R)	House (D) Senate (D)
1959	1.0	HTF	Eisenhower (R)	House (D) Senate (D)
1982	5.0	HTF	Reagan (R)	House (D) Senate (R)
1990	5.0	HTF and Treasury	Bush (R)	House (D) Senate (D)
1993	4.3	Treasury	Clinton (D)	House (D) Senate (D)

Source: James A. Dunn, Jr. *Driving Forces: The Automobile, Its Enemies, and the Politics of Mobility* (Washington, DC: Brookings Institution, 1998), 33.

The first modification in the earmarking principle came in the 1990 budget deal. After an acrimonious debate Congress agreed to reserve half the proceeds from a 5 cent increase in the gas tax for the general Treasury, with the other half earmarked for road building. In the 1993 budget package Congress broke even more sharply with past practice, treating the entire proceeds of a 4.3 cent gas tax increase as general revenues. Naturally, these moves were strongly condemned by highway user groups. But the politics of the deficit centralized the federal budgetary process, increasing the power of presidents, congressional party leaders, and budget controllers, and marginalizing program authorizers.[62]

Crafting safeguards

When the Highway Trust Fund was created in 1956, its spending was off-budget and immune to appropriations control, and gas tax revenues were dedicated exclusively for highways. By the mid 1990s trust fund spending was on-budget and subject to appropriations review, and a portion of gas tax receipts were being used for mass transit and deficit reduction. These procedural changes left the trust fund more vulnerable to the vicissitudes

---

[62] An amendment by Hank Brown (R-Colorado) requiring these revenues from the 1993 increase to be dedicated for transportation projects passed by a vote of 66–32, but was eliminated in conference committee. See Nivola and Crandall, *The Extra Mile*, 102–7.

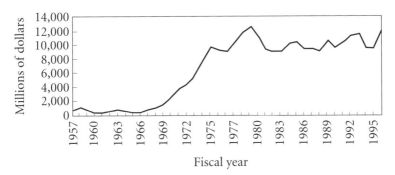

Figure 6.2 Highway Trust Fund cash balance, fiscal years 1957–1996
Note: Excludes mass transit account.
Source: Office of Management and Budget, *Budget of the United States Government* (Washington, DC: Government Printing Office, various years).

of ordinary politics. Highway advocates responded to this loss of insulation in two ways. First, they continued to defend the earmarking principle, arguing that a political contract existed between the government and highway users. Second, they pushed for the adoption of new procedural safeguards to restore the trust fund's autonomy.

Highway advocates were enormously advantaged by the fact that the trust fund had a cash balance of more than $10 billion in the early 1990s (figure 6.2). The existence of this balance put budget controllers on the defensive because it created the impression – which highway advocates did everything possible to encourage – that earmarked taxes were being illegitimately hoarded to hide the budget deficit. The true story was more complicated. Since 1956 the Highway Trust Fund has been maintained essentially on a pay-as-you-go basis, with trust fund spending generally about equal to the level of current revenues (figure 6.3). Indeed, the trust fund actually spent a bit *more* than 100 percent of its income during the 1980s and 1990s, meaning that its operations *contributed* slightly to annual federal budget deficits (table 6.2). Despite the erosion in the trust fund's procedural defenses and the tight budgetary climate, Congress continued to spend the system's earmarked revenues on road improvements; little if any hoarding of current trust fund taxes was taking place.

What then accounts for the massive buildup in the trust fund? The accumulated balance was largely a policy legacy of the temporary slowing of highway spending that occurred during the impoundment era of the late 1960s and early 1970s. This was the only period when the trust fund

Table 6.2. *Average trust fund spending as a percent of annual taxes and income, five-year periods between fiscal years 1957–1996*

Period	Average trust fund spending as a percent of annual tax receipts	Average trust fund spending as a percent of total income (including interest earnings)
1957–61	95	95
1962–6	100	100
1967–71	88	87
1972–6	89	83
1977–81	105	93
1982–6	117	103
1987–91	108	100
1992–6	103	99
1997–96	101	95

Source: Calculated from unpublished Congressional Budget Office data, and *Budget of the United States Government,* various years. Highway Account only. Excludes transition quarter.

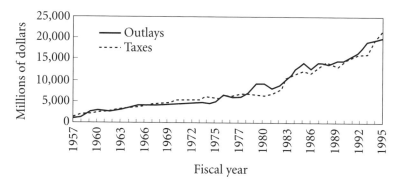

Figure 6.3 Highway Trust Fund taxes and spending, fiscal years 1957–1995
Note: Excludes mass transit account.
Source: Office of Management and Budget, *Budget of the United States Government* (Washington, DC: Government Printing Office, various years).

failed to spend at least 90 percent of its annual receipts (table 6.2). As I mentioned above, Congress terminated the impoundments in fairly short order. During the relatively brief period when trust fund spending was restrained, however, surpluses accumulated in the fund. These surpluses remained on the books of the Treasury. Over the years, the trust fund balance grew larger and larger because of the power of compound interest.[63]

To repeat: incumbent politicians during the 1980s and 1990s were fully funding the highway program. There was no hoarding of user tax revenues. The effect of trust fund accounting, however, was to keep current officeholders on the hook for the perceived budgetary misdeeds of their predecessors. At a time when other lobbies were having to mobilize against potential cutbacks, highway interests were arguing that the trust fund balance entitled them to increased spending. While highway advocates strategically portrayed themselves as victims of past mistreatment, their major objective was to stabilize the trust fund's political and financial future. Arguing that Congress had an obligation to "put the trust back in the trust fund," highway advocates pressed for the trust fund's removal from the unified budget, which would exempt the trust fund from the discretionary spending caps. The House narrowly defeated off-budget measures on three occasions between the mid 1980s and early 1990s.

But when the Republicans took over the House of Representatives in November 1994, incoming Transportation and Infrastructure Committee chairman Bud Shuster (R-PA), who referred to the Highway Trust Fund as "the original Contract with America," vowed to make the vote on off-budget treatment a "hypocrisy test" for the new GOP majority. A coalition of more than 100 transportation and business organizations calling itself "The Alliance for Truth in Transportation Budgeting" mobilized in support of the measure. A number of leading economists, including Federal Reserve chairman Alan Greenspan, came out in strong opposition against the proposal, arguing that it would narrow flexibility and signal a weakened political commitment to deficit reduction.[64]

As in the three previous House votes, support for the bill split along committee lines. The Public Works Committee members were virtually unanimous in their support, but they faced strong opposition from the Appropriations, Budget, and Ways and Means committees. In a *Dear Colleague* letter circulated to House members prior to the vote, the chairmen of the three budget control committees denied that highway users were being "cheated." Highway revenues, they emphasized, were

---

[63] The sizable balance also reflected a desire by states to avoid spending their full apportionment of highway funds in order to protect themselves against an uneven flow of federal assistance. See "Operations of and Outlook for the Highway Trust Fund," Statement of John W. Hill, Jr. Before the Subcommittee on Water Resources, Transportation, and Infrastructure, Committee on Environment and Public Works, United States Senate. May 9, 1990.

[64] *Congressional Record*, April 17, 1996, H3508–H3514.

currently being spent as quickly as they were collected.[65] The very fact that budget controllers felt compelled to emphasize this point demonstrated that Shuster had largely succeeded in framing the issue. While deficit politics had weakened the trust fund's autonomy, the fundamental idea that motorists were "owed" highway benefits by virtue of their earmarked contributions continued to resonate. The bill to take the trust fund off-budget passed easily, 284–143, with 162 Republicans and 123 Democrats voting for passage.[66] But the measure failed to gain momentum in the Senate and died for the session.

Building a firewall

In the end, the highway lobby was able to trade in its claims to the accumulated trust fund balance for a guarantee of funding security. In return for turning back to the US Treasury all but $8 billion – the amount needed to provide an adequate contingency reserve – of the $20 billion balance in the trust fund in 1998, highway advocates won adoption of a new "budgetary firewall" measure that locked-in more than $162 billion in future highway spending.[67] Just a year earlier, the highway lobby had been able to redirect the 4.3 cents per gallon gas tax enacted in the 1993 budget package to the trust fund. In the context of both a large trust fund balance *and* projected unified budget surpluses, it became virtually impossible for budget controllers not to accommodate the demands of highway advocates. "The people of this country deserve that the highway trust-fund money be spent on highways, and that's why it is very difficult to say we shouldn't have this program," said Senate Budget Committee chairman Pete Domenici (R-New Mexico).[68]

Under the new firewall mechanism, highway spending will be exempt from the discretionary spending limits. The appropriations panels will no longer get to set yearly obligation limits for the trust fund. Instead, each year's obligation limit will be automatically linked to the amount of user taxes collected by the trust fund during the prior year.[69] In one sense,

[65] "Where is the Truth in the 'Truth in Budgeting'," Dear Colleague Letter from John Kasich, Bob Livingston, and Bill Archer, March 21, 1996.

[66] See David Hosansky, "House Passes Bill to Remove Trust Funds From Budget," *Congressional Quarterly Weekly Report*, April 20, 1996, 1038–9.

[67] Highway advocates also gave up their right to future interest earnings. (Any future trust fund surpluses will be invested in non-interest bearing securities). It remains to be seen whether this was a significant concession.

[68] Quoted in Greg Hitt, "Senators Agree to Lift Highway Outlays by $26 Billion During the Next Six Years," *The Wall Street Journal*, March 3, 1998, A4.

[69] While there are ways to defeat the firewall, most analysts viewed the new protections as quite strong. For a detailed analysis, see American Road and

establishment of the firewall mechanism merely ratified past practice because a strong linkage between yearly highway revenues and outlays already existed. In another sense, however, it constituted a major structural reform because it promised to reduce future uncertainty.

Conclusions

Congress's unwillingness to establish an independent highway corporation with the authority to issue bonds – the major alternative to the trust fund design adopted in 1956 – should not be taken as evidence that lawmakers were unconcerned about policy durability. As Murray J. Horn notes, delegation of authority to an independent agency is most appealing as a precommitment strategy when the intended beneficiary group is diffuse and unlikely to dominate future political decisionmaking.[70] This did not obtain in the highway case because road contractors, if not ordinary voters, could be counted on to defend their particularistic interests.

The Highway Trust Fund has proved to be a highly effective vehicle both for locking-in distributive benefits and for recovering costs from highway users.[71] Because the Highway Trust Fund is based on an explicit exchange of specific taxes for related benefits, and because trust fund accounting ensures that any temporary underspending can be closely monitored, the highway lobby has been in the enviable position of being able to make aggressive budgetary demands even during times of general fiscal austerity.

But while the Highway Trust Fund has endured its operations have not gone unchallenged. As we have seen, the resilience of the trust fund has been challenged by the most basic forces of politics: interests (the mass transit lobby), ideas (the rise of environmentalism), and shifts in institutional configurations (the centralization of congressional budgeting). These forces have provided strategic openings for highway opponents and budget guardians to try and weaken the trust fund's autonomy and procedural defenses.

What accounts for the occasional willingness of politicians to stand up

---

Transportation Builders Association, "The Transportation Equity Act for the 21st Century," July 1998.

[70] Murray J. Horn, *The Political Economy of Public Administration: Institutional Choice in the Public Sector* (Cambridge: Cambridge University Press, 1995), 53.

[71] From 1956 through 1997, trust fund receipts totaled $367 billion while expenditures during the same period totaled $372 billion. See US Congress, Senate Budget Committee, "Budget Bulletin," 105th Congress, 2nd Session, March 30, 1998.

to the highway lobby? Although general budget pressures have played a contributing role, the most important factor is the relatively low degree of individual beneficiary reliance induced by the trust fund mechanism. While the Highway Trust Fund touches the lives of millions of Americans on a daily basis, it does not figure centrally in their future planning. Individual voters may support or oppose proposed changes in the trust fund's operations, but they do not react with anything like the alarm they display when proposed changes in Social Security or Medicare are discussed. The per capita stakes are much smaller, the underlying policy commitments far less sensitive.

   This is not to deny, however, that the Highway Trust Fund has generated massive *collective* lock-in effects for the nation as a whole. For better or worse, the building of the interstate system permanently altered the US social landscape. Trust fund spending has encouraged Americans to live in low-density suburbs and reinforced automobiles as the dominant transit mode. By the time the Highway Trust Fund was opened to transit projects in 1973, more than 80 percent of the interstate system was completed and another 16 percent was already under construction.[72] When Congress reauthorized the program in 1991, it gave state and local officials discretion to spend more than half of trust fund money on transit projects. Some environmentalists looked forward to the end of the "asphalt era." But Americans are so locked into driving as their mode of transportation that relatively few states took advantage of this unprecedented flexibility.[73] Whether the Highway Trust Fund continues for another five years or 50, there is little doubt that the American economic and social life will continue to be dominated by highways and automobiles, a legacy that the Highway Trust Fund helped to create.

[72] James J. Fink, *The Automobile Age* (Cambridge, MA: The MIT Press, 1988), 371.
[73] See Jonathan Walters, "The Highway Revolution That Wasn't" *Governing*, May 1995, 30–7. See also Nivola and Crandall, *The Extra Mile*, 115. State public policies also hamper change. In 31 states, state law limits gas taxes to highway projects only. See Surface Transportation Policy Project, "A Blueprint for ISTEA Reauthorization" (Washington, DC: STPP, 1997).

7

Airports

Created in 1970, the Airport and Airway (or Aviation) Trust Fund, like the Highway Trust Fund after which it was modeled, designates the proceeds of taxes collected from transportation users for transportation development programs. If the highway experience shows what happens when a preexisting trust fund structure is challenged by external political forces, the aviation case is the story of the tensions that arise when a trust fund is constructed to enforce conflicting promises.

From the very beginning there have been two diametrically opposed views of the Aviation Trust Fund's role. Program advocates on congressional authorizing committees, who have close ties to aviation clienteles, have viewed the trust fund primarily as a device for locking-in spending on aviation capital projects. In their view, the trust fund's earmarked revenues should be used to pay for airport development grants, procurement of high-tech navigation equipment, and other aviation capital improvements. Presidents and institutional budget guardians, in contrast, have argued that a large share of Aviation Trust Fund money should be used to finance the operating budget of the Federal Aviation Administration, including the enormous costs of running the nation's air traffic control system. Authorizers and aviation lobbyists insist that these routine bureaucratic costs should be paid substantially from general tax revenues. In one view, then, the Aviation Trust Fund is, or should be, a pure capital account; in the other, a true user pay system. The former conception implies that the trust fund's major purposes are to reduce political uncertainty and maximize aviation capital budgets, the latter to promote economic efficiency and safeguard the Treasury.[1]

The debate over the Aviation Trust Fund seems arcane, but there are large political stakes. To the extent officeholders treat the trust fund as a pure capital account, it increases the pot of money available for transportation infrastructure projects – particularistic benefits, such as airport expansions, for which members of Congress can claim electoral credit. But if FAA's operating expenses are *not* paid for out of the trust fund, ordinary taxpayers will be forced to subsidize wealthy owners and patrons of corporate jets and less money will be available to finance other discretionary spending needs. In sum, the conflict over the institutional role of the Aviation Trust Fund is about distributive benefits, "corporate welfare" in the US budget, and the tradeoff between policy commitment and discretion. As this debate has unfolded, both sides have sought to manipulate the trust fund's inherited design to advance their goals. No stable political equilibrium has ever been reached.

Rationales for trust funds and earmarked taxes

The Aviation Trust Fund built directly on the Highway Trust Fund experience. By the late 1960s the Highway Trust Fund was widely perceived to be an extremely effective instrument of budgetary precommitment. While the federal government had provided airport development grants to state and local operators since the 1940s, and while aviation users had long paid modest aviation fuel and ticket taxes, there was no linkage between aviation revenues and aviation spending.[2] In a clear example of "policy learning," the perceived success of the Highway Trust Fund taught aviation clienteles that they needed (and deserved) a dedicated transportation fund of their own.[3] This argument was made most forcefully by local airport operators, who placed a premium on funding stability. "A mechanism as secure as the one used so successfully

[1] See Congressional Budget Office, *The Status of the Airport and Airway Trust Fund* (Washington, DC: Government Printing Office, December 1988).

[2] These taxes included a 5 percent tax on air passenger tickets, a 2 cents per gallon tax on general aviation fuel, and taxes of 10 cents per pound on aircraft inner tubes and 5 cents per pound on aircraft tires. The ticket tax had originally been introduced in 1944 as a World War II revenue measure at a 15 percent level. The rate of the tax was subsequently lowered to 10 percent in 1954 and to 5 percent in 1962. The proceeds of the ticket tax went into general revenues, while the revenue from the gasoline, tire, and tube taxes was channeled into the Highway Trust Fund.

[3] On policy learning, see Hugh Heclo, *Modern Social Politics in Britain and Sweden* (New Haven, Conn.: Yale University Press, 1994).

in the highway program," said one airport executive, "is essential to assure that airport user revenues are not diverted to other aviation or Federal Government programs . . . unless new funds are available on a stable long-term basis, advance planning by airport operators will be very difficult."[4]

During the 1950s and 1960s, the growth of US air traffic greatly surpassed expectations. The FAA in both 1967 and 1968 had been forced to impose air traffic quotas for the nation's five busiest airports, "where delays caused backups in traffic throughout the system."[5] These delays, to borrow terms from John Kingdon, served as a "focusing event" that pushed aviation finance on the policy agenda, allowing the "problem" and "solution" streams to be joined.[6] Institutional budget guardians had floated proposals for increased aviation user charges since the 1950s. Historically, however, aviation interest groups, including the influential Aircraft Owners and Pilots Association, had adamantly opposed user tax hikes. Aviation industry lobbyists argued that aviation improvements should be funded from general tax revenues because the system had originally been built to support military aircraft and because aviation development spending benefited the entire nation through increased commerce and mobility. As we saw, policymakers rejected similar clientele arguments for general-fund financing of highway expansions in the 1950s. They were no more receptive to them now. Indeed, Ways and Means chairman Wilbur Mills flatly stated that an aviation expansion bill unaccompanied by a user tax increase was a political non-starter given the tight budgetary climate.[7]

By the late 1960s a number of aviation interest groups were signaling politicians that they *could* live with increased user charges – provided the money was set aside in a distinct trust fund. "The degree of the user's willingness to pay, and the amount of tax he is willing to accept, is *directly* affected by his approval of the use to which his money will be applied," stated a National Business Aircraft Association representative. "If the willingness of the taxpayer is to any degree a valid consideration, willingness to contribute to a trust fund would vastly exceed willingness to pay special use taxes into the general

4 US Congress, House of Representatives, "Aviation Facilities Maintenance and Development," Hearings Before the Committee on Interstate and Foreign Commerce, 91st Congress, 1st Session (1969), 273.
5 "Congress Passes Airport and Airway Development Act," *Congressional Quarterly Almanac* (1970), 169.
6 On focusing events, see John Kingdon, *Agendas, Alternatives and Public Policies* (Boston: Little Brown, 1984).
7 For Mills's views, see *Congressional Record*, November 6, 1969, 33283.

revenues of the United States."[8] In 1967, several aviation business groups drafted proposals for a new Airport Trust Fund. The Senate Commerce Committee immediately embraced the trust fund concept, but executive budget guardians were hostile.[9]

The Nixon Administration in June 1969 proposed a ten year, $5 billion aviation expansion program.[10] Under the plan, aviation user taxes would rise dramatically to cover 70 percent of federal aviation spending, up from the existing cost-recovery rate of under 25 percent. Both the FAA and Department of Transportation (DOT) argued that the proceeds of these revenues should flow into a new Aviation Trust Fund. But budget controllers at the Bureau of the Budget and Department of Treasury opposed the creation of an Aviation Trust Fund for two reasons. First, they argued that creation of an Aviation Trust Fund would set a dangerous precedent, encouraging every other industry that received special governmental benefits to lobby for trust fund status of their own. A second concern had to do with interest earnings. If the Aviation Trust Fund followed the Highway Trust Fund model, it would earn interest on any unspent balances. Yet the aviation bills passed by Congress assumed that the general fund would continue to underwrite a significant share of total federal aviation spending for years to come. Aviation users would thus be gaining the special privileges of trust fund financing on the cheap. The BOB argued that the right to interest earnings would give the aviation sector a wholly unnecessary advantage in the competition for budget support.[11]

Nixon's alternative: a "designated account"

As a compromise, the Administration offered to create a hybrid budget structure which it unfelicitously called a "designated account." The structure would be authorized to receive earmarked tax collections but would be ineligible for interest payments and of course would lack the

[8] National Business Aircraft Association Policy Statement: Development The National Airport System – June 1968, in US Congress, House of Representatives, "Aviation Facilities Maintenance and Development," 485.

[9] "1967 Developments," *Congressional Quarterly Almanac* (1967), 769. My discussion of the trust fund's origins draws on Erasmus Kolman, *Airport Trust Fund: DOT, Nixon, and the Congress*, ICP no. 130 (Syracuse: Inter-University Case Program, 1980).

[10] Robert B. Semple, Jr., "President Asks New User Taxes to Aid Airport," *The New York Times*, June 17, 1969, 1.

[11] Donald C. Winston, "Trust Fund Plan Hits Opposition," *Aviation Week & Space Technology*, April 7, 1969, 26–7; and Donald C. Winston, "Nixon User Tax Plan Drops Trust Fund," *Aviation Week & Space Technology*, May 19, 1969, 21–2.

symbolic power of the trust fund label. Transportation Secretary Volpe made a valiant effort to sell the concept to Congress.[12] Given "the total deficit which will occur over the life of the [aviation improvement] program," he said, "any fears that moneys received through user taxes will be diverted to non-aviation purposes are more theoretical than real. To the extent these fears are real, the establishment of a designated account would completely allay them."[13]

But if legislators were prepared to impose earmarked taxes on millions of citizens and a powerful industry in exchange for specific benefits, they needed to signal that funding promises would be kept. The key was the creation of a formal trust fund structure. "A 'designated account' arrangement, as proposed in the administration bill," stated Senator Jennings Randolph (D-W.Va.), "would not seem to me to give the taxpayers the assurance they must have that their special purpose payments will, indeed, be used for the special purpose for which they are levied."[14] Asked by a reporter to explain Congress's insistence on a trust fund structure, one committee aide explained: "This is really the only way to make a user charge palatable."[15]

Procedural safeguards

The Airport and Airway Development Act of 1970 was signed by President Nixon on May 21, 1970 after passing easily in both chambers.[16] This strong bipartisan show of support camouflaged a fundamental

---

[12] The Administration's designated account proposal was the subject of the very first question asked of Secretary Volpe when he testified before the House Commerce Committee in July 1969. Volpe was asked whether the money that would be raised would "go to a trust fund or the Treasury." Volpe assured the Committee that the money would indeed go into a "separate account" and tried to brush over the issue. See US Congress, House of Representatives, "Aviation Facilities Maintenance and Development," 89.

[13] US Congress, Senate, "Airport/Airways Development," Hearings Before the Subcommittee on Aviation of the Committee on Commerce, 91st Congress, 1st Session, Part 1 (1969), 4.

[14] US Congress, Senate, "Airport/Airways Development," 708.

[15] Quoted in Winston, "Nixon User Tax Plan Drops Trust Fund," 21.

[16] The House passed its version of the bill by a 337–6 roll call vote on November 6, 1969. Senate passage came by a 77–0 roll call vote on February 26, 1970. The conference report on the aviation bill was adopted by voice vote in the Senate and by a 361–3 roll call vote in the House. See "Congress Moves Toward Enactment of 10-Year Airport-Airways Plan," *National Journal*, November 15, 1969, 126–7; see also John L. Moore, "Senate Approval Moves Airport-Airways Expansion Plan Closer to Enactment," *The National Journal*, March 7, 1970, 492–3; "Transportation Legislation," *Congressional Quarterly Almanac*,

conflict over the trust fund's central purpose. In the view of the Nixon Administration and legislative budget guardians, the trust fund's user charges would greatly reduce the need for general fund spending on aviation in the future. According to the Ways and Means Committee, the goal was "for the civil part of the system to eventually become self-sustaining from air user taxes."[17] The unmistakable implication was that user taxes would finance the costs of routine FAA operations since these costs were the largest item in the total aviation budget. Program advocates on the authorizing panels accepted that aviation users would be contributing more. The major advantage of the trust fund from their perspective, however, was that it would free aviation capital expenditures "from having to compete for General Treasury funds, the basic reason for the funding uncertainties and inadequacies of the past."[18] Any use of trust fund money for routine operations "would be secondary."[19]

Authorizing committee members strengthened the trust fund's procedural integrity as a capital account in two ways. First, they ensured that airport development grants would be granted access to "backdoor" contract authority, the same privilege traditionally enjoyed by the Highway Trust Fund. Contract authority would enable FAA managers to enter into legally binding contracts with airport contractors without advance spending permission from the appropriations committees. The second safeguard was the adoption of a statutory floor on aviation capital spending levels. The Act mandated that not less than $530 million in capital outlays be spent from the trust fund by fiscal 1980. This provision reflected the Senate Commerce Committee's fear that aviation capital programs would not be adequately funded unless the executive's hands were tied. There was a legitimate reason for this belief. While federal spending on FAA operations increased significantly during the 1960s, executive budget guardians had consistently held down the level of capital investments. Outlays for new facilities and equipment fell every year between 1964 and 1968.[20] The Nixon Administration opposed both procedural safeguards but accepted them to get the bill.

pp. 657–63; and "Congress Passes Airport and Airway Development Act," *Congressional Quarterly Almanac*, 168–72.

[17] See House Interstate and Foreign Commerce Committee, *The Aviation Facilities Expansion Act of 1969*, H-Rept. 91–601.

[18] US Department of Transportation, *Fourth Annual Report* (Fiscal Year 1970), (DOT, 1971).

[19] Congressional Budget Office, *The Status of the Airport and Airway Trust Fund*, 2.

[20] Jeremy J. Warford, *Public Policy Toward General Aviation* (Washington, DC: Brookings Institution, 1971), 51.

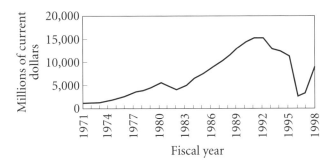

Figure 7.1 Aviation Trust Fund balance, fiscal years 1971–1998
Source: Office of Management and Budget, *Budget of the United States Government* (Washington, DC: Government Printing Office, various years).

Securing promises?

The conventional wisdom is that the Aviation Trust Fund has been a terrible deal for the aviation sector. Indeed, aviation trade association lobbyists regularly complain that their members are "not getting what they have already paid for."[21] As evidence for this alleged breach of faith, the lobbyists point to the cash balance in the trust fund, which climbed to more than $14 billion in the early 1990s, up from about $2 billion in 1975 (figure 7.1).

In his provocative recent book *Money for Nothing: Politicians, Rent Extraction, and Political Extortion*, public choice scholar Fred S. McChesney claims that the existence of a large balance in the Aviation Trust Fund demonstrates that government trust funds are inherently untrustworthy. "As the demand for these [aviation] projects has risen," he writes, "Congress has simply refused to keep its promise to release the money to finance them."[22] McChesney is of course correct that "Earmarking revenues for some future use gives the supposed beneficiaries no enforceable property rights in those funds."[23] But McChesney's outrage is misplaced. The real aviation scandal – if one exists – is not the size of the trust fund balance but the failure of Congress to impose reasonable fees on "general aviation" users (owners and patrons of corporate and recreational aircraft). While commercial airlines and their passengers

---

[21] Letter to the Editor from James D. Gormely, head of the General Aviation Manufacturers Association, *The Washington Post*, April 23, 1990, A10.

[22] Fred S. McChesney, *Money for Nothing: Politicians, Rent Extraction, and Political Extortion* (Cambridge, MA: Harvard University Press, 1997), 130.

[23] *Ibid.*, 125.

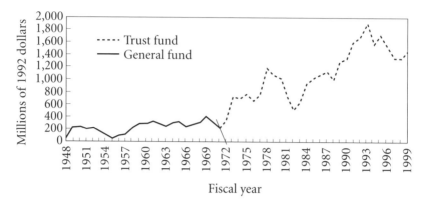

Figure 7.2 Real Federal Airport capital investment, fiscal years 1948–1999 (constant 1992 dollars)
Note: Table 9.6 (highway physical capital investment) and table 10.1 (total composite deflators).
Source: Office of Management and Budget, *Budget of the United States Government, Fiscal Year 2000 – Historical Tables* (Washington, DC: Government Printing Office, 1999).

have paid their fair share of the system's costs, general aviation users – who are disproportionately affluent – have historically received massive subsidies from average taxpayers. By law, these subsidies are not shown in the annual reports on the trust fund's financial status issued by the Treasury Department. In sum, the aviation case offers important lessons about the politics of trust funds and earmarked taxes, but these lessons are not quite what the common wisdom holds.

A quick look at the fund's performance

How well does the performance of the Aviation Trust Fund measure up against its designers' claims that the device would maximize aviation capital spending, reduce uncertainty, and protect the fisc? As the data in figure 7.2 show, the level of aviation capital spending increased dramatically following the trust fund's creation. During the ten years before the trust fund's enactment, annual federal airport capital investments averaged $286 million in constant 1992 dollars. It increased to $781 million over the next decade (figure 7.2). As in the highway case, the shift to trust fund status was thus followed by major expansions in transportation infrastructure spending.

Trust fund financing has been less successful in reducing political and

Table 7.1. *Standard deviation of annual real percentage change in air transportation budget during the decades immediately before and after trust fund creation*

Period	Standard deviation
Pre Trust Fund (FY 1961–1970)	0.112
Post Trust Fund (FY 1971–1980)	0.068

Note: Author's calculation based on real budget authority (constant FY 1996 dollars) for air transportation budget subfunction. Source: Budget Authority Data Set, Policy Agendas Project, Center for American Politics and Public Policy, University of Washington.

fiscal uncertainty, however. To be sure, the federal aviation budget did stabilize following the trust fund's adoption. As the data in table 7.1 show, the variance of annual changes in real budget authority for the air transportation budget declined during the trust fund's first decade of existence relative to its previous level. But this stability did not last. As I discuss below, conflict over the trust fund's governance role became so severe in the early 1980s that Congress was unable to maintain the trust fund's legal authority to collect taxes, causing the trust fund's current income to plummet from $1.8 billion in 1980 to only $21 million in 1981 (figure 7.3).[24] During the period in which its tax revenue stream was cut off, the Aviation Trust Fund was forced to spend down its reserves just to keep the aviation program going. In addition, as figure 7.2 shows, aviation capital spending experienced a temporary drop-off. This was hardly what aviation clienteles had intended when they lobbied for the trust fund's creation.

In contrast to the Highway Trust Fund, which has in general generated enough money to cover program budgets, the Aviation Trust Fund has not guaranteed effective cost recovery, although certainly its establishment represented an improvement over the *status quo ante*. At the direction of the Congress, the FAA and Transportation Department have regularly examined the allocation of the aviation system's costs. These

[24] Aviation taxes in place before 1970 continued at their pre-trust fund rates, with the proceeds deposited in the general fund (in the case of ticket tax revenues) or the Highway Trust Fund (in the case of aviation taxes on gasoline, tires, and tubes). For background, see "Airport Tax Development," *Congressional Quarterly Almanac* (1980), 267–9; and US Congress, House of Representatives, "Status of the Airport and Airway Trust Fund," Hearing Before the Committee on Ways and Means, 96th Congress, 2nd Session (1980).

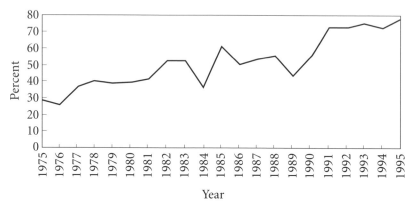

Figure 7.3 Percent of FAA spending paid from trust fund, fiscal years 1975–1995

Source: Congressional Budget Office, *The Status of the Airport and Airway Trust Fund* (Washington, DC: Government Printing Office, 1988) and J. F. Hornbeck, "Transportation Trust Fund Balances, Infrastructure Financing and the Federal Budget," CRS Report for Congress (Washington, DC: Congressional Research Service, Rpt 93–469E, 1993).

studies suggest that private users should collectively finance at least 85 percent of FAA spending, with public users (primarily military aircraft) responsible for the remaining 15 percent.[25] The Aviation Trust Fund has historically financed only about 60 percent of FAA spending, however, primarily because general aviation users have received massive subsidies. In 1985, for example, general aviation users were responsible for $1.4 billion of the FAA's costs but contributed only $100 million into the trust fund.[26] To sum up, the Aviation Trust Fund has been fairly successful in maximizing aviation capital investment, has had less success in reducing fiscal uncertainty, and been quite unsuccessful as an instrument of cost recovery.

Never-ending conflict, perpetual reform

The policy outcomes summarized above should not be reified. They are the result of conflict, not design – the product of a protracted struggle

[25] See, for example, US Department of Transportation,"Airport and Airway Cost Allocation Study Part I Report: Determination, Allocation and Recovery of System Costs" (Washington, DC: DOT, September 1973).
[26] "Paying for Highway, Airways, and Waterways", 43. Because aviation user charges do not correlate closely with marginal costs, they also fail to create an incentive for efficient use of air traffic control services.

between authorizing committee members and aviation lobbyists on the one hand, and presidents and budget guardians on the other. While the goals of these actors have largely been given by their institutional positions, the terms of engagement have been fundamentally shaped by the trust fund structure. The information refracted by the trust fund device has focused political attention on the trust fund's internal financial condition rather than on the size of the aviation budget relative to other domestic programs or on the economic costs of service provision. Because the trust fund has been "in surplus" throughout most of its history, budget controllers have not only found it difficult to control spending and increase user taxes. They have also been forced to fight off clientele demands for user tax *decreases*.[27]

The conflict over the Aviation Trust Fund's role has manifested itself in perpetual skirmishing over the arcane rules governing whether and how much trust fund money can be spent on routine FAA operations. While this conflict has been intensified by external fiscal pressures, it has been fueled mainly by the inability of lawmakers to reach a durable consensus on the trust fund's role and (especially after the 1980s) by the FAA's internal bureaucratic problems. This is not the story, then, of a preexisting trust fund facing stress from coalitional change, but rather of a deeply institutionalized conflict among existing political stakeholders.

The conflict starts

The conflict over the trust fund's role started almost as soon as the trust fund became operational. In 1971, President Nixon antagonized the aviation lobby by proposing to spend $700 million from the trust fund on routine FAA operations.[28] While this was a much higher level of operations spending than the 1970 statute contemplated, the Administration argued it was not bound to follow Congress's directives. "We know that it is not in the Act but that's what we felt is prudent to spend on airports at this date," said Transportation Under Secretary James M. Beggs.[29] Aviation lobbyists protested the Administration's move as an

---

[27] See Statement of Edward W. Stimpson, President of the General Aviation Manufacturers Association, in US Congress, House of Representatives, "Status of the Airport and Airway Trust Fund," Hearings Before the Committee on Ways and Means, 94th Congress, 2nd Session (1976), 49.

[28] Congressional Budget Office, *The Status of the Airport and Airway Trust Fund*, 5–6.

[29] Vera Hirschberg, "Congress Wrestles Over Use of Aviation Trust Funds," *National Journal*, February 13, 1971, 333–7.

outrageous "breach of faith," and demanded that Congress adopt a new rule prohibiting *any* future use of trust fund money for operations.[30]

At a hearing on the proposed change, House Commerce Committee member John Dingell (D-MI) scolded FAA executives for undermining the commitments authorizers had made to aviation clienteles. In a sense, Dingell was playing a two-level game, seeking simultaneously to reassure the aviation lobby that Congress's spending promises were credible and to constrain the fiscal discretion of the executive. "The reason we set up a trust fund, quite frankly, was because we didn't trust FAA and the Department of Transportation to administer the laws we had been putting out of this committee," said Dingell. "So we called it a trust fund because we didn't trust you folks. And you proved that we shouldn't and can't and don't!"[31] The bill prohibiting operating spending from the trust fund passed overwhelmingly. Nixon had little choice but to sign the measure.[32]

Elaborate safeguards

But the requirements of the new trust fund regime – no trust fund spending on FAA operations – proved so fiscally rigid that it soon generated pressure for further institutional reform. Between 1976 and 1990 authorizing committee members attempted to come up with a new trust fund design that would retain capital investment as the top priority while permitting limited operations spending from the trust fund. The complex fiscal design that emerged had two key elements. First, a *cap* was imposed on the maximum amount of trust fund money that could be used for operations in any given year. Second, a *penalty* clause reduced these maximum levels by two dollars for every dollar that actual investment spending fell below congressionally authorized levels.[33]

Yet despite these elaborate procedural safeguards, the balance in the trust fund continued to rise, frustrating authorizing committee members and aviation clients alike. When DOT officials testified on aviation legislation during 1981–2, committee members sought to extract an

---

[30] See US Congress, House of Representatives, "Airport and Airway Trust Fund," Hearings before the Subcommittee on Transportation and Aeronautics of the Committee on Interstate and Foreign Commerce, 92nd Congress, 1st Session (1971), 11. See also US Congress, Senate, "Airport and Airway Development and Revenue Act Amendments of 1971," Hearings Before the Subcommittee on Aviation of the Committee on Commerce, 92nd Congress, 1st Session on S. 1437 (1971).

[31] *Ibid.*, 22.

[32] "Airport Development," *Congressional Quarterly Almanac* (1971), 873.

[33] Congressional Budget Office, *The Status of the Airport and Airway Trust Fund*, 9.

explicit commitment from them to spend down the trust fund. In one particularly arresting exchange, Senator Bob Packwood (R-OR) pressed Transportation Secretary Drew Lewis and FAA Administrator J. Lynn Helms for an inviolable guarantee:

> Chairman Packwood: What I need is a pledge from you, and from Administrator Helms, that when we get this legislation in place the user fees will be used. And that we are not going to use them to mount up a surplus in the trust fund in order to help balance the budget. That is not the point of user fees. They are to be used for the purpose for which they are intended.

> Secretary Lewis: We agree completely. And if there is any way you can lock us in terms of the legislation, we would be pleased to be locked in so we are obligated, not only the two of us but whoever our successors should be. We feel very strongly the money is needed. We do not see that as a budget balancer. And I am sure that Mr. David Stockman, [the OMB Director] will work with us, because he has accepted the need for the airports. As a matter of fact, I should point out, at the time I accepted the job as Secretary of Transportation, I asked the President two questions. And one was: Was he willing to make a commitment to the needs of the airspace in the future. So not only do we have a commitment from OMB, but also from the President of the United States.

> Chairman Packwood: Thank you.

> Mr. Helms: Thank you. It was that specific commitment which Mr. Stockman made that we would draw down the surplus and not let it go back up.

> Chairman Packwood: Good.[34]

By 1986, however, aviation clienteles – with amplification from newspaper editorial boards – were complaining that the spending promises made four years earlier were not being kept.[35] As proof they pointed to the growing balance in the trust fund (figure 7.1). Said one aviation lobbyist:

> Every time you or I fly, we pay an 8 percent surcharge or "ticket tax" to the federal Airport and Airway Trust Fund. By law, Congress has pledged to spend these funds to improve our air travel system. But Congress has

---

[34] US Congress, Senate, "Airport and Airway System Development Act of 1981," Hearing Before the Subcommittee on Aviation of the Committee On Commerce, Science, and Transportation, 97th Congress, Second Session on S. 508 (May 21, 1982), 86–7.

[35] See, for example, "Close Calls in the Air," *The Washington Post*, April 24, 1987, A26.

failed to keep its promise and more than six billion dollars in unspent transportation taxes sit idle, while safety and capacity projects go unfunded . . . The simple fact of the matter is that we pay this ticket tax and elect our Senators. That gives us the right to demand our tax dollars be used for the purpose for which the tax was created – to improve our air transportation system.[36]

There are two leading explanations for Congress's failure to spend down the trust fund balance rapidly. The first – advanced by both aviation clienteles and authorizing committee members – is that institutional budget guardians were artificially creating trust fund surpluses to mask the true size of the deficit. "Despite the Airport and Airway Trust Fund's ever-increasing surplus and the fact that aviation users have paid the taxes in good faith, aviation's dedicated revenues continue to be surreptitiously used to avoid having to cut general fund programs," said Norman Y. Mineta (D-Ca), the chairman of the House Aviation Subcommittee.[37] The second explanation – offered by public choice scholar Fred S. McChesney – is that policymakers accumulated a large balance in the Aviation Trust Fund to force aviation interest groups to cough up more campaign contributions.[38]

It is certainly true that aviation groups have had an incentive to lobby relevant members of Congress. And deficit pressures no doubt gave appropriators an added incentive to restrain aviation spending during the 1980s and early 1990s.[39] Spending from the Aviation Trust Fund, like Highway Trust Fund spending, was subject to sequestration under Gramm-Rudman. It also counted against the limits on discretionary spending established by the Budget Enforcement Act of 1990.[40] But the

---

[36] Letter from the Partnership for Improved Air Travel, November 28, 1989; also cited in McChesney, *Money for Nothing*, 130.

[37] Quoted in Richard Witkin, "Aviation Leaders Eye Fund As Cushion for FAA Cuts, " *The New York Times*, January 20, 1986, A20.

[38] McChesney, *Money for Nothing*, 130.

[39] See Kurt C. Zorn, "The Airport and Airway Trust Fund: A Continuing Controversy," *Public Budgeting and Finance*, 10, Spring 1990, 23. The 1990 budget deal attacked the Aviation Trust Fund by temporarily reserving the revenues from a 2 percent increase in the airline ticket tax for deficit reduction. In the 1993 budget package, Congress retained the entire proceeds from a 4.3 cents a gallon tax on aviation fuel as general revenues. See "Bush Gets Parts of Aviation Package," *Congressional Quarterly Almanac* (1990), 384–8.

[40] As in the highway case, the shift to a more centralized budget process after the 1974 Budget Act gave appropriations committees the opportunity to begin setting yearly "obligation ceilings" on new capital spending commitments from the Aviation Trust Fund. See "Congress Sets Ceiling on Highway Spending," *Congressional Quarterly Almanac* (1976), 746–54.

two leading hypotheses for the Aviation Trust Fund balance are too simplistic. A close examination of the political and financial history of the Aviation Trust Fund reveals that the balance grew primarily because of unforeseen bureaucratic problems and unintended institutional design consequences.[41]

Beginning in the early 1980s, the FAA sought to implement a $16 billion plan to modernize the nation's antiquated air traffic control system. To put it mildly, the agency's efforts did not go smoothly. The FAA found it extraordinarily difficult to integrate new computer and radar equipment. As the FAA slipped further behind its procurement schedule, appropriators had no choice but to reduce capital spending levels, causing revenues in the trust fund to build up. Congressional appropriators provided $945 billion less for air traffic equipment between 1982 and 1987 than President Reagan requested.[42]

This set off the penalty clause in the appropriations law. As a result, trust fund spending for *operations* also had to be reduced, further accelerating the surplus buildup. The penalty clause thus had exactly the opposite result from what was intended. Instead of forcing the trust fund balance to decline, the penalty mechanism (which of course would not have existed in the absence of the conflict over the permissible uses of trust fund money) caused the balance to *increase*. The penalty mechanisms and accumulated interest were responsible for almost 80 percent of the trust fund balance over the 1980s.[43]

The General Accounting Office concluded that the FAA could not have effectively spent any more than it did given its technological and administrative problems.[44] Nonetheless, the growing trust fund balance created the definite impression that aviation users were being "cheated." To repeat: this impression was false. General aviation users in particular continued to benefit from massive general fund subsidies. Indeed, if such users had been forced to pay their full share of the system's costs, the

---

[41] See James C. Miller III, "Airport Woes and Trust Fund's 'Surpluses'" *The Wall Street Journal*, September 15, 1987, 34.

[42] See Robert D. Hershey, "A Fight Builds Over Money Not Spent," *The New York Times*, September 4, 1987, A14.

[43] J.F. Hornbeck, "Transportation Trust Funds: Economic and Policy Issues," Congressional Research Service Issue Brief, IB90057, updated February 20, 1992.

[44] The General Accounting Office issued countless reports on the FAA's administrative troubles. See, for example, General Accounting Office, "FAA Budget: Agency Faces Key Management Challenges on Major Issues," Statement of Kenneth M. Mead, Director, Transportation Issues, Resources, Community, and Economic Development Division, Testimony Before the Subcommittee on Transportation and Related Agencies, Committee on Appropriations, House of Representatives, April 19, 1994, GAO/T-RCED-94-101.

balance in the trust fund would actually have been *negative*.[45] But the Treasury's own numbers showed a massive balance in the trust fund, making it virtually impossible for budget guardians to control the agenda. Unsurprisingly, aviation clienteles and congressional authorizers refused to accept the judgment of the GAO, and insisted that the FAA *could* handle a higher level of capital spending. Their next strategy was to push for the trust fund's removal from the unified budget. Off-budget proposals came within ten votes of passage on the House floor twice between 1985 and 1987, with nay votes from budget controllers responsible for the narrow defeats.[46]

Taxes are fungible

Probably the only conceivable way to force budget guardians to increase capital spending levels (beyond what most experts said the FAA could feasibly handle) was to eliminate the aviation taxes altogether. In 1987 spending advocates tried exactly this tactic. They created yet another precommitment device: a "trigger tax" mechanism that would automatically reduce aviation tax rates by 50 percent if capital outlays fell below 85 percent of authorized levels.[47] Because the amount of revenue that would be lost to the government through activation of this trigger mechanism exceeded the level of new capital spending demanded, any effort to use surplus trust fund for deficit-reduction purposes would become self-defeating.[48] If officeholders failed to spend aviation taxes on new capital as promised, the aviation taxes would be killed.

Implicit in the trigger tax device was a threat: aviation proponents would prefer sacrificing earmarked taxes rather than allow their capital spending demands to go partly unmet. By their actions, however, budget guardians demonstrated that they considered the threat not to be credible. In its baseline deficit calculations, OMB assumed that the trigger tax mechanism would not go into effect.[49] Moreover, appropriations for

---

[45] Congressional Budget Office, *The Status of the Airport and Airway Trust Fund*, 28.

[46] In the 1987 vote, for example, Appropriations Committee members voted 1–49 against. Budget Committee members voted 7–25 against. Public Works and Transportation Committee voted 45–3 for passage. See "Airport Reauthorization Bill Enacted," *Congressional Quarterly Almanac* (1987), 106–H.

[47] See "Airport Reauthorization Bill Enacted," *Congressional Quarterly Almanac*, 339–44.

[48] The trigger mechanism kicked in if the sum of the obligation limits for airport grants and appropriations for facilities and equipment and research and development for 1988 and 1989 was less than 85 percent of the total amounts authorized by Congress.

[49] Meyers, *Strategic Budgeting*, 133.

capital programs were kept to only 80 percent of authorizations for 1988–9.[50]

The trigger tax and penalty mechanisms were abolished after an accommodation was reached between authorizers and appropriators late in the 1990 congressional session.[51] Authorizers agreed to eliminate the procedural restrictions on the trust fund in exchange for a commitment from appropriators to increase aviation capital spending by $1 billion over five years. After years of steady increases, the balance in the trust fund finally began to decline (figure 7.1). The elimination of the penalty clause meant the trust fund would cover about 75 percent of total FAA outlays and about 50 percent of the agency's routine operations. These levels were approximately achieved in fiscal years 1991–5 (figure 7.4).

The political agreement underlying this cost-sharing arrangement remained fragile, however. Some congressional budget guardians hoped to see the general fund contribution permanently reduced to 15 percent. In 1998 the Clinton Administration proposed eliminating general fund spending on FAA services altogether. Under the Administration's plan, aviation spending would be financed through a more economically efficient system of user fees based on marginal costs. Congressional authorizers naturally opposed this move, seeking to preserve not only the trust fund itself but also the traditional general fund subsidy.[52] In sum, three decades after its creation, the basic conflict over the Aviation Trust Fund's function remains unresolved.[53]

---

[50] Paul Starobin, "Obscure Trigger-Tax Provision Imperils Aviation Budget," *Congressional Quarterly Weekly Report*, April 8, 1989, 745–6.

[51] Mike Mills, "Trust Fund 'Sanctity' Crumbling Under Pressure From Budget," *Congressional Quarterly Weekly Report*, October 20, 1990, 3503–4.

[52] Quoted in Mark Murray, "Another Year, Another Trust Fund Fracas," *National Journal*, February 27, 1999, 550–1. See also "The Aviation Money Grab," *The Washington Post*, March 24, 1999, A26.

[53] The trust fund balance would have been about $5 billion larger but for the lapse of the aviation taxes for nearly eight months in 1996 and for another two months in 1997. The first lapse was an unintended consequence of the larger budget battle between President Clinton and the Gingrich Republicans. A timely reauthorization of the aviation taxes was passed by Congress in 1995, but the measure was included in an omnibus budget package that Clinton vetoed, leading to a government shutdown. The second lapse reflected an effort by lawmakers to game budget enforcement rules. Under the CBO's rules, the aviation taxes counted as "new" revenue each time they were renewed, meaning they could be used to offset new mandatory spending and tax cuts. See Michael Wines, "With Budget Bills in Limbo, a Lapsed Airline Tax Fuels a Growing Deficit," *The New York Times*, April 24, 1996, A20. On the budget gaming, see the statement by Senator Bob Graham (D-FL), *Congressional Record*, February 27, 1997, S1772.

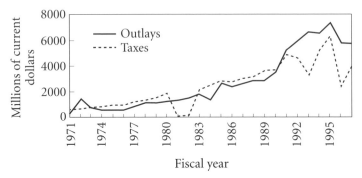

Figure 7.4 Aviation Trust Fund, fiscal years 1971–1997
Source: Office of Management and Budget, *Budget of the United States Government* (Washington, DC: Government Printing Office, various years).

Conclusions

Just as the Hospital Insurance Trust Fund is often compared to Social Security, so the Aviation Trust Fund is often compared to the Highway Trust Fund, its institutional predecessor. Generally the conclusion drawn is that the Aviation Trust Fund has been the less successful of the two transportation funds. Robert Kuttner, for example, argues that one of the reasons why airports became "such a mess" during the Reagan years, even while the highway program prospered, is because highway spending "is financed by a more ironclad trust fund."[54] This argument is correct as far as it goes but it fails to probe the historical and institutional roots of the Aviation Trust Fund's relative weakness.

Most of the Aviation Trust Fund's incapacities trace back to tensions contained in its original enabling statute.[55] While trust funds are often designed to serve more than a single objective, the multiple goals underlying the creation of the Aviation Trust Fund have proved particularly difficult to reconcile. The preexistence of a large general fund aviation program in 1970, coupled with the inescapable costs of air traffic control,

[54] Robert Kuttner, "Reaganism, Liberalism, and the Democrats," in Sidney Blumenthal and Thomas Byrne Edsall, eds., *The Reagan Legacy* (New York: Pantheon Books, 1988), 129.

[55] Another difference between the two transportation trust funds has to do with the geographic distribution of benefits. While there is an interstate highway project in practically every district, airports dot the landscape less evenly. Still, the Aviation Trust Fund has sparked legislative conflict more along committee than along geographic lines.

left open the question of what proportion, if any, of trust fund money could be used for routine FAA operations. Because aviation users do make significant earmarked contributions, aviation lobbyists feel entitled to protest loudly whenever trust fund surpluses accumulate, even if for unavoidable bureaucratic reasons. Yet because federal aviation taxes do not remotely cover total aviation spending, budget controllers are particularly adamant about retaining some flexibility over how money flowing into the Aviation Trust Fund is used.[56] In sum, the exchange of special taxes for special benefits in the aviation case has been perceived by budget controllers (if not by aviation lobbyists themselves) as one-sided, not reciprocal. In the highway case, the question has been whether it is acceptable to divert some highway revenues to non-highway uses. In the aviation case, the question has been whether it breaks a moral commitment to withdraw billions of *general fund* subsidies.

The conflict over the permissible use of aviation revenues has clearly reduced the trust fund's capacity to reduce political uncertainty. Yet it must be emphasized that trust fund financing has strengthened, not weakened, the aviation lobby's claim on the public fisc by keeping public and media attention on trust fund balances and capital investment promises, rather than on equitable or efficient cost sharing. "It's not because of the way I comb my hair," said Transportation Committee chairman Bud Shuster in 1999 of his power in aviation budget fights, "it's because the [aviation] needs are there, and the facts are on our side, and the integrity of the trust fund is there."[57] To the extent the integrity of the Aviation Trust Fund as a capital account is respected, of course, general aviation users get a virtual free ride and the rest of the domestic budget becomes more turbulent.

[56] The Highway Trust Fund supports the Federal Highway Administration's operating expenses, but these expenses are too small (2 percent of total trust fund spending in 1991) to spark much controversy.

[57] Quoted in Juliet Elperin, "Transportation a Winner Again: Committee Leader Uses Threat to Push Airport Proposal," *The Washington Post*, March 26, 1999, A08.

8

Superfund

The very nature of environmental policymaking makes crafting durable policy commitments challenging. While the benefits of environmental policies are often long-term and diffused, the costs may be immediate and concentrated on influential interests. Hence the initial passage of a major new environmental program in the United States often requires some perceived scandal or "crisis."[1] If environmental policies are difficult to enact they may be even harder to sustain. Industry opponents will constantly be on the lookout for opportunities to reverse preexisting arrangements. Environmental activists thus have their work cut out for them. Yet while these conditions are constraining, the Superfund case shows how strategic advocates can use fiscal design to enhance the political durability of an environmental program.[2]

Established in December 1980 by a lame-duck Democratic Congress and a lame-duck Democratic President (Jimmy Carter) following the shocking discovery of a leaking toxic waste dump in the suburb of Love Canal, New York, the Superfund Trust Fund pays for cleanup of

---

[1] See James Q. Wilson, ed., *The Politics of Regulation* (New York: Basic Books, 1980). Superfund is thus an example of what Wilson labels "entrepreneurial politics." It must be recalled that what matters in Wilson's framework are the *perceived* costs and benefits of policies, not the actual economic incidence.

[2] My analysis in this chapter is heavily indebted to two excellent studies of Superfund: Mark K. Landy, Marc J. Roberts, and Stephen R. Thomas, *The Environmental Protection Agency: Asking the Wrong Questions From Nixon to Clinton*, Expanded Edition (New York: Oxford University Press, 1994); and John A. Hird, *Superfund: The Political Economy of Environmental Risk* (Baltimore: Johns Hopkins University Press, 1994).

abandoned hazardous waste sites primarily from taxes on the chemical and petroleum industries.[3] The underlying premise of Superfund's design is that if the true cost of cleaning up the nation's hazardous waste sites were made explicit to voters, the political commitment to completing the job would be weaker and less secure.

The key to strengthening this commitment, policy entrepreneurs at the Environmental Protection Agency believed, was sheltering the program from budgetary competition and minimizing its need for general tax revenues. This was accomplished in two steps. First, the law created a stringent private liability regime to force parties with some connection to particular waste sites (e.g., waste generators, transporters, dump site operators) to pay for site cleanups themselves, out of their own pockets. Spending under this liability regime is considered "off-budget." Second, to pay for site cleanups where no legally responsible party could be found or was solvent ("orphan sites"), special taxes on industry were levied, with the money funneled into the Superfund Trust Fund, which gives the overall program its popular name.[4]

Both the liability regime and the trust fund structure are based on the idea of "polluter pays." This is in a sense the mirror opposite of the "contributory insurance" or "user pay" doctrines upon which the social insurance and transportation trust funds are based. The trust fund structures and earmarked taxes in those cases are meant to reinforce a sense of reciprocity, the idea that recipients have specifically paid for their (desired) benefits and that the government in turn has an obligation to make good on its spending promises. But in the Superfund case the policy message is that someone *else* – the polluters – are paying to solve an unpleasant social problem.[5]

Rationales for dedicated taxes and trust fund

Many economists support the use of "liability charges" to internalize negative externalities like pollution.[6] By charging firms for the harms

---

[3] The trust fund was originally named the Hazardous Substance Response Trust Fund. It was renamed the Hazardous Substance Superfund Trust Fund in 1986. I use the more familiar Superfund name throughout the chapter.

[4] Trust fund money could also be used to undertake work at particularly dangerous sites where responsible parties could be identified but simply refused to pay. After cleanup work began, however, the government would attempt to recoup the money. Cost recoveries would then get plowed back into the trust fund.

[5] On the messages contained in policy designs, see Anne Schneider and Helen Ingram, "Social Construction of Target Populations: Implications for Politics and Policy," *American Political Science Review*, 87, June 1993, 334–47.

[6] See, for example, Pechman, *Federal Tax Policy*, 195.

their activities impose on society, the government can compensate for damages and simultaneously create incentives for pollution reduction. At first blush, the Superfund taxes would seem to be a textbook application of liability charges since they are levied against the chemical and petroleum industries, the very economic sectors responsible for most hazardous waste contamination. Moreover, the revenues are legally earmarked for a related spending activity. In fact, however, the taxes make almost *no* contribution to efficiency. First, the taxes are "imposed on some, but not all, hazardous chemicals, and not on the waste produced in either manufacturing or using them."[7] Firms thus have no direct incentive to reduce their waste generation. Second, the money is used to cope with environmental problems that occurred *before* the taxes were enacted. The taxes therefore cannot function as true insurance payments.[8]

Opposition from economists and budget guardians

These features are clearly undesirable from an economist's perspective. But they were *not* accidental. They were in fact deliberate choices made by the architects of the Superfund design, who simply had different priorities. The most important architects were policy entrepreneurs inside the EPA itself. The agency's overriding goal was to lock-in spending for a major hazardous waste cleanup effort. EPA officials feared that once the publicity surrounding the Love Canal scandal died down, the public (and the media) would focus its limited attention elsewhere. Any large-scale hazardous waste cleanup program would be expensive and the federal budget climate was becoming increasingly tight. Congressional appropriations committees, EPA executives believed, were not likely to provide adequate resources for a major cleanup initiative from general revenues.[9] "We just didn't think they'd make the spending commitments," reflected Thomas Jorling, Assistant Administrator for Water and Waste Management under President Carter.[10]

The EPA fashioned a two-pronged design to generate a stable flow of revenues and lower the risk that future politicians would fund the program inadequately. First, it proposed a liability regime to force

---

[7] Congressional Budget Office, "The Growth of Federal User Charges" (Washington, DC: Government Printing Office, August 1993b), 7.
[8] The Superfund liability scheme is similar in this regard because it seeks to recover costs for past, not current, damages.
[9] Landy, Roberts and Thomas, *The Environmental Protection Agency*, 144.
[10] Interview with Thomas Jorling, former EPA Assistant Administrator, February 22, 1999.

responsible parties to assume the cost of most site cleanups themselves. Second, to recover the costs of site cleanups where the liability regime failed to produce the needed resources, the EPA called for new excise taxes (which it called "fees") on petroleum oil and chemical raw materials (feedstocks).[11] This "polluter pay" approach quickly won strong support from the environmental community. "Without an industry-based fee this legislation would be nothing more than an authorization bill – congressional permission to ask OMB and the Appropriations Committees for money," said Blakeman Early of the Sierra Club in congressional testimony. "It is mere folly to expect Congress and the executive branch, in the age of balanced budget fervor, to appropriate, out of the general treasury, the amount of money recognized by all of us as necessary to solve this problem."[12]

The Council of Economic Advisers (CEA), the Department of Treasury, and the OMB all came out against the dedicated funding proposal, however. Former CEA senior staff economist Lawrence J. White recalls the reasons for the Council's opposition:

> Fees on chemicals would lead to distortions and inefficient substitutions of chemical inputs . . . Perhaps present or past chemical users were the sources; perhaps past chemical companies that had gone out of business were the sources . . . Also, we reminded the others, the chemical companies would likely not be the ultimate payers; rather it was the final consumers of chemical products who would largely bear the cost. The creation of the super fund (sic) itself meant that a pot of money would come into existence, with greater pressures to spend it. Congress would scrutinize these expenditures less closely than expenditures out of general revenues.[13]

The most economically efficient approach would be to tax hazardous waste directly. But the EPA rejected such a "waste-end" tax in 1980 on the grounds that it would be difficult to implement. Directly taxing waste would require an extensive enforcement system since there were at least 260,000 waste generators across the nation. By contrast, targeting

---

[11] Testimony of Thomas C. Jorling, US Congress, Senate, "Hazardous Waste Disposal," Joint Hearings before the Subcommittees on Environmental Pollution and Resource Protection of the Committee on Environment and Public Works, 96th Congress, 1st Session (1979), 50.

[12] US Congress, House of Representatives, "Superfund," Hearings Before the Subcommittee on Transportation and Commerce of the Committee on Interstate and Foreign Commerce, 96th Congress, 1st Session, (1979), 445–6.

[13] Lawrence J. White, *Reforming Regulation* (Englewood Cliffs: Prentice Hall, 1981), 149.

chemical producers required less than 1,000 collection points.[14] "We were seeking to mobilize revenues, not to change corporate behavior," explained Jorling.[15] With but one significant exception every top OMB official opposed the dedicated fee proposal on the grounds it would narrow budgetary discretion. The exception was Eliot Cutler, assistant director for energy and environment and a former aide to Senator Ed Muskie (D-MN). Cutler made a strong pitch for the dedicated fee approach but was overruled by his OMB superiors. But President Carter sided with Cutler at a final White House planning meeting, agreeing that the proposal would be more compelling if the costs were targeted against industry rather than taxpayers.[16]

Unsurprisingly, the chemical industry vehemently opposed the fees, contending that the whole program should be paid out of general revenues. More interesting is the reason for its opposition. The industry's concern was not that the fees would directly hurt its bottom line. Chemical lobbyists recognized, as did the EPA itself, that the fees would be substantially passed through to consumers. Rather, their main objection was that the symbolic linkage to toxic waste dumps created by the earmarked taxes would reinforce a negative public image of the industry, tarnishing the reputations even of feedstock companies that had disposed of their wastes properly. As one reporter observed, the leading chemical industry trade group "never argued that the money would in any way endanger its business, only that the fund seemed to require the innocent to pay for the sins of the guilty."[17]

But the very symbolism that distressed the chemical industry was extremely appealing to lawmakers seeking to avoid blame for new taxes.[18] While the costs would be borne by every purchaser of chemical products, individual consumers would be paying these costs only a few pennies at a time. Few people were likely to notice these negligible price increases, and fewer still to mentally connect them to the passage of the Superfund law. In sum, Superfund's costs would not be politically "traceable" (to borrow

---

[14] Harold C. Barnett, *Toxic Debts and The Superfund Dilemma* (Chapel Hill: University of North Carolina Press, 1994), 63.

[15] Jorling interview.

[16] Cutler interview; and Landy, Roberts and Thomas, *The Environmental Protection Agency*, 149.

[17] See Joanne Omang, "House Approves Fund to Cleanup Chemical Wastes," *The Washington Post*, September 24, and Landy, Roberts and Thomas, *The Environmental Protection Agency*, 145.

[18] On blame avoidance, see R. Kent Weaver, "The Politics of Blame Avoidance," *Journal of Public Policy* 6, October–December 1986, 371–98.

R. Douglas Arnold's term).[19] Congress ultimately created a $1.6 billion trust fund, with $1.38 billion coming from excise taxes on the chemical and oil industries. Only $220 million (14 percent) would come from the general revenue pool.[20] As environmental policy expert John A. Hird writes, "In short, members of Congress were well aware that Superfund costs would ultimately be borne by consumers, yet the size of the cleanup fund they envisioned could come only from industry in the face of substantial budget deficits. There was simply little room for appropriations out of general revenues, although hidden taxes were apparently politically acceptable."[21]

Addition of a formal trust fund

As the Superfund bill was being incubated in Congress, its supporters regularly spoke in terms of creating a *trust fund*. Indeed, when industry representatives questioned the fairness of taxing current producers of hazardous waste materials for the failures of the past, environmentalists were quick to invoke the precedent of the Black Lung Disability Trust Fund, which had been created in 1977 to collect fees from "currently active coal miners to provide benefits for miners who got black lung before the Act was passed."[22] Yet when Carter's Superfund proposal emerged from OMB review, it called for the creation of a special fund. But, just as Congress had transformed Nixon's original aviation proposal for a "designated account" into the Airport and Airway Trust Fund (chapter 7), so it made the symbolic point of creating a formal trust fund structure to pay for Superfund cleanups.

The Ways and Means Committee was responsible for this change and it seems to have had three goals in mind: (1) to protect its institutional prerogatives; (2) to assure the chemical and petroleum industries that their future tax liabilities would be contained; and (3) to safeguard the Treasury. Originally, the EPA sought the authority to levy the industry "fees" itself. But this proposed delegation greatly disturbed the chemical

---

[19] R. Douglas Arnold, *The Logic of Congressional Action* (New Haven: Yale University Press, 1990).

[20] The bill passed in the House during one of the last legislative days of the 96th Congress by a vote of 274–94 under suspension of the rules (246 votes were needed to pass). Final passage in the Senate had come earlier by voice vote. See "Congress Clears 'Superfund' Legislation," *Congressional Quarterly Almanac* (1981) 584–93.

[21] Hird, *Superfund*, 195.

[22] Statement of Kenneth S. Kamlet, US Congress, House of Representatives, "Superfund," 601.

industry, and it urged Ways and Means to retain jurisdiction on the grounds that the revenues were not voluntary fees but compulsory taxes.[23] This the Committee was happy to do.[24] Once Ways and Means asserted its authority, it was natural for it to create a formal trust fund structure. The tax-writing panel emphasized that trust fund financing would give the affected industries confidence that they would not be taxed indiscriminately. As Ways and Means Committee chair Al Ullman (D-Oregon) stated on the House floor:

> It has been the custom of the Committee on Ways and Means, when we are asked to raise revenue from a narrow segment of the economy for specific purposes related to the activities of that segment of the economy, to put the revenues so raised into a trust fund. The purpose of these trust funds is to give some assurance to the particular industry that the monies taken from them will be used for the intended purposes. In the absence of a trust fund the revenues would go into the general fund and might never be spent for the purposes originally intended. In return for the guarantee offered by the trust fund mechanism, we have found industries are less opposed to the new taxes.[25]

Ullman added that the Superfund trust fund would assure industry groups that "they will not receive a surprise tax increase in later years."[26] In short, even though Superfund was not based on the reality or appearance of reciprocal exchange, paying earmarked taxes into a federal trust fund still created a certain expectation of fairness. It established a kind of standing for the chemical and petroleum industries before the tax-writing panel, even as they were being stigmatized as "dirty polluters."

Finally, the trust fund embodied a promise of fiscal responsibility from Ways and Means to the full House chamber. According to Ullman, the

---

[23] On the industry's desire for Ways and Means to claim jurisdiction, see "Closer to a Cleanup Superfund," *Business Week*, July 14, 1980, 74.

[24] Ways and Means Committee members had only one serious reservation about creating the Superfund Trust Fund. Within the House, the tax-writing panel would possess legislative jurisdiction only over the revenue side of the fund. The Commerce Committee would control spending. The last thing Ways and Means wanted was to create the expectation that it would establish new trust funds whenever an authorizing committee put forward a spending need. But Ullman concluded that the split-jurisdictional arrangement for Superfund was consistent with the treatment of a number of other trust funds including highways and airports, and that it could be managed effectively. *Congressional Record*, September 19, 1980, 26347.

[25] Statement of Congressman Ullman, *Congressional Record*, September 23, 1980, 26797.

[26] *Ibid.*

creation of the trust fund should "assure all our colleagues that when we promise to fund a program out of specific tax receipts, we will not be forced in later years to finance the program out of general fund revenues."

Securing promises?

Trust fund financing was clearly meant to stabilize Superfund's legislative and financial future. Specifically, it was hoped that the trust fund would provide a sure source of dedicated revenues, protecting toxic waste cleanups from tradeoffs with other budget needs. The trust fund would also assure the chemical and petroleum industries that their future tax liabilities would be contained. Finally, the system would safeguard the fisc by reducing the need for future Congresses (in Ullman's words) to "invade general revenues."[27]

These specific trust fund commitments, considered on their own terms, have been more honored than broken since 1980. Superfund budgets grew dramatically during the early Reagan years, even as EPA's operating budget was being targeted for major cutbacks. When more money has been needed for Superfund cleanups, Congress has tried to minimize the drain on general revenues. The chemical industry's tax liability has not been dramatically increased. And Congress has refused to divert Superfund taxes to other uses.

Yet despite this basic fidelity to the trust fund commitments, Superfund's policy development has been extraordinarily volatile. In part, this volatility stems from the larger political conflict over environmental policy in America. But four specific features of Superfund's inherited design have contributed to the program's instability.

First, the size of the original trust fund was clearly inadequate. Superfund's creators failed to resolve how the program would be financed over the long haul. Second, the Superfund Trust Fund has enjoyed relatively few procedural advantages. Spending from the trust fund has always been on-budget and considered discretionary, legislative jurisdiction over the trust fund has been divided among multiple committees, and the trust fund's taxing authority must be periodically renewed. Third, the private liability regime component of the design has inadvertently spawned a morass of litigation by giving potentially responsible parties an incentive to sue every other firm that might have contributed to the mess, and their insurers, instead of agreeing to early settlements.[28] The result has been

---

[27] *Congressional Record*, September 23, 1980, 26797.
[28] The courts have ruled that liability under Superfund is strict, joint and several,

both to increase private sector transaction costs and to breed corporate resistance.

The final reason that Superfund has been unstable is because its inherited policy design has stimulated only modest beneficiary "lock-in" effects. To be sure, influential interests, including environmental contractors and trial attorneys, have a large stake in the existing program. Moreover, once physical construction work begins at a waste site, it must be completed in a safe and orderly manner (although the work can be done quite expeditiously if cleanup standards are relaxed). But most citizens' reliance on the continuity of Superfund spending is extremely modest relative to their dependence on programs like Social Security and Medicare. As a result, Superfund's dedicated taxes could lapse twice, and the program's operations could come to a virtual standstill for more than a year, without devastating repercussions for officeholders.

Super assaults, shielded budgets

Trust fund financing clearly did help secure Superfund's claim on the federal budget during the program's early years. This is noteworthy since a major reason for Superfund's hasty adoption in December 1980 was that congressional Democrats were anxious about what a conservative Reagan Administration might portend for environmental policy.[29] Reagan didn't disappoint. Neither of his two main appointees for Superfund – EPA Administrator Anne Gorsuch and program chief Rita M. Lavelle – could remotely be described as sympathetic to the program. Gorsuch enraged the environmental lobby by stating she saw no need for Superfund to continue beyond its initial five-year authorization.[30] A major scandal erupted in 1982 when Reagan's environmental team were charged by congressional Democrats with negotiating "sweetheart deals"

and retroactive. This means that a single company can be held responsible for the entire costs of cleaning up a site even if it contributed only a negligible amount of the waste *and* broke no laws at the time the dumping took place. On the Superfund liability regime, see Lewis A. Kornhauser and Richard L. Revesz, "Evaluating the Effects of Alternative Superfund Liability Rules," in Richard L. Revesz and Richard B. Stewart, eds., *Analyzing Superfund: Economics, Science, and Law*, (Washington, DC: Resources for the Future, 1995) and Katherine N. Probst, Don Fullerton, Robert E. Litan, and Paul R. Portney, *Footing the Bill for Superfund Cleanups* (Washington, DC: Brookings Institution and Resources for the Future, 1995), 12.

[29] Hird, *Superfund*, 9.

[30] Steve Cohen, "Defusing the Toxic Time Bomb: Federal Hazardous Waste Programs," in Norman J. Vig and Michael E. Kraft, eds., *Environmental Policy in the 1980s: Reagan's New Agenda*, (Washington, DC: CQ Press, 1984), 285.

with corporations for quick-and-dirty cleanups instead of bringing suits against them to obtain better compliance. When Gorsuch refused to turn over subpoenaed Superfund documents sought by two House subcommittees, Congress cited her for contempt.[31] Eventually both Gorsuch and Lavelle were forced from office.[32]

Yet despite the Reagan Administration's antagonism toward Superfund, spending from the trust fund grew rapidly over the early 1980s. What makes this growth all the more remarkable is that it occurred during an era of retrenchment in environmental policy. Spending for environmental and national resource programs, which had increased from 1.5 percent of the federal budget in 1970 to 2.4 percent in 1980, dropped to 1.2 percent by 1984. As one analyst notes, "Few environmental programs, whether for conservation of resources, construction of pollution control facilities, demonstration of technologies, acquisition and management of land, or regulation of environmentally harmful activities, escaped the Reagan budget scalpel (or meat ax)."[33] Superfund was the major exception to this anti-environmental putsch.[34] After adjusting for inflation, EPA's budget authority (excluding Superfund) fell 40 percent between fiscal year 1980 and fiscal year 1984. In contrast, Superfund's real budget authority increased 890 percent in the four years after fiscal year 1981 (table 8.1). This trend cannot be attributed simply to congressional decisions. Reagan's *own* budgets over the early 1980s generally proposed significant increases for Superfund, even as he was requesting cuts in other environmental activities.[35] As Superfund outlays grew, and other environmental spending stagnated, the trust fund became a larger and larger share of the EPA's total budget (figure 8.1).[36]

---

[31] Maureen Dowd, "Superfund, Supermess," *Time*, February 23, 1983, 14.

[32] Lavelle was also sentenced to a six-month jail term for obstructing Congress.

[33] Robert V. Bartlett, "The Budgetary Process and Environmental Policy," in Norman J. Vig and Michael E. Kraft, eds., *Environmental Policy in the 1980s: Reagan's New Agenda* (Washington, DC: CQ Press, 1984), 121.

[34] This is not to suggest, however, that many site cleanups were completed during the early Reagan years. In fact, progress on the ground was painfully slow. The Reagan Administration's opposition to the program was one important factor. Another was the insistence of environmentalists on "gold plated" cleanups. Most trust fund spending during this period actually went for scientific and engineering studies.

[35] "Federal Budget Stresses 'Efficiency' at Agencies," *Chemical Engineering*, February 21, 1983, 31.

[36] As Hird correctly notes, this comparison presents a somewhat misleading picture of Superfund's relative size because many other EPA programs are largely regulatory in nature. Hird, *Superfund*, 7.

Table 8.1. *Budget Authority for Superfund and EPA operations during early 1980s*
(Budget Authority in millions, constant 1987 dollars)

Fiscal year	EPA (excluding Superfund)	Superfund
1980	6615.1	0
1981	3839.6	51.8
1982	4181.1	216.2
1983	3984.7	253.4
1984	3961.1	512.1

Source: Office of Management and Budget, *Budget of the United States Government, Fiscal Year 1995 – Historical Tables* (Washington, DC: Government Printing Office, 1994), table 5.2.

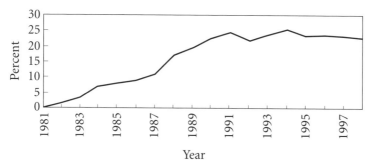

Figure 8.1 Superfund outlays as a percent of EPA spending, fiscal years 1981–1998
Sources: Superfund outlay data from unpublished Congressional Budget Office data set on file with author. Total EPA outlay data from Office of Management and Budget, *Budget of the United States Government, Fiscal Year 1999 – Historical Tables* (Washington, DC: Government Printing Office, 1998), table 4.1.

Taxing choices: efficiency or predictability?

When politicians have faced the decision of what tax sources to target for Superfund cleanups, they have consistently opted for stable resource mobilization over economic efficiency. The political and administrative stability of Superfund has still suffered, however, because the decision-making process leading to the selection of these earmarked taxes has been incredibly drawn out and contentious.

In 1984, politicians were compelled to reexamine Superfund's revenue base because the trust fund's taxing authority was due to expire late the next year. By this time even Reagan acknowledged that Superfund would have to be extended. Most policymakers believed a significantly larger trust fund was needed. The EPA had already committed two-thirds of the trust fund's original $1.6 billion authorization, and half of the 500 sites on its existing priority list were still not receiving attention.[37] Some 1,400 and 2,200 additional waste dumps were also thought to exist.[38] The EPA projected that the government's Superfund bill could ultimately reach $16 billion.[39]

In considering how to stock a larger trust fund, Congress faced a key redesign question: whether to use the trust fund structure as a vehicle for imposing true liability charges. The appeal of this approach was not lost on lawmakers. "The current Superfund today is a textbook case for distorted economic incentives," said Rep. Ron Wyden (D-Oregon).[40] In 1985, the House passed a $10 billion reauthorization bill that genuinely took a stab at promoting efficiency. The bill's major innovation was a new levy on hazardous-waste disposal itself.[41] This "waste-end" tax would give corporations a powerful incentive to reduce their toxic pollutants. In a partial reversal of its position in 1980, the EPA now concluded that a waste-end tax was indeed feasible, provided the agency was given money to beef up its enforcement staff.

But Congress again opted for fiscal stability over economic efficiency. Some lawmakers continued to question the feasibility of a direct tax on waste. Senator Lloyd Bentsen, for example, said the waste-end tax would create an "administrative nightmare for the IRS."[42] But the major criticism was that using a direct tax on waste to finance Superfund could lead to perverse budgetary results.[43] "If a waste-end tax does have the proper incentives, then in theory it will dry up the revenue source, and

---

[37] Office of Technology Assessment, *Superfund Strategy* (Washington, DC: OTA, 1985), 3.

[38] The Office of Technology Assessment put the figure at 10,000 sites. See "House, Senate Pass Superfund Authorization," *Congressional Quarterly Almanac* (1985), 191.

[39] While this was obviously a major expansion in the program's scope, it would be inaccurate to suggest, as many have, that Superfund was originally a modest program that suddenly took on a life of its own. In fact, many lawmakers in 1980 knew that the original $1.6 billion trust fund would prove inadequate, and that additional sums would have to be authorized later.

[40] Quoted in Warren Richey, "Superfund Tax Would Urge Recycling, Not Dumping," *The Christian Science Monitor*, April 26, 1985, 3.

[41] The House bill passed on December 10 by a vote of 391–33.

[42] *Congressional Record*, October 3, 1986, 28421.

[43] Barnett, *Toxic Debts*, 222.

then we will not have the money to clean up the hazardous-waste sites of the past," said a lobbyist for the public interest group Congress Watch.[44]

In the end, Congress adopted a new broad-based corporate tax levied against virtually every big company in the nation.[45] This "corporate environmental income tax" was expected to generate $2.5 billion. The reauthorization measure (which was not passed until 1986 because of the conflict over revenue sources) also featured $2.75 billion in petroleum taxes, $1.4 billion in feedstock taxes, and a $1.25 billion general fund subsidy. Although much larger in dollar terms, the general fund subsidy in the 1986 bill accounted for about the same proportion (14 percent) as the general fund contribution in the original 1980 Act.[46]

More than 500 corporations and trade associations lobbied against the broad-based corporate tax, protesting that they bore no responsibility whatever for the toxic waste problem.[47] But taxing industry, broadly defined, for a problem deemed to be industry's fault was close enough to "polluter-pays" for most legislators. The broad-based tax appealed to Congress because it avoided the need for even higher taxes on the petroleum and (especially) the chemical industries. The chemical industry emerged as the major winner under the 1986 reauthorization. Not only did the feedstock tax remain unchanged, but the reauthorization included certain provisions to facilitate its pass-through to consumers. While the petroleum industry as a whole did take a significant hit, domestic refiners were deliberately protected through special tax breaks.[48] In sum, Congress's overriding goal in 1986, as it had been six years earlier, was not to allocate Superfund's costs in proportion to the amount of damage particular business sectors had actually created. Rather, it was to guarantee stable financing without antagonizing general taxpayers. When Congress renewed Superfund for another five years in 1990, it preserved the 1986 tax schedule.[49]

Yet if Congress's substantive tax policy decisions have shown a clear

---

[44] Quoted in Richey, "Superfund Tax," 3.

[45] The Senate bill passed an 86–13 vote on September 26, 1985. See "House, Senate Pass Superfund Authorization," *Congressional Quarterly Almanac*, 191.

[46] The measure also created a Leaking Underground Storage Tank Trust Fund.

[47] Congress adopted the conference report by 386–27; the Senate by 88–8. See "Reagan Signs 'Superfund' Waste-Cleanup Bill," *Congressional Quarterly Almanac* (1986), 111. The broad-based tax temporarily drew a presidential veto threat, but Reagan ultimately bowed to Congressional pressure and signed the bill. See Michael Weisskopf, "White House Backs Off Superfund Veto Threat," *The Washington Post*, October 17, 1986, A03.

[48] See Barnett, *Toxic Debts*, 234.

[49] Debra K. Rubin, "Superfund Gets New Lease on Life," *Engineering News-Record*, 225(19) November 8, 1990, 8.

preference for political stability over economic efficiency, policymaking for Superfund has been anything but consensual. Indeed, Congress has not even been able to maintain the trust fund's authority to collect earmarked taxes from industry. The program's initial taxing authority expired on September 30, 1985. The reauthorization bill, however, was not signed until more than a full year later. As a result, the trust fund's tax collections plummeted to $15 million in 1986 from $273 million in 1985. The linkage between yearly trust fund taxing and spending that had existed up to this point was thus broken (figure 8.2). While trust fund outlays continued at their existing rates, budget appropriations – a better measure of current policy – plummeted to $406 million in 1986 from $620 million in 1985.

With only a small ($130 million) unobligated balance in the trust fund to draw down, EPA Administrator Lee M. Thomas in 1985 warned that he would be forced to terminate site contracts if Congress did not provide new funding authority.[50] Congressional leaders wished to keep Superfund going, but believed that the prospect of the trust fund's depletion would compel conferees to produce a quick deal. Accordingly, Congress adopted two stop-gap resolutions that gave the trust fund temporary authority to receive repayable advances from the general fund. This was quite similar to the deliberate decision, in 1982, to grant only temporary borrowing authority to the Social Security Trust Fund. As I mentioned in chapter 4, that move had produced an imminent solvency crisis, which in turn had created pressure for a major Social Security overhaul in 1983.

But the effort to construct a Superfund Trust Fund solvency crisis to force a political consensus on the program's renewal failed. What accounts for this? A delay in the pace of Superfund cleanups may have been an irritant to lawmakers, but it simply did not instill the same electoral fear, and thus the same willingness to compromise, as did the prospect of late Social Security checks. When Superfund's emergency loan authority expired in September 1986, no agreement was at hand. The program did not resume full operations until 1987. This interruption had definite administrative consequences on the ground. The EPA was forced to halt cleanup work at some 375 sites across the nation, leading some private-sector contractors to lay off employees.[51] But, while environmental groups expressed concern about the delays, the reaction of the public was generally muted.

---

[50] Rochelle L. Stanfield, "Hill Stalemate Imperils the Superfund," *National Journal*, February 8, 1986, 342.
[51] Quoted in Joseph A. Davis, "Congress Clears 'Superfund,' Awaits President's Decision," *Congressional Quarterly*, October 11, 1986, 2532.

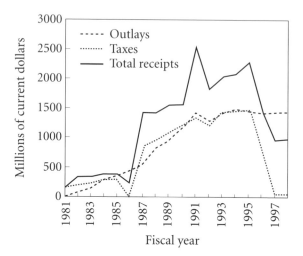

Figure 8.2 Financial history of Superfund, fiscal years 1981–1998
Note: Tax revenues include fines.
Sources: unpublished Congressional Budget Office data on file with author for years 1981–1995; Office of Management and Budget, *Budget of the United States Government* (Washington, DC: Government Printing Office, 1998) for later years.

Symbols have costs

In one sense, Superfund's fiscal design has been a tremendous success. The private liability scheme in particular has succeeded beautifully in "minimizing direct government implementation of cleanups and therefore the cost to the trust fund."[52] And trust fund financing has reduced the program's drain on general revenues. But Superfund's design has decidedly *not* guaranteed political stability. While Superfund costs have been shifted onto the private sector, just as its political architects intended, these costs have nonetheless been very steep, intensifying business opposition to the program. By the late 1990s, the average Superfund site was generating bills of $30 million.[53] While Superfund costs climbed rapidly, cleanup progress was slow. By 1990, only 33 waste

---

[52] Probst *et al.*, *Footing the Bill for Superfund Cleanups*, 17.
[53] Mark Reisch, "Superfund Reauthorization Issues in the 105th Congress," *CRS Report for Congress* (Washington, DC: Congressional Research Service, Updated April 2, 1998).

sites had been remedied out of more than 1,200 on the EPA's priority list.[54]

A major reason for Superfund's high costs and slow progress is that massive legal costs were being incurred by firms to avoid liability. A 1992 Rand Corporation study found that between 1986 and 1989, 92 percent of the $1.3 billion spent by insurers on Superfund went for legal bills.[55] Superfund liability carries a hefty price tag in large measure because environmentalists and the courts have insisted on, and Congress has adopted, stringent cleanup standards.[56] Many experts question whether these standards would pass a cost–benefit test. Superfund's inherited fiscal design, however, positively *discourages* Congress from explicitly confronting the policy tradeoffs. As Marc Landy observes, the program's dedicated taxes and off-budget liability regime were deliberately structured to create the impression that "rights are being protected at no great cost to the public."[57]

Ironically, Superfund conceivably would be less litigious if the whole program were financed through a larger governmental trust fund. If more of the program were paid from public taxes, there would be less need for businesses to fight over liability for specific dump sites. Social insurance could provide a cheaper substitute for "adversarial legalism."[58] The Clinton Administration in 1994 proposed the creation of a new governmental trust fund to provide assistance to parties that agreed to submit to arbitration, with the money coming from a new commercial liability insurance tax. While the proposal won the backing of chemical manufacturers, major insurance companies, and many environmental groups, it infuriated small insurance companies with few Superfund claims against them, and the measure failed to reach the floor in either chamber.[59] After

---

[54] Frank Vivano, "How Superfund Became a Mess," *The San Francisco Chronicle*, May 20, 1991, A1.

[55] Jan Paul Acton and Lloyd Dixon, *Superfund and Transaction Costs* (Santa Monica, CA: Rand Institute, 1992). See also "The Toxic Mess Called Superfund," *Business Week*, May 11, 1992, 32.

[56] Under the 1986 reauthorization, all Superfund cleanups must meet every "applicable or relevant and appropriate" state and federal environmental air and water quality standard. In practice, this means that even sites in the middle of filthy industrial parks must be restored to a pristine condition.

[57] Marc Landy, "The New Politics of Environmental Policy," in Marc Landy and Martin Levin, eds., *The New Politics of Public Policy* (Baltimore: Johns Hopkins University Press, 1985), 213.

[58] On US reliance on adverserial legalism in lieu of social insurance, see Robert A. Kagan, "Adverserial Legalism and American Government," in Marc Landy and Martin Levin, eds., *The New Politics*.

[59] "No Floor Action on Superfund Bill," *Congressional Quarterly Almanac* (1994), 231–6.

Republicans took over Congress in 1995, the business community pushed for a better bargain. But environmentalists refused to accept any deal that would let polluters "off the hook," and no bargain was reached.[60]

Hostage games

So, at the end of 1995, the existing trust fund's taxing authority expired yet again, the second such lapse in a decade. Superfund's tax collections fell rapidly from $1.5 billion in 1995 to just $75 million in 1997 (see figure 8.2). But unlike the situation in 1985–6, when there was no money in the trust fund to draw down, Superfund in 1996 had an uncommitted balance of about $2 billion.[61] CBO figures showed that the trust fund balance could keep the program going at current spending rates through the year 2000.[62] As a result, there was no immediate funding crisis. Still, each day the Superfund levies were not collected meant a loss of about four million dollars to the government.

While Superfund's fiscal design may have been originally intended to ensure continuity of funding, the expiration of the trust fund provided an opening for conservative opponents to take the program's future tax revenues hostage. Ways and Means Chairman Bill Archer (R-TX) ruled out any renewal of the earmarked taxes without reforms that weakened Superfund's existing liability regime.[63] Archer's hostage-seizing strategy could work, however, only if the Superfund taxes were kept off-limits from poachers. But these levies were an inviting target for would-be spenders in a time of fiscal stress. Indeed, the Clinton Administration in both 1994 and 1995 attempted, without success, to divert Superfund taxes to other executive initiatives, including welfare reform and implementation of tariff reductions under the GATT treaty. Treasury Secretary Lloyd Bentsen argued that the proposals merely involved "budget scorekeeping." But the contemplated diversions drew sharp opposition from environmentalists and, perhaps surprisingly, the corporate sector. It was not that business groups suddenly were Superfund proponents.

---

[60] Karen Florini, senior attorney, Environmental Defense Fund, quoted in Timothy Noah, "Superfund Plan is Revised by GOP for Senate Action," *The Wall Street Journal*, March 25, 1995, B10.

[61] Although fresh tax revenues weren't coming in, the trust fund was being replenished by cost recoveries from responsible parities, which had increased to $350 million in 1998 from $7.9 million in 1985 under tougher EPA enforcement.

[62] See Mark Reisch, "Superfund Reauthorization Issues in the 105th Congress."

[63] See Margaret Kriz, "War Over Wastes," *National Journal*, May 11, 1996, 1042–6; and Allan Freedman, "Congress Prepares New Assault on Troubled Superfund Sites," *Congressional Quarterly*, June 28, 1997, 1502–7.

Rather, they saw their future tax payments as a valuable resource in the larger battle over liability reform. Invoking the moral language of trust fund financing, a Chemical Manufacturing Association spokesman argued that the "industry has always felt that Superfund taxes should go for cleanups, that they shouldn't be diverted to other activities. If you start taking money and using it for other things, it defeats the whole purpose of the trust fund."[64] The ultimate value of the earmarked taxes as a hostage will not be known until the Superfund Trust Fund's coffers are empty.

Conclusions

Like the other cases examined in this book, the Superfund Trust Fund was created to lock-in taxing and spending promises. The only actors who consistently believed that the design's revenue structure should be used to promote efficiency and encourage pollution reduction have been professional economists and their advice has been flatly rejected.

Trust fund financing (and the liability regime) were intended to conceal Superfund's costs to voters. Key to this masking has been the polluter-pay symbolism. As a framework for guiding policymaking, the polluter-pay concept has proved to be simultaneously constraining and elastic, not unlike the doctrine of contributory insurance under Social Security. The perception that the costs are borne by private industry has clearly given the environmental lobby more leverage in opposing efforts to relax cleanup standards. At the same time, however, the doctrine has been sufficiently malleable to generate the revenues for major program expansions. When Congress found it needed more money to pay for a bigger Superfund trust fund in 1986, it simply redefined polluters to include virtually every major American corporation. There is no evidence that politicians feared that citizens would grasp that this was tantamount to a general increase in consumer prices. In sum, Superfund presents yet another example of the strategic use of trust funds and earmarked taxes.

Despite these important points of similarity, however, there are crucial differences between the Superfund Trust Fund and the social insurance and transportation funds examined in the preceding chapters. Superfund is of course unique in being residual to a private liability regime. But the most important differences stem from the divergent nature of the underlying policy commitments themselves. The first key difference is that the establishment of Superfund has not created the same level of beneficiary

---

[64] Quoted in "Chemical Industry Opposed Clinton Superfund Tax Plan," *Chemical Marketing Reporter*, December 18, 1995.

reliance as have the major social insurance funds. As both a practical and normative matter, politicians have not been quite so anxious to maintain the program's continuity. The trust fund has been allowed to lapse on multiple occasions, and even the normally cautious Congressional Budget Office has suggested that policymakers give serious thought to terminating the program once the trust fund is empty.[65]

A second important difference is that Superfund's earmarked taxes are not based on the idea of reciprocal exchange. While the trust fund structure was meant to give the chemical and petroleum industries some assurance that they would not be taxed indiscriminately, the tax-paying industries do not intrinsically value Superfund spending. Indeed, they view the trust fund and the earmarked taxes as a threat to their good name. While corporations have made use of the trust fund symbolism when it serves their strategic purposes, the truth is they would just as soon see the entire program repealed. Superfund's complex fiscal design did help seal the initial bargain over program enactment and it did help the program survive some early budget onslaughts. These are indeed significant legacies. But given the relatively low level of reciprocity upon which it is based, and its failure to induce a high degree of promisee reliance, the Superfund Trust Fund remains relatively vulnerable to major change or even dismantling.

---

[65] "Spend the Remaining Balance of the Superfund Trust Fund and Terminate the Program," in Congressional Budget Office, "Maintaining Budgetary Discipline: Spending and Revenue Options" (Washington: Government Printing Office, April 1999b), 69.

9

Barriers to trust fund adoption: the failed cases of energy security and lead abatement

Political institutions – even mechanisms as arcane as trust fund structures – do not arise automatically. They must be created. What policy actors fail to do is thus at least as theoretically important as what they do. This chapter briefly explores two cases – the Energy Security Trust Fund and the Lead Abatement Trust Fund – where Congress considered proposals to establish new government trust funds but ultimately rejected them. The analysis provides further evidence that trust funds are not casual or inadvertent creations; politicians oppose and support these devices with a purpose. In the final section, I draw some conclusions about the politics of trust fund adoption from the cases examined here and in the preceding five chapters.

Energy security trust fund

When proposals to create new trust funds fail, Congress typically rejects both the substantive expenditure program and any accompanying dedicated tax. Yet Congress in 1980 *accepted* a Carter Administration proposal to levy a windfall profits tax on oil industry profits but spurned its request to dedicate the revenues for an Energy Security Trust Fund. The Energy Security case is an excellent limiting case to explore for two reasons. First, there is evidence that the public was receptive to this idea. Indeed, a Harris Survey found that 85 percent of respondents favored the proposal, with only 10 percent opposed (5 percent were not sure).[1]

---

[1] Harris Survey, December 12, 1977.

Second, much of the debate over the proposal in Congress focused explicitly on the appropriateness of trust fund financing.

Background

The windfall profits tax and proposed Energy Trust Fund comprised key elements of the Carter Administration's response to the energy crisis of the late 1970s.[2] Domestically produced oil was then subject to price controls, weakening the incentive for energy conservation.[3] In April 1979, Carter announced an end to oil price controls in a major presidential address. Experts projected that the price of US oil would climb from $9.50 to $16 a gallon. To avoid jarring the economy, and infuriating consumers, Carter recommended that the price increases be phased-in over two years. Oil companies stood to gain $26 billion to $31 billion in added revenues as controls were lifted.[4] Arguing that oil companies had no right to such "huge and undeserved windfall profits," the president asked for a new oil industry tax to claim most of these revenues for the government.[5]

Rationales for trust fund

In an effort to increase the appeal of the tax and to generate resources for his spending initiatives, Carter proposed that nearly all of the $140 billion expected to be generated from the windfall profits tax between 1980 and 1990 be targeted for an Energy Security Trust Fund.[6] The money would be used, Carter said, "to protect low-income families from energy prices increases, to build a more efficient mass transportation system, and to

[2] For background, see "Energy Policy," *Congress and the Nation, Vol. V* (Washington, DC: Congressional Quarterly, 1981); especially 451–6 and 493–5. See also Joseph A. Yager, "The Energy Crisis of 1979" in Craufurd D. Goodwin, ed., *Energy Policy in Perspective* (Washington, DC: The Brookings Institution, 1981), 601–6.

[3] President Nixon had originally imposed oil price controls in 1971 as part of his general wage-and-price controls to curb inflation.

[4] Ann Pelham, "Carter Pledges Oil Decontrol, Wants Windfall Profits Tax," *Congressional Quarterly Weekly Report*, April 7, 1979, 619.

[5] Quoted in "Energy Policy," *Congress and the Nation, Vol. V*, 483. Carter's windfall profits tax proposal had two parts. The first was a temporary 50 percent tax on the additional profits the oil industry would reap from already flowing oil after price controls were lifted. The second part was a permanent OPEC tax. Any time the oil cartel boosted the market price of oil, half of the new revenues of US companies would go to the government.

[6] Judy Sarasohn, "Proposed Energy Trust Fund: Will It Work?" *Congressional Quarterly Weekly Report*, August 18, 1979, 1709–14.

put American Genius to work solving our long-range energy problems."[7] The lion's share ($88 billion) of the trust fund would be dedicated for an Energy Security Corporation, which would subsidize development of synthetic fuels. Other significant trust fund expenditures would include mass transit improvements ($10 billion), research on automotive fuel economy ($6.5 billion), and programs to help the poor pay their heating bills ($2.4 billion).[8]

Initial political reaction to the plan was favorable.[9] The main appeal for oil-state legislators was price decontrol itself. For liberals, the proposal held out the tantalizing promise of forcing the oil industry to finance programs targeted for inner cities and the economically disadvantaged.

As in the Superfund case, the Energy Security Trust Fund was accepted by executive budget guardians reluctantly. In testimony before the Ways and Means Committee, OMB director James T. McIntyre, Jr. acknowledged that he was "generally opposed to the establishment of statutory funds and earmarking tax revenues." But McIntyre nonetheless endorsed the trust fund proposal, arguing that it would lower the risk of "overspending and increased budget deficits."[10] The OMB's goal was for the trust fund eventually to be self-financing.[11]

Interest group lobbying

Carter warned that his energy package would be threatened by the attempts of oil companies to "keep the profits which they have not earned" and by "the inevitable scrambling by interest groups for a larger share of these revenues."[12] In this, Carter proved to be an excellent prognosticator. The tax did come under fire from much of the oil industry, and scores of lobbies tried to claim a share of the money. What Carter failed to foresee, however, was that Congress would ultimately accept the tax, and enact a multi-billion dollar energy initiative, but reject

---

[7] "Carter Broadcast Energy Address," *Congressional Quarterly Weekly Report*, April 7, 1979, 661.

[8] The trust fund would also finance solar energy programs and tax expenditures for special fuels. See Sarasohn, "Proposed Energy Trust Fund," 1714.

[9] For background, see Richard Halloran, "Schlesinger Victory Seen in Energy Program," *The New York Times*, April 7, 1979, D11.

[10] Statement of James T. McIntyre, Jr., Director, Office of Management and Budget. US Congress, House of Representatives, "Windfall Profits Tax and Energy Trust Fund," Hearings Before the Committee on Ways and Means, 96th Congress, 1st Session, (1979), 175–7.

[11] *Ibid.*

[12] "Carter Broadcast Energy Address," *Congressional Quarterly Weekly Report*, April 7, 1979, 662.

his proposal to link the revenues and spending through the trust fund structure.

Most Democratic tax-writers supported the trust fund concept. In May, the Ways and Means Committee reported a bill that authorized the creation of a trust fund. But Al Ullman (D-Oregon), the committee chairman, made a strategic decision to put off a decision on how money in the trust fund would be spent in order to permit early Senate action on the measure. Rather than expediting the trust fund's legislative progress, however, this move merely encouraged the divisive lobbying contest that Carter feared. More than 100 different organizations, including the AFL-CIO, the NAACP, and the American Public Transit Association, begged Congress for a piece of the trust fund pie.[13]

Witnessing this clientele frenzy, the League of Women Voters' energy policy specialist argued that it would be better to keep windfall profits tax revenues in the operating budget, thus allowing Congress to make calmer and more rational spending decisions.[14]

The trust fund also drew opposition from the oil industry, and from some conservative lawmakers, on the ground that it would lock-in the windfall profits tax. "In the future, there will be pressure to continue to have the tax in place whether it makes sense or not," warned Bill Grandson (R-Ohio). "I do not like trust funds, I don't like earmarked funds. We are setting up an empty sack and are going to fill it," agreed Barber B. Conable Jr (R-NY). But a Republican-led effort to strip the trust fund from the Ways and Means bill failed in committee by a vote of 20–16.[15]

Eliminating the trust funds

It was during Senate floor debate that the trust funds were stripped from Carter's energy package. The Senate Finance Committee had reported a bill earmarking windfall tax revenues for two new trust funds: one for mass transit and a second for low-income energy assistance. The Committee refused, however, to precommit profits tax revenues for synthetic fuels development, which many members regarded as an enormously risky venture.

By a vote of 82–13, the Senate approved an amendment to the Finance Committee measure, sponsored by Appropriations Committee chairman

---

[13] Richard Corrigan, "Who'll Get the Largest Slices of the $1 Trillion 'Windfall Profits' Pie?" *National Journal*, November 10, 1979, 1885–8.

[14] "Windfall Profits Tax," *Congressional Quarterly Almanac (1979)*, 614.

[15] Ann Pelham, "House is About to Approve a Windfall Profits Tax, But Question is on the Rule," *Congressional Quarterly Weekly Report*, June 23, 1979, 1277.

Warren G. Magnuson (D-Washington), and actively supported by Budget Committee chairman Edmund S. Muskie (D-Maine), eliminating both the transit and energy assistance trust funds. Magnuson argued that these trusts would "tie the hands" of current and future lawmakers, forcing the government to maintain these programs even if the energy problem later faded in national importance. "This bill contains the worst kind of spending, spending that mortgages the future, spending that prevents any future Congress having any leeway and it is the type of spending that must be stopped if Congress is ever to achieve some kind of balance in the Federal budget," he said.[16] Muskie emphasized that the proposed energy trust funds violated accepted norms of institutional design, arguing that "these are not trust funds in any sense of the word."

> Under basic principles of Federal budgeting, revenues are raised from various sources and distributed among programs based on a congressional determination of national need. The trust funds concept is an exception to the basic rule. In the past, real trust funds have been established when Congress determined that if it was appropriate to give special benefits for programs, such as highways, airports, and social security, it was also appropriate to tax the users to pay for the special benefits. No such purpose is served by these so-called trust funds that collect the windfall tax from the oil companies and make payments from those receipts to unrelated but worthy beneficiaries. Indeed, there is nothing to distinguish the proposed scheme from the normal budget principle and, therefore, no reason to divorce the revenue and payments scheme from the normal congressional procedures.[17]

With but one exception, Muskie was accurate in claiming that virtually all major federal trust funds in existence in 1979 conformed to the user pay or insurance model. The exception was the General Revenue Sharing Trust Fund, which had been established in 1972 to convert stipulated levels of general revenue sharing grants from annual appropriations into mandatory spending. The General Revenue Sharing Trust Fund (whose subsequent evolution will be discussed in the next chapter) was a special case because it had no specific earmarked funding source; it depended entirely on general fund transfers for its income. Very much like Carter's Energy Security Trust Fund proposal, the General Revenues Sharing Trust Fund sparked vehement opposition from budget guardians when it was first proposed.[18] House Appropriations Committee chairman

---

[16] *Congressional Record*, November 29, 1979, 33579.
[17] *Ibid.*, 33580.
[18] A key exception was Ways and Means chairman Wilbur D. Mills. While he originally opposed the bill, Mills became a program supporter around the time

George Mahon (D-Texas) argued that it constituted "a rank perversion of the trust fund concept."[19] But opponents were unable to defeat the trust fund's adoption. One reason is because proponents were able to make a coherent argument that the program's effectiveness hinged on trust fund financing and entitlement status. If federal grants were subject to annual appropriations control, they claimed, state and local officials would be unable to plan ahead for using shared revenues.[20]

But key lawmakers challenged the idea that Carter's energy proposals warranted special protection. "I am concerned about the trust funds because I am not convinced that the programs described by the Finance Committee need the long-term security that a trust fund provides," said Senator S. I. "Sam" Hayakawa (D-CA).[21] The CBO argued that the trust fund design was particularly inadvisable because the amount of windfall profits tax revenues that would enter the fund in future years would be "extremely sensitive to future OPEC prices, which are very difficult to predict."[22] This uncertainty could lead to the wrong level of investment in energy initiatives. "We could easily find ourselves with two or three times as much money available to spend on low-income fuel assistance as we are currently planning on, with no way to transfer it to other top priority uses," argued Senator Lawton Chiles (D-Florida).[23] In sum, opponents challenged the substantive importance of Carter's energy proposals, the inherent need of these programs for institutional reinforcement, and the capacity of the proposed trust fund mechanism to reduce uncertainty.

The House and Senate conferees did suggest that 25 percent of windfall profits tax revenues be used to aid low-income families, 60 percent to finance income tax reductions, and 15 percent for energy and transportation programs.[24] They also recommended that synthetic fuel devel-

he was considering running for president. So three important trust fund developments occurred during the brief period Mills was exploring the presidential waters: the indexing of Social Security benefits; the indexing of the Medicare Part B premium; and the adoption of the General Revenue Sharing Trust Fund.

[19] *Congressional Record*, June 21, 1972, 21727.

[20] Bruce A. Wallin, *From Revenue Sharing to Deficit Sharing: General Revenue Sharing and Cities* (Washington, DC: Georgetown University Press, 1998).

[21] *Congressional Record*, November 29, 1979, 33581.

[22] Congressional Budget Office, *The Windfall Profits Tax* (Washington, DC: Government Printing Office, 1979), 50.

[23] Statement of Sen. Lawton Chiles, *Congressional Record*, November 27, 1979, 33585.

[24] "Final Vote on Windfall Profits Provisions Is Expected Soon in Senate and House," *Congressional Quarterly Weekly Report*, March 8, 1980, 668–9.

opment be financed with the proceeds of the additional federal income taxes that oil companies would be paying under decontrol. Although not legally binding, these recommendations provoked criticism from legislators who still wished to designate windfall profits tax revenues for energy programs.[25] But the House rejected, by a 201–215 vote (Republicans vote 23–130; Democrats 178–85), a purely symbolic resolution that would have called on future Congresses to spend 50 percent of profits tax revenues on energy items.

Aftermath

Ironically, the huge revenue pot on which Carter's trust fund proposal was predicated never materialized. The windfall profits tax did generate $23 billion for the federal government in 1981. But oil prices declined steadily over the next few years. In 1986 the oil market collapsed entirely. By the end of 1986, only $80 billion in total federal receipts had been generated, far less than the $300 billion that had been predicted. Congress finally repealed the profits tax in 1988.[26]

Optimistic projections about future synthetic fuels development also proved inaccurate. It was hoped that the Synthetic Fuels Corporation would churn out energy equivalent to 2 million barrels of oil per day by 1992. But the corporation never came anywhere close to achieving this level of production. From its inception the synthetic fuels program was a technological and managerial disaster. Congress finally abolished the program in 1985.[27] The Synthetic Fuels Corporation was founded on an extremely fragile legislative coalition between liberal Democrats and free-market conservative Republicans. The coalition came together in response to the energy crisis of 1979. Once the crisis ended, the coalition fell apart. Some government programs arguably do merit protection from the vicissitudes of ordinary politics. The synfuels program was clearly not one of them.

[25] Ann Pelham, "Congress Clears Landmark Oil Profits Tax," *Congressional Quarterly Weekly Report*, March 29, 1980, 843.

[26] The repeal came in the Omnibus Trade and Competition Act of 1988. On the politics, see Joseph A. Davids, "'Windfall Profits Tax Headed for Extinction," *Congressional Quarterly Weekly Report*, November 7, 1987, 27247–8.

[27] See Linda R. Cohen and Roger G. Noll, "Synthetic Fuels from Coal," in *The Technology Pork Barrel*, Linda R. Cohen and Roger G. Noll, eds. (Washington, DC: Brookings Institution, 1991), 297. See also "Congress Dismantles Synthetic Fuels Program," *Congressional Quarterly Almanac (1985)*, 212–14.

Lead abatement trust fund

The Lead Abatement Trust Fund presents a second case of an "unsuccessful" trust fund proposal. The basic concept was to use the revenues from a new excise tax on lead to finance lead cleanup and removal programs. Unlike Carter's Energy Security Trust Fund, the Lead Abatement Trust Fund was not a high-profile presidential initiative. Indeed, it failed to reach the floor of either chamber. The Lead Abatement Trust Fund thus died the relatively quiet death experienced by most legislative proposals.

Background

Lead poisoning has been a significant public health concern since the 1930s.[28] By the late 1970s, compelling evidence had emerged linking lead poisoning in children with lower intelligence, hyperactivity, and behavior problems.[29] This encouraged Congress to ban lead-based paint for residential use and to gradually phase out leaded gasoline. But lead poisoning remained a problem in many places. Most homes built before 1950 contained substantial amounts of lead-based paint. As many as 3,000,000 children under age six were believed to have low-level lead poisoning. Minorities and children in inner cities were disproportionately affected.

Rationales for a lead abatement trust fund

In 1988, the Centers for Disease Control issued a report that characterized childhood lead poisoning as a national epidemic. The CDC report received extensive media and public attention, creating an opening for legislative action. But the tight budgetary climate of the late 1980s posed a significant obstacle to the enactment of a major federal lead abatement initiative. Public health advocates recognized that to be "politically feasible" any program would have to "respond to current budgetary realities."[30] In 1990, the Environmental Defense Fund (EDF) released a report entitled *A Legacy of Lead* that proposed the creation of a National

---

[28] See "Lead Poisoning," *The Congressional Quarterly Researcher*, 2(23), June 19, 1992, 525–48. For a skeptical view of the severity of the lead problem, see Ellen Ruppel Shell, "An Element of Doubt," *The Atlantic*, December 1995, 24–8, 36–9.

[29] This study was conducted by Herbert Needleman of the Alliance to End Childhood Lead Poisoning. Cited in Ellen Ruppel Shell, "An Element of Doubt," *The Atlantic*, December 28.

[30] Environmental Defense Fund, *Legacy of Lead: America's Continuing Epidemic of*

Lead Paint Abatement Trust Fund. The purpose of the trust fund was no more and no less than bringing a major new government program into existence and protecting its funding stream.[31]

The EDF believed it could sell the trust fund as an application of the "polluter pays" concept, which had been successfully used during the 1980s to justify passage of the Superfund and the Leaking Underground Storage Tank and Oil Spill Liability funds. Under the EDF proposal, the Lead Paint Abatement Trust Fund would support matching grants to state and local governments for the inspection of residential structures and child care centers, abatement of identifiable lead hazards, and training of contractors. Grants to eligible agencies would be given entitlement status to allow them to bypass the regular appropriations process and escape the discretionary spending caps of the Budget Enforcement Act. The trust fund itself would be fed by an excise tax on the production or sale of lead of 75 cents per pound for newly mined lead and 37 cents per pound for recycled lead. This tax structure was expected to produce about $1 billion annually, enough to meet projected spending needs.[32]

Ben Cardin (D-MD) of the Ways and Means Committee introduced the measure in the House in July 1991.[33] By June 1992, the bill had picked up 44 cosponsors. At a congressional hearing on the measure Cardin argued that the trust fund embodied the "polluter pays" doctrine, was deficit neutral, and would protect the priority of lead abatement spending.[34] The EDF's Karen Florini testified that trust fund financing was crucial to reducing uncertainty "Instead of relying on annual appropriations that are almost certain to be inadequate and that will be difficult to predict, the use of a dedicated ten-year trust fund will allow rational long-term planning. Once abatement workers are trained and specialized equipment is purchased, it makes no sense to scale back abatement of priority units simply because of fluctuations in annual appropriations."[35] Florini further argued that the proposed tax on lead was appropriate because it would "internalize externalities, albeit imper-

---

Childhood Lead Poisoning, March 1990, excerpted in "Lead Poisoning," *CQ Researcher*, (23), June 19, 1992, 541.

[31] Phone interview with Karen Florini, Environmental Defense Fund, April 1, 1996.

[32] Based on information from the Alliance to End Childhood Lead-Poisoning's web site: www.aeclp.org/4/lead_hazards_in_housing.

[33] *Congressional Record*, July 17, 1991, E2586–E2588.

[34] US Congress, House of Representatives, "Lead-Based Paint Hazard Abatement Act," Hearing Before the Subcommittee on Select Revenue Measures of the Committee on Ways and Means, 102nd Congress, 2nd Session on H.R. 2922 (1992).

[35] *Ibid.*, 152.

fectly across intervening decades."[36] A study of the Joint Committee on Taxation had concluded that demand for lead is generally inelastic, and that a lead tax would therefore cause little economic distortion.[37]

Arguments against the trust fund

Inevitably, lead industry representatives strongly challenged these claims, arguing that society as a whole had benefited from inexpensive lead and that any lead abatement program should therefore be paid for out of general revenues. Lead industry groups also contested the Joint Committee on Taxation's claim that the tax would not create significant economic hardship. A battery industry trade association testified that the tax would leave small battery manufactures with "no choice but to close their doors."[38]

The Bush Administration came out strongly against the bill. The Administration's spokesman on the measure, Deputy Assistant Treasury Secretary for Tax Analysis R. Glenn Hubbard, testified that trust fund financing was inappropriate because there was "no connection between the desired spending on the abatement programs and the amount of funds raised by the tax." The trust fund failed as an efficiency mechanism, he said, because the revenues would be used "to correct problems caused by past, rather than current uses of lead." He also argued that the two-tiered structure of the tax, which was intended to encourage lead recycling, would put domestic lead companies at a competitive disadvantage. Finally, Hubbard argued that trust fund financing would reduce flexibility.[39]

The measure picked up three more cosponsors following the hearing for a total of 47. The bill's legislative progress then stalled. But when Congress reauthorized federal housing programs in 1992, it incorporated the language from a separate lead paint bill that had been introduced without the trust fund structure. As signed into law, the Lead-Based Paint Poisoning Prevention Act gave the EPA the authority to regulate lead abatement and inspection contractors and authorized federal grants to states for regulatory enforcement. In addition, real estate agents were required to alert occupants of older homes to the presence of lead.[40] In

---

[36] Ibid., 144–5.   [37] Cited in Ibid., 49.

[38] Statement of Celwyn E. Hopkins, Executive Secretary, Independent Battery Manufacturers Association, Ibid., 174.

[39] Testimony of R. Glenn Hubbard, Deputy Assistant Secretary (Tax Analysis), US Department of Treasury, Ibid., 58–66.

[40] Shell, "An Element of Doubt," 48; see also Susan Kellam, "Conferees Get the Lead Out," Congressional Quarterly Weekly Report, October 3, 1992, 3058.

sum, Congress established a *regulatory* regime for lead inspection and abatement, one that was entirely in keeping with the precedents established in its previous regulation of lead paint and leaded gasoline. Advocates viewed this latest regulatory move as an "interim" measure. Nonetheless, the legislation did represent a significant federal response to the lead poisoning problem, and it received the enthusiastic endorsement of many of the same groups that had backed the trust fund proposal.[41]

In 1993, Cardin introduced a revised version of the trust fund bill. He emphasized that without a trust fund, the new federal lead-abatement programs would be underfunded. But the bill generated little support, picking up four fewer cosponsors than the earlier version.

In a strange coda, the proposal briefly reemerged in 1994 during the national health care reform debate. The comprehensive health care bill reported out by the Subcommittee on Health authorized the creation of a Lead Abatement Trust Fund. The bill's spending provisions were basically the same as in the Cardin proposal. Much to the surprise of the lead abatement lobby, however, the trust fund's revenue source was changed during subcommittee markup from an excise tax on lead to sales tax on the purchase of small cigarettes in order to accommodate members from lead-producing states.[42] In the words of one public health lobbyist, "With one move the 'polluter pay' rationale of the bill went out the window."[43] Ultimately, of course, the health reform bill died. The Lead Abatement Trust Fund was thus another casualty of Clinton's 1994 health care debacle. After Republicans took over Congress in November 1995, Cardin and the public health lobby essentially gave up on the bill.[44]

[41] Cited in Shell, "An Element of Doubt," 38.

[42] US Congress, House of Representatives, "Report on H.R. 3600," Subcommittee on Health of the Committee on Ways and Means, Washington, DC, April 15, 1994, at 124. See also Alissa J. Rubin, "Clinton's Main Tenents Drive New Movement on Health," *Congressional Quarterly Weekly Report*, March 26, 1994, 737–40.

[43] Phone interview with Anne M. Guthrie, Director of Health Policy, Alliance to End Childhood Lead Poisoning, February 8, 1999.

[44] By the mid 1990s, the case for a Lead Abatement Trust Fund was objectively tougher to make. Because of federal regulations of leaded gasoline and paint, and the legislation enacted during the Bush Administration, the number of children with lead poisoning had declined from 2.3 million in the early 1990s to around 890,000 in 1997, although significant problems remained in minority neighborhoods. *Ibid.* See also information presented on the Alliance to End Childhood Lead Poisoning's web site; and General Accounting Office, "Lead Poisoning: Federal Health Care Programs Are Not Effectively Reaching At-Risk Children," Report to the Ranking Minority Member, Committee on Government Reform, GAO/ HEHS-99–18 (Washington, DC: Government Printing Office, January 15, 1999).

The politics of trust fund adoption

This brief exploration of the unsuccessful attempts to establish trust funds for Energy Security and Lead Paint, together with the findings of the previous case study chapters, make clear that trust fund financing is never a simple technocratic exercise in budget accounting. Political forces, as mediated by the incentives of influential lawmakers and clientele groups, crucially shape the fate of trust fund proposals. But the trust fund design process turns on more than raw political strength. In his insightful study of indexation of federal programs, Kent Weaver argues that new structural mechanisms must clear a series of "hurdles" if they are to survive the legislative process.[45] My analysis suggests that trust funds must surmount similar obstacles to win adoption. Four hurdles emerge from the case studies as crucial to an understanding of the politics of trust fund adoption.

The first hurdle that trust fund proposals must clear is *establishing a base of support for the underlying expenditure program*. In all of the cases examined in this book, successful trust fund adoptions were predicated on a consensus among policymakers that the government should provide (or expand) a particular public service. Some groups of politically relevant actors, generally a combination of officeholders and interest groups, must be willing to expend scarce resources to get the spending proposal on the agenda. This pattern holds even when the spending program and earmarked revenue source are both already in existence. The highway and aviation funds, for example, were adopted only after policymakers agreed on the need to vastly expand preexisting transportation infrastructure programs.

A second hurdle is *establishing the plausibility of the trust fund financing mechanism*. The plausibility of a given trust fund proposal is shaped by two factors: the existence of a precedent for the specific type of trust fund being considered and the availability of an appropriate revenue source.

The findings of the case study chapters, along with the tendency for trust funds to diffuse across policy sectors over time (discussed in chapter 2), suggest that the chances for successful trust fund adoption rise considerably if proponents can identify an institutional precedent. Thus, advocates of the Airport and Airway Trust Fund pointed to the prior existence of the Highway Trust Fund, and proponents portrayed the Medicare Hospital Insurance Trust Fund as medical care "through Social Security." When, as in the energy case, no clear precedent for a given

---

[45] See Weaver, *Automatic Government*, especially chapter 10.

trust fund exists, opponents can more easily question the proposal's legitimacy. To be sure, the existence of a precedent does not guarantee that a particular trust fund proposal will win adoption. Advocates for the Lead Paint Abatement Trust Fund, for example, claimed that the trust fund was based on the Superfund model. But having the weight of precedents on one's side generally increases the chances for adoption, everything else being equal.

The availability of a plausible revenue source is also important. A plausible revenue source does not necessarily need to be economically correlated with the spending program. But politicians do have to believe there is a *political* connection between trust fund income and outgo. Historically, federal policymakers have found two types of linkages most appealing: "user pays" and "polluter pays." The need to identify a plausible revenue source has traditionally been a significant barrier to the creation of trust funds with explicitly redistributive purposes: charging poor people for their benefits obviously defeats the purpose.[46] But if general fund subsidies can be tapped as an income source, trust fund financing for redistributive programs becomes more feasible. One of the reasons why the General Revenue Sharing Trust Fund (which was intended to be mildly redistributive) was adopted in 1972 was that the federal government was in good fiscal shape at the time.[47] In 1999, President Clinton proposed channeling a small portion of emerging unified budget surpluses into a new trust fund for Head Start and other children's programs.

Another important plausibility test is whether the trust fund's designated income source is expected to produce an adequate and stable flow of revenues. One important reason why the Energy Security Trust Fund failed to win adoption is because the CBO warned that windfall profits tax revenues would be extremely sensitive to unpredictable developments in the world oil market. Similarly, policymakers rejected the waste-end tax for Superfund in large part because they feared it was incapable of producing the desired level of resources.

A third hurdle is *demonstrating that trust fund financing is necessary to make the program work*. It is generally not sufficient for policymakers

---

[46] Of course the social insurance trust funds also involve redistribution but the transfers are largely hidden within the program's universalism. On this income redistribution tactic, see Theda Skocpol, "Targeting within Universalism: Politically Viable Policies to Combat Poverty in the United States," in Theda Skocpol, ed., *Social Policy in the United States* (Princeton: Princeton University Press, 1995), chapter 8. Most low-income entitlements in the US budget are paid out of general revenues.

[47] See Wallin, *From Revenue Sharing to Deficit Sharing*, chapter 2.

to support the underlying spending program; they also must believe that the program merits special budget protection. This hurdle is easiest to clear when reasonably coherent arguments can be made that the program could not be enacted without the trust fund mechanism or that continuity of funding is critical for the measure to achieve its policy objectives. When, as in the case of Carter's energy proposal, such arguments can be effectively challenged, the case for trust fund financing weakens. It also is generally necessary to show that no better, feasible alternative exists to the contemplated trust fund design. Thus the Highway Trust Fund was accepted only after two funding alternatives – bonds and tolls – were rejected on political and administrative grounds. The presumptive funding mechanism in US budgeting is general fund appropriations, and trust fund proponents generally must show why this will not work. As we have seen, policymakers explicitly rejected general fund financing in the highway, aviation, and Superfund cases, largely because budget guardians wished to promote cost recovery.

A final hurdle is *neutralizing any opposition to the trust fund proposal*. Opposition to trust funds tends to arise from two categories of actors: trust fund payers, and budget controllers. When would-be payers are also intended trust fund beneficiaries, the group's posture will depend on its assessment of the trust fund's expected net benefits (including the advantages of increased predictability). In contrast, payers will tend to oppose trust funds from which they expect to derive little benefit. Thus the chemical industry opposed the creation of the Superfund and the lead industry opposed the establishment of the Lead Paint Trust Fund. Whether politicians can effectively neutralize this opposition will depend both on the appeal of the designated spending to other clienteles and on whether a plausible case can be made that it is reasonable for society to target these particular industries.[48]

Budget controllers, as we have seen, often oppose the creation of trust funds in order to preserve flexibility. Their initial opposition may be partly neutralized, however, when they can be convinced that narrowing their formal discretion will promote cost recovery and protect the Treasury (the highway and aviation cases), expand or protect their institutional prerogatives (Social Security and Superfund), placate tax-paying industries (Superfund), or prevent expensive new spending

---

[48] For an excellent discussion of this point, see Nonna A. Noto and Louis Alan Talley, "Excise Tax Financing of Federal Trust Funds," *Congressional Research Service Report for Congress* (Washington, DC: Government Printing Office, January 5, 1993), 93–6 E.

promises from damaging preexisting fiscal commitments (Medicare). The fact that budget controllers agree to create trust funds provides no guarantee, however, that they or their institutional successors will not attempt to take back this budgetary discretion later on.

10

Conclusions: the structure and normative challenges of promise-keeping

The complex reality of trust funds in the United States budget contradicts two arguments that are often simplistically advanced by social scientists.[1] One is that precommitments are impossible to sustain through time in democratic politics because any prior law can always be repealed; the other offers the opposite idea that policy inheritances all but eliminate flexibility of choice in the present. My analysis of the experience with trust funds and earmarked taxes in American national budgeting reveals both the limits and possibilities of statutory mechanisms for binding future politicians.

As we have seen, the trust fund device gives a distinctive cast to policymaking. Trust fund financing empowers budget claimants to use the symbolically explosive language of moral rights and often affords designated programs a level of protection from normal processes of fiscal control. But trust funds have historically been weak instruments for prefunding. Government trust funds have compelled politicians to make good on long-term commitments, but they have not actually segregated the economic resources to pay for those commitments. Overall, the trust fund experience suggests that statutory precommitment devices work best when they are used to harness, rather than to override, the natural incentives of officeholders. While devices like trust funds do not rule out future political conflicts, they do shape what the debates are about. The remainder of this chapter discusses some broader implications of my analysis, presents a framework for understanding observed differences

---

[1] This formulation was suggested by an anonymous reviewer.

188

across the case study chapters, and projects the normative challenges and future prospects of trust fund financing in American government.

Implications of the main findings

Christopher Howard, in his excellent account of tax expenditures for social purposes in the US budget, suggests that many tax subsidies are created with little foresight.[2] In sharp contrast, trust funds are nearly always created with long-term goals in mind, even if trust funds may sometimes produce unintended consequences. As the case studies have demonstrated, trust funds are often adopted only after alternative funding mechanisms have been explicitly or implicitly rejected. The relatively greater degree of foresight evident in trust fund adoptions does not mean that trust funds are substantively more important than tax expenditures, many of which have far-reaching effects on economic activity and income distribution. Rather, it reflects the trust fund device's greater visibility and more obvious role as a long-term commitment device.

Chapter 2 outlined four distinct rationales for the creation of trust fund structures: making users pay, maximizing budgets, reducing uncertainty, and guarding the Treasury. While each of these objectives has influenced policymakers' decisions on some occasions, reducing political uncertainty has been the most important. In every case examined in this book, including the two unsuccessful efforts to establish new trust fund structures (discussed in chapter 9), locking-in future budget promises was a major objective of trust fund proponents. This pattern reflects the strong desire of politicians, interest groups, and plain citizens for a measure of predictability in government amidst the turmoil of democratic politics.

When trust funds are created for preexisting spending programs, proponents are often motivated by a desire both for more certainty *and* for larger budget shares. The goal of making users pay has generally been intended to achieve other policy objectives. In both the highway and aviation cases, for example, user tax increases drew support from politicians and clientele groups because these levies promised to recover program costs, stabilize future revenue flows, and finance higher levels of infrastructure investment. Proposals for technically efficient *pricing* mechanisms (e.g., tolls in the highway case, waste-end taxes for Superfund) tend not to command support outside of professional economists. Trust

---

[2] Christopher Howard, *The Hidden Welfare State: Tax Expenditures and Social Policy in the United States* (Princeton, NJ: Princeton University Press, 1997), 189.

fund user taxes are generally set too low, and rarely do liability charges properly internalize externalities.[3] To the extent the creation of trust fund financing improves microeconomic efficiency from what it otherwise would be, then, it generally does so as byproduct of other legislative objectives. This is not surprising. For better or worse, democratic politics is more about helping one's friends than it is about "getting prices right." The trust fund device, in and of itself, does not alter this reality.

Crucial role of fiscal conservatives

Several research findings are more surprising, however. One is that trust funds have been adopted as much to restrain program spending, and safeguard the Treasury, as to maximize government outlays. Without denying the importance of program advocates in the trust fund creation process, what is striking is how often trust funds have elicited support from fiscal conservatives, who view dedicated funding as a mechanism both to discipline spending demands and to prevent unbalanced budgets.[4] The original creation of a separate Old-Age Reserve Account for Social Security reflected the preference of Franklin Roosevelt and Henry Morgenthau for "sound financing." As chapter 5 showed, Wilbur Mills designed the Medicare trust funds not only to distinguish Medicare from welfare, but also to forestall future health care expansions and protect the financial stability of the preexisting Social Security system. Mills also insisted on the creation of the Airport and Airway Trust Fund as a condition of his support for increased aviation spending. The Ways and Means Committee under Al Ullman (D-Oregon) embraced trust fund financing of the Superfund program in part to limit the program's drain on general revenues. And it was Eisenhower's fiscally conservative Treasury Security George Humphrey whose endorsement helped win bipartisan support for the Highway Trust Fund in 1956. In sum, trust fund financing has traditionally elicited support not only from liberal proponents of big government but also from committed fiscal conservatives. A focus on trust funds and earmarked taxes thus helps explain how massive federal programs like Social Security, Medicare, and the interstate

---

[3] On this point, see Congressional Budget Office, *Paying for Highways, Airways, and Waterways: How Can Users Be Charged* (Washington, DC: CBO, May 1992b); see also McChesney, *Money for Nothing*, chapter 6. While McChesney's account of the Aviation Trust Fund is flawed because it ignores the aviation lobby's access to general fund subsidies (see chapter seven), McChesney is correct about the lack of efficient user charging in federal budgeting.

[4] On the importance of fiscal conservatism in American policymaking, see Zelizer, *Taxing America*.

highway program were enacted and sustained despite the fragmentation of the US system and the aversion of policymakers to general tax hikes and deficit spending.

Concentration of trust funds across missions

Given the strong appeal of federal trust funds to US politicians of diverse ideological persuasions, the real surprise may be the fact that the device has not been used more extensively than it has.[5] To be sure, the scope of trust funds in the US budget *has* expanded since the early 1970s, as we observed in chapter 2 (figure 2.2). The trust fund device has come to be used in a number of policy sectors where it was previously not employed, including the environmental and natural resource area. Still, one might well have anticipated an even greater level of diffusion of the trust fund device, particularly given the fiscal austerity of the 1980s and 1990s. Inspection of congressional data bases reveals scores if not hundreds of trust fund proposals that were introduced during this period but not enacted. For example, during the 100th Congress alone, there were bills introduced to create federal trust funds for marine research, public funding of elections, compensation of accident victims, organ transplantation, anti-smoking programs, housing programs, public broadcasting, and other purposes.

In fiscal 1995, earmarked revenues set aside for trust funds accounted for 31 percent of total federal budgetary resources (including budget authority, contract authority, and borrowing authority). These trust fund receipts, however, were highly concentrated across the federal government's 17 substantive "mission areas" (table 10.1). Trust funds provided the dominant share of budgetary resources for three missions (Social Security, Medicare, and transportation) but made up 1 percent or less of resources in seven other missions (defense, administration of justice, commerce, agriculture, energy, education and training, and general administration). What accounts for this relative concentration? Two key factors have served to limit the growth of trust funds across policy sectors. First, as we have seen, the very process of creating trust funds is path dependent. Trust funds tend to be adopted in sectors (e.g. transportation) where use of the device is already well established. In policy sectors, where other fiscal instruments are more common, trust fund proponents cannot point to an existing precedent and thus may have a more difficult time overcoming the obstacles to adoption. As chapter 9 showed, one reason why the Lead Paint Trust Fund proposal failed to win

---

[5] Robert Reischauer stimulated me to think about this point.

Table 10.1. *Trust fund resources by federal missions, fiscal year 1995*

Federal mission	Trust fund resources in thousands of dollars (Percentage of mission resources)
Administration of justice	172,446 (0.6%)
Agriculture	325,259 (1.0%)
Commerce and housing credit	404,914 (0.3%)
Community and regional development	2,042,382 (10.4%)
Education, training, employment, and social services	1,567,238 (2.3%)
Energy	2,039 (0.0%)
General government	62,033 (0.1%)
General science, space, and technology	39,360 (0.2%)
Health	22,650,790 (14.3%)
Income security	132,938,469 (42.8%)
International affairs	14,549,447 (13.7%)
Medicare	177,273,679 (81.0%)
National Defense	789,093 (0.2%)
Natural resources and environment	3,992,450 (10.4%)
Social Security	341,339,280 (98.6%)
Transportation	48,340,460 (70.8%)
Veterans benefits and services	15,147,434 (25.3%)
Total	761,636,773 (30.8%)

Source: General Accounting Office, *Budget Account Structure: A Descriptive Overview* (Washington, DC: Government Printing Office, September 1995) GAO/AIMD-95–179, figure II.5, 44–5. Federal missions correspond to Office of Management and Budget subfunctions.

adoption is because the federal government has traditionally responded to the lead poisoning problem through social regulation rather than through direct spending paid from earmarked taxes.

The relative concentration of trust funds reflects more than historical development, however. It also reflects a genuine desire among policymakers to preserve their discretion over program funding, particularly where the advantages from locking-in promises are less apparent. "As a matter of policy and practice," stated an internal 1972 Treasury Department memorandum, "the Federal Government has made limited use of trust funds financed by taxes or the earmarking of tax revenues. Essentially, this is the result of the feeling on the part of the Congress and the Executive that trust funds or earmarking prevent effective and efficient budget control . . ."[6]

Both external and internal controls have checked the propensity of lawmakers to expand trust funds to new missions. The most important external control is the existence of the CBO and OMB. These central budget offices have historically been well-positioned to challenge efforts to restrict budget flexibility. In his fascinating book *Strategic Budgeting*, former CBO analyst Roy T. Meyers portrays these agencies as struggling mightily to preserve discretion in the face of intense pressure from spending proponents seeking a bye in the yearly competition for budget support.[7] But while central budget controllers may feel beleaguered, there would surely be even *more* promiscuous use of devices like trust funds if these agencies did not exist. The political puzzle is not that central budget agencies sometimes lose but that they win as often as they do.

In addition, Congress itself seems to exercise a degree of collective self-restraint. The case accounts testify that lawmakers, especially members of the three key fiscal control committees (Appropriations, Budget, and Ways and Means) fully understand that trust fund financing typically entails a loss of flexibility. As the Lead Paint case demonstrates, members also seem to recognize that use of the trust fund device can be more or less appropriate depending on the linkage between revenues and benefits, the predictability of the revenue source, and, especially, the inherent need for credibility and long-term planning. In sum, members of Congress have reasonably coherent ideas about what constitutes proper use of the trust fund device, even if they do not always abide by these principles. Such policy understandings about the advantages and disadvantages of

---

[6] Memorandum on H.R. 16141, General Records of the Department of Treasury, Office of Tax Policy, Subject File, August 8, 1972. I am indebted to Prof. Jim Wooten for sending me this memo.

[7] Meyers, *Strategic Budgeting*.

the trust fund device themselves constitute a kind of budget institution, although one can legitimately question its current strength and durability.

Trust funds and transaction cost models

This last point touches on an important scholarly debate about the efficiency of public sector institutions (which is distinct from the issue of efficient *pricing* of specific services). Very roughly, the literature on political transaction costs divides into two camps. Oliver Williamson and his followers, including Avinash K. Dixit, argue that political institutions are generally efficient, not only from the narrow standpoint of the politicians who create them, but also from a more global perspective. According to this view, if unusual governmental arrangements (such as federal trust funds) exist, the (rebuttable) premise is that they represent the most feasible way to cope with the unavoidable transaction costs of making and enforcing political agreements.[8] An emphatically opposed view is offered by scholars who work out of a public choice framework. According to economist Charlotte Twight, the public sector is inimical to efficiency reasoning. Indeed, Twight argues that government officials systematically *increase* the political transaction costs facing voters in order to enhance their own power.[9] While Williamson stresses that high political transaction costs are inherent to many of the tasks that government performs, Twight contends that high political transaction costs are often artificially 'contrived' by officeholders.

Which of these accounts is true – or more nearly true – clearly depends on the effectiveness of the political process in which new institutions are crafted. Yet neither the Williamsonian camp nor the public choice camp gives adequate attention to the nature and quality of policymakers' deliberations over institutional design choices. My research on trust funds suggests that the process does not always work well enough to guarantee that socially efficient design choices are made, but it usually ensures that the key design issues – such as the tradeoff between commitment and discretion – are at least flagged and discussed.[10]

---

[8] Oliver E. Williamson, "Public and Private Bureaucracies: A Transaction Cost Economics Perspective," *Journal of Law, Economics, and Organization*, 15 (1), March 1999, 306–42; see also Dixit, *The Making of Economic Policy*.

[9] See Charlotte Twight, "Book Review of Dixit, The Making of Economic Policy," *The Independent Review: A Journal of Political Economy*, 111 (1) Spring 1998, 132–5.

[10] While policymakers care deeply about locking-in benefits, and about how particular clienteles will react to their institutional design choices, they show little

To be sure, policymakers' deliberations are not infrequently subject to informational distortions. As we have seen, trust fund architects often seek to camouflage the true costs of programs to current and future taxpayers (e.g., the nominal splitting of social insurance taxes between employees and employers; the pretense that Superfund taxes are not passed on to consumers). The effect is to deny citizen-voters the very information they need to send politicians the proper signals. Although the US electoral process is highly competitive, it is not clear that constructing such "fiscal illusions" poses serious risks for incumbent politicians; if it did we would see fewer of them. Score one for the public choice perspective.

Yet we have also seen that trust fund advocates rarely can win merely by asserting their narrow material interests. They are generally forced to convince their colleagues, including skeptical budget guardians, that the trust fund device is necessary to make the underlying budget transaction work and to show why alternative funding approaches are infeasible or somehow less desirable.[11] To repeat, politicians are forced to justify budgeting structures in relatively public-spirited terms for primarily self-interested reasons. Given the multiplicity of veto points in the US system, it is difficult for a coalition to gets its structural projects enacted without fairly broad support, and other factions cannot be expected to share the former group's parochial interests.[12] Even when such appeals are primarily instrumental, however, they do narrow somewhat the range of institutional designs that can be successfully sold. In sum, the institution-

interest in easing the administrative burdens on bureaucratic agencies. See Martha Derthick, *Agency Under Stress* (Washington, DC: Brookings Institution, 1990).

[11] Elsewhere I have shown that permanent appropriations in the US budget are largely reserved for sensitive income transfer programs and debt repayment and that "long-term appropriations" are seldom used to finance cabinet departments, such as Justice, State, and Treasury, whose budgets create potential agency problems because dominated by hard-to-monitor operating expenses. See Eric M. Patashnik, "The Contractual Nature of Budgeting: A Transaction Cost Perspective on the Design of Budgeting Institutions," *Policy Sciences*, 29 (3), 1996, 189–21. In a similar vein, Joseph White has argued that use of the entitlement form in American national budgeting has been largely policy driven. See White, "Entitlement Budgeting vs. Bureau Budgeting," 510–21.

[12] On this point, see Robert Goodin, "Institutions and Their Design," in Robert Goodin, ed., *The Theory of Institutional Design* (Cambridge: Cambridge University Press, 1996), 42. See also David Luban, "The Publicity Principle," in the same volume. On deliberation over design choices in US welfare policy, see Eugene Bardach, "Exit Equality, Enter Fairness," in Marc Landy, Martin Levin, and Martin Shapiro, eds., *Durability and Change: Policymaking in the 1990s* (Johns Hopkins University Press, forthcoming).

al design process is hardly an exercise in neutral social planning yet neither is it without certain (perhaps minimal) constraints.

Varieties of promise keeping

A final intriguing and somewhat surprising finding is that, while trust funds are typically designed to promote programmatic and financial stability, many trust fund programs have in fact been quite unstable. At a fundamental level, this instability stems from the impossibility of ever extracting governmental commitments from "permanent dependence" on the political process, which is inevitably buffeted by economic and social developments.[13] One proximate cause of the instability experienced by trust funds has been the frictions that have been generated when new budget rules and procedures with conflicting logics have been layered atop old trust fund mechanisms.[14] In the highway case, for example, the trust fund's financial autonomy was temporarily weakened by the passage of centralizing budget reforms and deficit control measures. Most scholars who have studied budget process reforms have examined whether these changes have worked on their own terms. My analysis suggests, however, that it is also crucial to explore how such reforms affect the operations of preexisting institutional arrangements.

Ironically, the instabilities exhibited by trust funds also reflect the dynamics set in motion by the trust funds themselves. As we have seen, there are numerous potential threats to the procedural and financial integrity of trust fund arrangements. Trust fund outlays can be trimmed for general fiscal reasons. Earmarked revenues can be diverted to other uses. Trust funds can go bankrupt or even be dismantled. What makes certain trust funds more or less susceptible to these and other risks?

Many budget scholars would draw a fundamental distinction between trust funds whose expenditure programs have entitlement status and those which do not. While this distinction points to an important difference in the funds' spending automaticity, it cuts too deeply. Both the Hospital Insurance Trust Fund and the Supplementary Medical Insurance Trust Fund are considered entitlements (and provide benefits to largely the same clientele group), but only the former trust fund has

---

[13] Heclo here makes the important point that even long-term commitments which are implemented in the private sector, such as privatized Social Security accounts, are ultimately dependent on governmental frameworks for their sustainability. In this sense, political risks are inescapable. See Heclo, "A Political Science Perspective," quoted at 71.

[14] On institutional layering, see Orren and Skowronek, "Beyond the Iconography of Order."

been threatened with bankruptcy. Spending from both the Highway Trust Fund and the Superfund Trust Fund is considered discretionary. Yet during the late 1990s Congress kept the highway fund well-stocked while refusing even to activate Superfund's taxing authority.

To make sense of variations in trust funds' susceptibility to cutbacks, diversions, and other political and fiscal hazards, it is crucial to examine the "strategic structure" (to borrow a phrase from Russell Hardin) of each of the underlying political promises.[15] I have argued throughout that trust funds can be distinguished according to (1) whether their underlying promises are based on a reciprocal exchange of specific tax payments now in return for desired benefits later and (2) whether individual beneficiaries subsequently become reliant on the government. These dimensions are continuous rather than dichotomous. The more trust fund payers and beneficiaries overlap (even across time), the tighter the connection between spending and revenues, and the less the program is subsidized by general fund transfers, the more the trust fund promise is based on *reciprocal exchange*. The more that individual beneficiaries are induced into making long-term commitments, and the more personally vulnerable they become to governmental reneging, the higher the level of *subsequent reliance*.[16]

Trust funds can thus be located on a map consisting of two axes – reciprocity and reliance – with each varying from low to high (figure 10.1). Before mapping the cases, two points should be stressed. First, discussions of more or less reciprocity should not be interpreted to mean that the promises are more or less *political*. All federal trust funds rest on government coercion. Policy images notwithstanding, none is based on voluntary self-help. And, even in a relatively high reciprocity case, the linkage between individual payments and benefits is never perfect. Differences among trust funds in their underlying exchange relationships

---

[15] See Russell Hardin, *Morality within the Limits of Reason* (Chicago: University of Chicago Press, 1988), especially 59–65. Hardin distinguishes between "exchange" promises, which are explicitly a reciprocal part of an exchange relation, and "gratuitous" promises, which are made without any reciprocal benefit to the promiser.

[16] The overwhelming majority of federal trust funds in the budget could be situated in this map. The only hard case would be the federal and military retirement funds. These funds clearly induce a high level of beneficiary reliance. The reciprocity of the exchanges underlying the trust funds is more complex. Employee contributions account for none (in the case of the military pension system) or only a small portion (in the case of the civilian system) of the trust funds' income; general fund transfers make up the difference. Both of these trust fund systems, however, rest on an implicit exchange of public service for pension benefits.

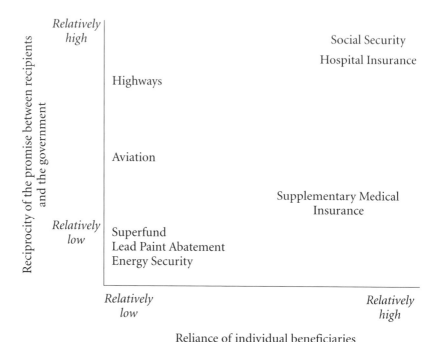

Figure 10.1 The strategic structure of trust fund promising: case studies by reciprocity and reliance

are nonetheless important. Various positions in the map should therefore be interpreted as different kinds of political relationships. Second, as in James Q. Wilson's framework for categorizing policies, it is the *perceived* reciprocity of trust fund promises, not the actual economic incidence of costs and benefits, that matters politically.[17]

In the top right-hand corner, where both reciprocity and reliance are relatively high, are the Social Security and Hospital Insurance Trust Funds. Workers make substantial earmarked contributions, benefit payments constitute a very large share of the average recipient's income, and people take into account the existence of the programs when making their private retirement and investment decisions. These factors contribute to the overall strength and integrity of the systems, generally inhibiting blame-avoiding politicians from explicitly diverting earmarked revenues to other uses or imposing major cutbacks outside of internally defined trust fund solvency crises.

[17] James Q. Wilson, *Political Organizations* (New York: Basic Books, 1973).

Ironically, however, the very sensitivity of the underlying promises leaves these trust funds vulnerable to certain kinds of attacks. Precisely *because* individual payers make such substantial contributions, and are so vulnerable to the consequences of unreliability by the government, ideological opponents of the commitments may seek to instill fears by warning future beneficiaries that they do not actually possess individual contractual rights to their benefits, that the government cannot be trusted to keep its hands off any reserves, and that their money would earn more and be safer in the private sector. In sum, the sensitivity of the underlying promises generally inhibits opponents from making frontal attacks on the trust funds themselves, but invites them to undermine beneficiaries' confidence in the systems' future credibility.

The Highway Trust Fund is a relatively high reciprocity/low reliance case. The fact that motorists contribute every time they fill up, and that annual trust fund revenues more or less cover the costs of federal highway spending, enables the trust fund's defenders to cast any effort to divert gas tax revenues to non-highway purposes as a "breach of faith." But while the building of the interstates fundamentally transformed American economic and social life, individual citizens are much less reliant on the Highway Trust Fund for their personal economic security than on, say, the social insurance trust funds. As we have seen, this low degree of promisee reliance has led budgetary guardians to support procedural changes that will reduce the trust fund's spending automaticity and isolation from normal fiscal pressures.

The Aviation and SMI Trust Fund are mixed cases. In both, the level of reciprocity is contested. Payers feel entitled to their benefits because they do make substantial earmarked contributions. But both trust funds are heavily subsidized by general tax revenues. The different patterns exhibited by the two trust funds largely reflect differences in their respective levels of promisee reliance. As we have seen, the combination of modest reciprocity/ low reliance has been extremely destabilizing for the Aviation Trust Fund, leading to endless battles over the level and permissible uses of aviation tax revenues. There have been ongoing efforts to reduce aviation capital spending below the level favored by the trust fund's payers. By contrast, the SMI Trust Fund has been much more stable. The high degree of reliance of current and future beneficiaries on physicians' services makes program spending hard to cut, and the trust fund's access to unlimited general fund transfers eliminates the possibility of a distinct trust fund solvency crisis.

Finally, located in the lower left-hand corner are Superfund and the (not enacted) trust funds for Lead Paint Abatement and Energy Security. These trust funds are (or would have been) characterized by low reciprocity and low reliance. The linkage between taxes and spending is weak, the attitude of the targeted payers is at best indifferent and at worst hostile, and individual beneficiaries are not terribly dependent on the programs' continuation (though these activities may well have committed interest group supporters).

Trust fund promises based on low reciprocity and low reliance should be the most vulnerable to dismantling. In fact, the only major federal trust fund I could identify that has been terminated – the General Revenue Sharing Trust Fund, which was abolished in 1986 – would be classified in the lower left-hand corner.[18] As I mentioned in chapter 9, the General Revenue Sharing Trust Fund had no specific earmarked funding source, just a slice of the general fund pie. At the time of the trust fund's original enactment in 1972, the federal government was relatively flush. But, when federal budget deficits emerged in the 1980s, the federal government had no more general revenues to share. The General Revenue Sharing Trust Fund was also vulnerable because it failed to induce reliance. Indeed, the benefits were spread so thinly across society that citizens hardly noticed they were being withdrawn.[19] One might well have expected state and local officials to have become addicted to the benefits. But revenue sharing grants constituted a very small share of state and local budgets. Moreover, the trust fund and entitlement status of the grants notwithstanding, state and local officials considered the revenue sharing program's future highly uncertain from the outset, in part because the program was originally authorized for only five years. Most deliberately refrained from incorporating the grants into their long-term budget plans, viewing the money as a one-time cash windfall. As a result,

---

[18] I could identify three other trust funds which have been dismantled but none was operational at the time of its repeal. The Recreational Trails Trust Fund was terminated in 1998. The trails fund was originally adopted in 1991 to earmark the revenues from recreational fuels (e.g., gasoline used by off-road motorcycles and snowmobiles) for restoration of recreational trails. Although the trails program received general fund appropriations during this period, the trust fund mechanism itself was never triggered. Still, the trails lobby remained in a strong bargaining position because of their user tax payments. With its approval, and the acquiescence of the road lobby, the trails spending program and related user taxes were eventually folded into the Highway Trust Fund. Two other trust funds were repealed before they became operational. The Deep Seabed Revenue Sharing Trust Fund was established in 1979 to collect the revenue from taxes on certain minerals, but the tax expired before any deep seabed mining had occurred. The Post-Closure Liability Trust Fund was established in 1980 but was repealed in 1986 for mainly technical reasons before any of its revenues were appropriated. Amounts paid into the trust fund were refunded to payers who submitted claims. See Noto and Talley, "Excise Tax Financing," 93–6 E.

[19] Arnold, *The Logic of Congressional Action*, 137.

the political consequences of terminating the General Revenue Sharing Trust Fund were less than devastating.[20]

Normative challenges

As Brian Hogwood and Guy Peters point out, while there are often good reasons for revenue earmarking, the practice can also lead to certain policy pathologies.[21] My analysis suggests that these pathologies are importantly mediated by the strategic context of promise keeping. Although reciprocity and reliance are continuous variables, different combinations of them give rise to qualitatively distinct normative challenges (figure 10.2).

1 *Inappropriate adoption.* Establishing trust funds for low reciprocity/low reliance promises constitutes a blatant misuse of the trust fund device. The user fee or social insurance logic is tenuous at best; the need for credibility weak. Indeed, the rationale for trust fund financing is simply to evade normal budgetary control. The normative challenge here is to maintain or increase the barriers to trust fund adoption.

2 *Misallocation of resources.* Use of the trust fund device is more legitimate for high reciprocity/low reliance promises. The user fee logic justifies a statutory linkage between revenues and spending. Still, trust fund arrangements can take on a life of their own, making it harder for budget controllers to reallocate resources as priorities change. As we saw, budget controllers were able to shift some Highway Trust Fund money into public transit modes during the energy crises, but arguably less than these programs deserved. Similarly, budget controllers had to fight hard to gain control over aviation capital investment spending levels, even after the FAA experienced severe technological problems. The main normative challenges here are to maintain a reasonable economic linkage between taxes and spending, to preserve opportunities for regular legislative review, and to provide the minimum level of procedural safeguards possible. In general, this means that the trust funds should remain on-budget and (contrary to current highway finance practice) subject to meaningful appropriations control.

---

[20] Wallin, *From Revenue Sharing to Deficit Sharing.*
[21] For an excellent discussion of the pathologies of tax earmarking, see Brian W. Hogwood and B. Guy Peters, *The Pathology of Public Policy* (Oxford: Clarendon Press, 1985), 119–22. My contribution here is to link specific earmarking problems to variations in the structure of the underlying policy commitments.

Beneficiary reliance

	Relatively high	*Relatively low*
Relatively high	Greatly reduced chances for policy termination	Misallocation of resources
Relatively low	Uncontrollable spending	Inappropriate adoption

Reciprocity of promise

Figure 10.2 Problems by level of reciprocity and reliance

3 *Uncontrollable spending.* As the Medicare Part B case showed, trust fund promises in which reliance is high but reciprocity low create severe problems of fiscal control. Promisees are heavily dependent on the program's continuation, but do not make adequate contributions to the system's financing. The weakness of the connection between earmarked contributions and spending attenuates the fiscal discipline that would otherwise be associated with trust fund financing. The normative challenge is to get spending under control and withdraw general fund subsidies for beneficiaries who do not need them.

4 *Limited scope for policy termination.* Finally, trust funds based on high reciprocity/high reliance (such as Social Security) severely limit the scope for dismantling existing arrangements. Promisees can legitimately argue that they have an earned right to future benefits, and any effort to abolish the current system overnight would trigger massive social disruptions.

There is a legal doctrine of reliance that holds that when people have made long-term plans on the basis of a prior act of promising, those expectations should generally not be disappointed. This doctrine seems no less applicable to social contracts than to private agreements, particularly when the social contracts are explicitly part of a reciprocal exchange between citizens and the government. Indeed, a government that systematically breaks promises on which citizens have been compelled to depend not only will be the object of public scorn but will ultimately damage its own capacity to govern. This is not to suggest, however, that the ideal society is one in which every citizen is reliant on the government for everything or that once clienteles do become reliant no reforms should ever be made. But when there is previous reliance, it is morally (and not merely practically) incumbent upon reformers to phase-in changes gradually, thereby preventing citizens from being left out on a limb.[22] This requirement will, of course, raise the "transition costs" of policy reform, but these are costs that society ethically must pay.

Future prospects

What are the future prospects of trust fund financing in the American welfare state? Will the massive Social Security and Medicare trust funds continue indefinitely? Will they be fundamentally reformed? The theory of budgetary incrementalism suggests that it is a safe bet that tomorrow's budgets will closely resemble yesterday's. As we have seen, however, incrementalism pays scant attention to institutional design and the politics of precommitment. My analysis of trust funds suggests that important modifications in current social insurance arrangements are indeed possible, although it is difficult to predict the precise direction these changes will take.

The aging of the baby boom generation will place severe pressure on the Social Security and Hospital Insurance trust funds. The deep reliance of millions of Americans on these programs rules out a total abandon-ment of the government's protective role. Nonetheless, the threat of trust fund insolvency may well keep reform on the policy agenda. The policy ideas, such as the insurance imagery, long used to market these programs, encourage comparison with private sector investment alternatives, which might give individual recipients a greater sense of personal control over their money.

The emergence of large but temporary unified budget surpluses potentially gives policymakers an opportunity to choose between two radically different long-range reform approaches without having to impose short-term costs on their constituents. The first approach, endorsed by the Clinton Administration in 1999, would shore up the Social Security and Hospital Insurance trust funds by injecting large amounts of general fund transfers into them. An alternative approach would be to shift to a privatized system of individual asset accounts, using federal budget surpluses (including the surpluses generated by Social Security itself) to finance the costs of the transition. Each of these approaches carries with it distinctive political risks. A careful assessment of these risks would require another book.

One risk applies no matter what reform path institutional designers

---

[22] A possible exception would be where gradualism seems certain to undermine the entire reform effort, in which case compensation schemes might be in order.

take: the risk of hubris. A sense of humility is always appropriate in making public policy but never more so than when commitments and institutions are being crafted for the long run. The experience with federal trust funds demonstrates that the future of a polity can indeed be shaped through institutional design. Yet the preferences of future leaders and citizens, and the conditions they will inhabit, cannot be known with certainty. Binding the government to unsustainable, imprudent promises leads eventually to cynicism and disillusionment. Only by endeavoring to leave successor generations a decent policy inheritance, including the freedom to make important choices of their own, will officeholders be worthy of the public trust they hold.

Bibliography

Aaron, Henry J. and Reischauer, Robert D. 1995. "The Medicare Reform Debate: What Is the Next Step?" *Health Affairs*, 14

Ackerman, Bruce A. 1991. *We the People*. Cambridge, MA: Harvard University Press

Acton, Jan Paul and Dixon, Lloyd. 1992. *Superfund and Transaction Costs*. Santa Monica, CA. Rand Institute

Adams, Rebecca. 1999. "Lawmakers Envision a Medicare System Greater Than the Sum of Its Parts," *Congressional Quarterly Weekly Report*, April 27

Advisory Council on Social Security. 1938. "Final Report," reprinted in 1985 *The Report of the Committee on Economic Security of 1935*. 50th Anniversary Edition. December 10. Washington, DC: National Conference on Social Welfare

Alt, James E. and Lowery, Robert C. 1994. "Divided Government, Fiscal Institutions, and Budget Deficits: Evidence From The States," *American Political Science Review*, 88

Altmeyer, Arthur. 1966. *The Formative Years of Social Security*. Madison: University of Wisconsin Press

    1949. "Old-Age, Survivors, and Disability Insurance," *Social Security Bulletin*, April

The American Enterprise. March/April, 1990

American Road and Transportation Builders Association. 1998. "The Transportation Equity Act for the 21st Century." Washington, DC, July

Angell, Homer D. 1951. "Statement," *Congressional Record*, September 19

Arnold, R. Douglas. 1990. *The Logic of Congressional Action*. New Haven: Yale University Press

Ball, Robert M. 1978. "The 1977 Amendments to the Social Security and

Financing Social Security," Testimony Before the Subcommittee on Social Security, Senate Finance Committee, April 6

1988. "Panel on Formulating a Deficit Reduction Package: What is the Role of Social Security," in Henry J. Aaron (ed.), *Social Security and the Budget*. Washington, DC: National Academy of Social Insurance

1995. "What Medicare's Architects Had In Mind," *Health Affairs*, 14(4), Winter, 62–72

Ball, Robert M. and Bethell, Thomas N. 1997. "Bridging the Centuries: The Case for Traditional Social Security," in Eric R. Kingson and James H. Schultz (eds.), *Social Security in the 21st Century*. New York: Oxford University Press

Bardach, Eugene. 1976. "Policy Termination As A Political Process," *Policy Sciences*, 7

Forthcoming. "Exit Equality, Enter Fairness," In Marc Landy, Martin Levin, and Martin Shapiro (eds.), *Durability and Change: Policymaking in the 1990s*. Baltimore: Johns Hopkins University Press

Barlett, Robert V. 1984. "The Budgetary Process and Environmental Policy," in Norman J. Vig and Michael E. Kraft (eds.), *Environmental Policy in the 1980s: Reagan's New Agenda*. Washington, DC: Congressional Quarterly Press

Barnett, Harold C. 1994. *Toxics Debts and The Superfund Dilemma*. Chapel Hill: University of North Carolina Press

Baumgartner, Frank R. and Jones, Bryan D. 1993. *Agendas and Instability in American Politics*. Chicago: University of Chicago Press

Berkowitz, Edward D. 1996. "Social Security and the Financing of the American State," in W. Elliot Brownlee (ed.), *Funding the Modern American State, 1941–1995: The Rise and Fall of the Era of Easy Finance*. Cambridge and Washington, DC: Cambridge University Press and Woodrow Wilson Center Press

Blais, Andre and Dion, Stephane. 1991. "Are Bureaucrats Budget Maximizers?" *The Budget-Maximizing Bureaucrat: Appraisals and Evidence*. Pittsburgh: University of Pittsburgh Press

Blendon, Robert J. *et al.*, 1997 "What Do Americans Know About Entitlements?" *Health Affairs*, September/October

Blinder, Alan S. 1998. "Shrewd Politics, Sound Policy," *The New York Times* March 3

Bogert, George Gleason and Bogert, George Taylor. 1973. *Handbook of the Law of Trusts*. Fifth Edition. St. Paul, Minnesota: West Publishing

Bracewell-Milnes, Barry. 1991. "Earmarking in Britain: Theory and Practice," *The Case for Earmarked Taxes: Government Spending and Public Choice*. London: Institute of Economic Affairs

Breach, John S. 1923. "Provision for Retirement Employees," *The Congressional Digest*, April

Brown, J. Douglas. 1977. *Essays on Social Security*. Princeton: Princeton University Press

Buchanan, James M. 1963. "The Economics of Earmarked Taxes," *Journal of Political Economy*, 71

Buck, Mr. 1939. "The Social Security Act – Old-Age Reserve Account," *Congressional Record*, April 6

Burnham, John C. 1961. "The Gasoline Tax and the Automobile Revolution," *The Mississippi Valley Historical Review: A Journal of American History*, 98, December

Business Week. 1980. "Closer to a Cleanup Fund," July 14
  1992. "The Toxic Mess Called Superfund," May 11

Cates, Jerry R. 1983. *Insuring Inequality*. Ann Arbor: University of Michigan Press

Chemical Engineering. 1983. "Federal Budget Stresses 'Efficiency' at Agencies," February 21

Chemical Marketing Reporter. 1995. "Chemical Industry Opposed Clinton Superfund Tax Plan," December 18

Chisman, Forrest P. 1988. "Social Security Reserves and the Budget Deficit," in John R. Gist, ed., *Social Security and Economic Well-Being Across Generations*. Washington, DC: American Association of Retired Persons Public Policy Institute

Cloud, David S. 1991. "Moynihan Tries Again," *Congressional Quarterly Weekly Report*. Washington, DC: Government Printing Office, January 26

Cogan, John F. 1994. "The Dispersion of Spending Authority and Federal Budget Deficits," in John F. Cogan, Timothy J. Muris, and Allen Schick (eds.), *The Budget Puzzle*. Palo Alto: Stanford University Press

Cohen, Linda R. and Noll, Roger G. 1991. "Synthetic Fuels From Coal," in Linda R. Cohen and Roger G. Noll (eds.), *The Technology Pork Barrel*. Washington, DC: Brookings Institution

Cohen, Steve. 1984. "Defusing the Toxic Time Bomb: Federal Hazardous Waste Programs," in Norman J. Vig and Michael E. Kraft (eds.), *Environmental Policy in the 1980s: Reagan's New Agenda*. Washington, DC: Congressional Quarterly Press

Committee on Economic Security. 1985. "Report of the Committee on Economic Security of 1935," *The Report of the Committee on Economic Security of 1935*. 50th Anniversary Edition. Washington, DC: National Conference on Social Welfare

Concord Coalition. 1998. "How To Measure Social Security's Financial Status: Facing Facts Alert," June 15
  1999. "Issue Brief: The 1999 Report of the Social Security and Medicare Trustees" May 20

Congress and the Nation. 1981. "Energy Policy," Washington, DC: Congressional Quarterly Press

Congressional Budget Office. 1979. *The Windfall Profits Tax.* Washington,
    DC: Government Printing Office
    1988. *The Status of the Airport and Airway Trust Fund.* Washington, DC:
    Government Printing Office
    1990. *The Economic and Budget Outlook: Fiscal Years 1991–1995.*
    Washington, DC: Government Printing Office, January
    1992a. *The Economic and Budget Outlook: Fiscal Years 1993–1997.*
    Washington, DC: Government Printing Office
    1992b. *Paying for Highways, Airways, and Waterways: How Can Users Be
    Charged.* Washington, DC: Government Printing Office, May
    1993a. *Federal Debt and Interest Costs.* Washington, DC: Government
    Printing Office
    1993b. *The Growth of Federal User Charges.* Washington, DC: Government
    Printing Office, May
    1999a. *An Analysis of the President's Budgetary Proposals for Fiscal Year
    2000.* Washington, DC: Government Printing Office, April
    1999b. *Maintaining Budgetary Discipline: Spending and Revenue Options.*
    Washington, DC: Government Printing Office
Congressional Quarterly Almanac. Washington, DC
    1954.
    1955. "Highway Proposals."
    1956. "13 Year Highway Program."
    1967. "1967 Developments."
    1969. "Transportation Legislation."
    1970. "Congress Extends Interstate Highway System."
    1970. "Congress Passes Airport and Airway Development Act."
    1971. "Airport Development."
    1973. "Highway Act: Compromise on Mass Transit Funds."
    1975. "Highway Act Extension Sent to Congress."
    1976. "Congress Sets Ceiling on Highway Spending."
    1979. "Windfall Profits Tax."
    1980. "Airport Tax, Development."
    1981. "Congress Clears 'Superfund' Legislation."
    1983. "Social Security Rescue Plan Swiftly Approved."
    1985a. "House, Senate Pass Superfund Authorization."
    1985b. "Congress Dismantles Synthetic Fuels Program."
    1986. "Reagan Signs 'Superfund' Waste-Cleanup Bill."
    1987. "Airport Reauthorization Bill Enacted."
    1990. "Effort to Shift Social Security Taxes Fails."
    1990. "Bush Gets Parts of Aviation Package."
    1994. "No Floor Action on Superfund Bill."
Congressional Quarterly Weekly Report. Washington, DC: Congressional
    Quarterly Service, 1972, 1975, 1977, 1979, 1980

Congressional Record. 1953, 1954, 1955, 1956, 1965, 1969, 1972, 1975, 1978, 1979, 1980, 1986, 1991, 1996, 1997

Cordes, Joseph J. 1996. "How Yesterday's Decisions Affect Today's Budget and Fiscal Options," in C. Eugene Steuerle and Masahiro Kawai (eds.), *The New World Fiscal Order: Implications for Industrialized Nations.* Washington, DC: The Urban Institute

Corrigan, Richard. 1979. "Who'll Get the Largest Slices of the $1 Trillion 'Windfall Profits' Pie?" *National Journal*, 10, November

Cox, Gary W. and McCubbins, Mathew. 1991. "Divided Control of Fiscal Policy," in Gary W. Cox and Samuel Kernell (eds.), *The Politics of Divided Government.* Boulder, CO: Westview Press

Crain, W. Mark and Muris, Timothy J. 1995. "Legislative Organization of Fiscal Policy," *Journal of Law and Economics*, 38

Cruikshank, Nelson H. 1978. "A Philosophy for Social Security." Paper Delivered at the Social Security Administration, Third Robert M. Ball Lecture, Baltimore, Maryland. December 12

Davis, Joseph A. 1986. "Congress Clears 'Superfund,' Awaits President's Decision," *Congressional Quarterly*, 11, October

1987. "Windfall Profits Tax Headed for Extinction," *Congressional Quarterly Weekly Report*, November 7

Dentzer, Susan. 1990. "Paycheck Politics," *US News and World Report*, January 29

Derthick, Martha. 1979. *Policymaking for Social Security*, Vol. II. Washington, DC: Brookings Institution

1990. *Agency Under Stress.* Washington, DC: Brookings Institution

Forthcoming. "The Evolving Old Politics of Social Security," in Marc Landy, Martin Levin, and Martin Shapiro (eds.), *Durability and Change: The New Politics of Public Policy*, Vol. II. Baltimore: John Hopkins University Press

Dicey, A. V. 1959. *Study of the Law of the Constitution.* 10th Edition. London: MacMillian Press

Dixit, Avinash K. 1996. *The Making of Economic Policy: A Transaction-Cost Politics Perspective.* Cambridge, MA: MIT Press

Dowd, Maureen. 1983. "Superfund, Supermess," *Time*, February 23

Dunleavy, Colleen A. 1992. "Early Railroad Policy," in Sven Steinmo, Kathleen Thelen, and Frank Longstreth (eds.), *Structuring Politics: Historical Institutionalism in Comparative Analysis.* Cambridge: Cambridge University Press

Dunn, James A. 1981. *Miles to Go: European and American Transportation Policies.* Cambridge, MA: MIT Press

1998. *Driving Forces: The Automobile, Its Enemies, and the Politics of Mobility.* Washington, DC: Brookings Institution

Economic Indicators Handbook. Detroit: Gale Research, 1992

The Economist. 1989. "Put Not Your Trust In Congress," November 11

Eliot, Thomas H. 1961. "The Legal Background of the Social Security Act," Speech delivered at general staff meeting at Social Security Administration Headquarters. Baltimore, Maryland, February 3

Elperin, Juliet. 1999. "Transportation a Winner Again: Committee Leader Uses Threat To Push Airport Proposal," *The Washington Post*, March 26

Elster, John. 1979. *Ulysses and the Sirens: Studies in Rationality and Irrationality*. Cambridge: Cambridge University Press

Elster, Jon and Rune Slagstad, eds., *Constitutionalism and Democracy*. Cambridge: Cambridge University Press

Environmental Defense Fund. 1990. *Legacy of Lead: America's Continuing Epidemic Of Childhood Lead Poisoning* exerpted in "Lead Poisoning," *Congressional Quarterly Researcher*, 2(23), June 19, 1992

Feldstein, Martin. 1997. "The Case for Privatization," *Foreign Affairs*, July/ August

Final Breaux-Thomas Medicare Reform Proposal. 1999. Http://thomas.loc.gov/medicare

Fink, James J. 1988. *The Automobile Age*. Cambridge, MA: MIT Press

Frant, Howard. 1996. "High-Powered and Low-Powered Incentives in the Public Sector," *Journal of Public Administration Research and Theory*, 3

Freedman, Allan. 1997. "Congress Prepares New Assault on Troubled Superfund Sites," *Congressional Quarterly*, 28, June

General Accounting Office. 1988a. "Budget Issues: Trust Funds and Their Relationship To the Federal Budget." GAO/AFMD-88-55. Washington, DC: Government Printing Office

    1994. "FAA Budget Agency Faces Key Management Challenges on Major Issues," Statement of Kenneth M. Mead, Director, Transportation Issues, Resources, Community, and Economic Development Division, Testimony Before the Subcommittee on Transportation and Related Agencies, Committee on Appropriations House of Representatives, April, GAO/T-RCED-94-101

    1995. "Budget Account Structure: A Descriptive Overview," GAO/AIMD-95–179. Washington, DC: Government Printing Office

    1998. "Financial Audit: 1997 Consolidated Financial Statements of the United States Government," GAO/AIMD-98–127. Washington, DC: Government Printing Office

    1999. "Lead Poisoning: Federal Health Care Programs Are Not Effectively Reaching At-Risk Children: Report to the Ranking Minority Member Committee on Government Reform," GAO/HEHS-99–18. Washington, DC: Government Printing Office

Gilmour, John B. 1995. *Strategic Disagreement*. Pittsburgh: University of Pittsburgh Press

Gist, John (ed.) 1988. *Social Security and Economic Well-Being Across*

Generations. Washington, DC: American Association of Retired Persons Public Policy Institute

Gleckman, Howard. 1990. "Social Security's Dirty Little Secret," *Business Week*, January 29

Goetz, Charles J. 1968. "Earmarked Taxes and Majority Rule Budgetary Processes," *The American Economic Review*, 58

Goodin, Robert. 1996. "Institutions and Their Design," in Robert Goodin (ed.), *The Theory of Institutional Design*. Cambridge: Cambridge University Press

Gordon, Margaret S. 1988. *Social Security Policies in Industrial Countries: A Comparative Analysis*. Cambridge: Cambridge University Press

Gormely, James D. 1990. "Letter to the Editor," *The Washington Post*, April 23

Governing. 1991. "The Earmarks of a Solution," *Governing*, March

Haas, Lawrence J. 1988. "Paying As You Go," *National Journal*, 22, October

Hager, George. 1991a. "Domenici vs. Sasser," *Congressional Quarterly Weekly Report*, April 20

   1991b. "Senate Oks Fiscal Blueprint, Rejects Payroll Tax Cut," *Congressional Quarterly Weekly Report*, April 27

Hall, Peter A. and Taylor, Rosemary C.R. 1996. "Political Science and the Three New Institutionalisms," *Political Studies*, 44

Halloran, Richard. 1979. "Schlesinger Victory Seen in Energy Program," *The New York Times*, April 7

Hardin, Russell. 1988. *Morality within the Limits of Reason*. Chicago: University of Chicago Press

Heclo, Hugh. 1994. *Modern Social Politics In Britain and Sweden*. New Haven: Yale University Press

   1998. "A Political Science Perspective on Social Security Reform," in R. Douglas Arnold, Michael J. Graetz, and Alicia Munnell (eds.), *Framing the Social Security Debate*. Washington, DC: Brookings Institution

Hershey, Robert D. 1987. "A Fight Builds Over Money Not Spent," *The New York Times*, September 4

Hibbs, Douglas. 1987. *The American Political Economy*. Cambridge, MA: Harvard University Press

Hill, John W. Jr. 1990. "Operations of and Outlook for the Highway Trust Fund." Statement before the Subcommittee of Water Resources, Transportation, and Infrastructure, Committee on Environment and Public Works, US Senate, May 9

Hird, John A.1994. *Superfund: The Political Economy of Environmental Risk*. Baltimore: Johns Hopkins University Press

Hirschberg, Vera. 1971. "Congress Wrestles Over Use of Aviation Trust Funds," *National Journal*, February 13

Hitt, Greg. 1998. "Senators Agree to Lift Highway Outlays by $26 Billion During the Next Six Years," *The Wall Street Journal*, March 3

Hogwood, Brian W. and Peters, B. Guy. 1983. *Policy Dynamics*. New York: St. Martins Press

1985. *The Pathology of Public Policy*. Oxford: Clarendon Press

Holmes, Stephen. 1988. "Precommitment and the Paradox of Democracy," in Jon Elster and Rune Slagstad (eds.), *Constitutionalism and Democracy*. Cambridge: Cambridge University Press

Hosanky, David. 1996. "House Passes Bill to Remove Trust Funds From Budget," *Congressional Quarterly Weekly Report*, April 20

Horn, Murray J. 1995 *The Political Economy of Public Administration: Institutional Choice in the Public Sector*. Cambridge: Cambridge University Press

Hornbeck, J.F. 1992. "Transportation Trust Funds: Economic and Policy Issues," Congressional Research Service Issue Brief. IB 90057. 20 February

House Interstate and Foreign Commerce Committee," The Aviation Facilities Expansion Act of 1969," H. Rept. 91-601

House Report. 1956. "The Highway Revenue Act of 1956," 84th Congress. 2nd Session. Number 1899

1969. "The Aviation Facilities Expansion Act of 1969," 91st Congress. 2nd Session. Number 91–601

Howard, Christopher. 1997. *The Hidden Welfare State: Tax Expenditures and Social Policy in the United States*. Princeton, NJ: Princeton University Press

Hubin, Donald C. 1986. "Of Bindings and By-Products: Elster on Rationality," *Philosophy and Public Affairs*, 15

Jacobs, Lawrence. 1993. *The Health of Nations*. Ithaca: Cornell University Press

Jacobs, Lawrence R. and Shapiro, Robert Y. 1998a. "Myths and Misunderstandings about Public Opinion toward Social Security," in R. Douglas Arnold, Michael J. Graetz, and Alicia H. Munnell (eds.), *Framing the Social Security Debate* Washington, DC: Brookings Institution

1998b. "Myths and Misunderstandings about Public Opinion toward Social Security: Knowledge, Support and Reformism," in R. Douglas Arnold, Michael J. Graetz, and Alicia H. Munnell (eds.), *Framing the Social Security Debate*. Washington, DC: Brookings Institution

Julnes, George and Mohr, Lawrence B. 1989. "Analysis of No-Difference Findings In Evaluation Research," *Evaluation Review*, 13

Kagan, Robert A. 1985. "Adversarial Legalism and American Government," in Marc Landy and Martin Levin (eds.), *The New Politics of Public Policy*. Baltimore: Johns Hopkins University Press

Kahn III, Charles. 1998. "Comment," in Robert D. Reischauer, Stuart Butler, and Judith R. Lave (eds.), *Medicare: Preparing for the Challenges of the 21st Century*. Washington, DC: National Academy of Social Insurance

Kahneman, Daniel and Tversky, Amos. 1984. "Choices, Values and Frames," *American Psychologist*, 39

Kamlet, Mark S. and Mowery, David C. 1987. "Influences on Executive and Congressional Budgetary Priorities, 1955–1983," *American Political Science Review*, 81

Kasich, John, Livingston, Bob, and Archer, Bill. 1996. "Truth in Budgeting." Dear Colleague Letter

Kaufman, Herbert. 1976. *Are Government Organizations Immortal?* Washington, DC: Brookings Institution

Kellam, Susan. 1992. "Conferees Get The Lead Out," *Congressional Quarterly Weekly Report*, October 3

Kingdon, John. 1984. *Agendas, Alternatives and Public Policies*. Boston, MA: Little, Brown

Koitz, David. 1988. "The Social Security Surplus: A Discussion of Some of the Issues," CRS Report for Congress. Washington, DC: Congressional Research Service, November 21, 88–709 EPE
    1991. "Medicare Financing," CRS Report for Congress. Washington, DC: Congressional Research Service, 91–517 EPW

Koitz, David, Nuschler, Dawn, and Winters, Philip. 1990. "Trust Funds and the Federal Deficit," Congressional Research Service Report for Congress, February 26, 90–106 EPW
    1996. "Federal Trust Funds: How Many, How Big, and What Are They For?" *Congressional Research Service Report for Congress*, CRS 96–686 EPW

Kolman, Erasmus. 1980. *Airport Trust Fund: DOT, Nixon, and Congress*, ICP, No. 130. Syracuse. Inter-University Case Program

Kornhauser, Lewis A. and Revesz, Richard L. 1995. "Evaluating the Effects of Alternative Superfund Liability Rules," in Richard L. Revesz and Richard B. Stewart (eds.), *Analyzing Superfund: Economics, Science, and Law*. Washington, DC: Resources for the Future

Krehbiel, Keith. 1998. *Pivotal Politics*. Chicago: University of Chicago Press

Kriz, Margaret. 1996. "War Over Wastes," *National Journal*, May 11

Kuttner, Robert. 1988. "Reaganism, Liberalism, and the Democrats," in Sidney Blumenthal and Thomas Byrne Edsall (eds,), *The Reagan Legacy*. New York: Pantheon Books
    1990. "Thanks for Tossing that Grenade, Mr. Moynihan," *Business Week*, February 5

Landy, Mark. 1985. "The New Politics of Environmental Policy," in Marc

Landy and Martin Levin (eds.), *The New Politics of Public Policy*. Baltimore: Johns Hopkins University Press

Landy, Mark K., Roberts, Marc J., and Thomas, Stephen R. 1994. *The Environmental Protection Agency: Asking the Wrong Questions From Nixon to Clinton*. Expanded Edition. New York: Oxford University Press

Langbein, John H. 1995. "The Contractarian Basis of the Law of Trusts," *Yale Law Journal*, 625

Leonard, Herman. 1986. *Checks Unbalanced. The Quiet Side of Public Spending*. New York: Basic Books

1990. "In God We Trust – The Political Economy of Social Security Reserves," in Carolyn Weaver (ed.), *Social Security's Looming Surpluses*. Washington, DC: American Enterprise Institute

Levi, Margaret. 1988. *Of Rule and Revenue*. Berkeley: University of California Press

Light, Paul. 1985. *Artful Work: The Politics of Social Security Reform*. New Haven: Random House

Loftus, Joseph A. 1955. "Eisenhower Gets 101 Billion Federal-State Road Plan," *The New York Times*, January 12

Lubin, David. 1996. "The Publicity Principle," in Robert Goodin (ed.), *The Theory of Institutional Design*. Cambridge: Cambridge University Press

Majone, Giandomenico. 1996. "Public Policy and Administration: Ideas, Interests, and Institutions," in Robert E. Goodin and Hans-Dieter Klingermann (eds.), *A New Handbook of Political Science*. New York: Oxford University Press

Malbin, Michael J. 1973. "Long Deadlock Ends In Compromising Opening Highway Trust Fund For Mass Transit," *National Journal*, August 11

Marmor, Theodore R. 1973. *The Politics of Medicare*. Chicago: Aldine
Forthcoming. *The Politics of Medicare*. 2nd Edition

Martin Jr., John M. 1956. "Proposed Federal Highway Legislation in 1955: A Case Study In The Legislative Process," *The Georgetown Law Journal*, 44

Mayhew, David R. 1990. *Divided We Govern*. New Haven: Yale University Press

McChesney, Fred S. 1997. *Money for Nothing: Politicians, Rent Extraction, and Political Extortion*. Cambridge, MA: Harvard University Press

McKissick, Gary. 1997. "Issue Manipulation: Interest Group Lobbying and the Framing Of Policy Alternatives," Ph.D. Dissertation. University of Michigan

Meriam, Lewis and Schlotterbeck, Karl. 1950. *The Cost of Financing Social Security*. Washington, DC: Brookings Institution

Meyers, Roy T. 1994. *Strategic Budgeting*. Ann Arbor: University of Michigan Press

1999. "Federal Financing for Medical Research Through Trust Fund and Entitlements." Paper Presented at the American Association for the

Advancement Science Workshop, "How to Fund Science: The Future of Medical Research," Wye River Conference Centres, Queenstown, Maryland, February 14–16

Miller, Gary J. and Moe, Terry M. 1983. "Bureaucrats, Legislators, and the Size of Government," *American Political Science Review*, 77

Miller III, James C. 1987. "Airport Woes and Trust Fund's 'Surpluses'" *The Wall Street Journal*, September 15

Miller, Matthew. 1985. National Public Radio Commentary, October 16

Mills, Mike. 1990. "Trust Fund 'Sanctity' Crumbling Under Pressure From Budget," *Congressional Quarterly Weekly Report*, October 20

Moe, Terry M. 1990a. "Politics Institutions: The Neglected Side of the Story," *Journal Of Law, Economics, and Organization*, 6

　1990b. "The Politics of Structural Choice: Toward a Theory of Public Bureaucracy," in Oliver Williamson (ed.), *Organization Theory From Chester Barnard to the Present and Beyond*. New York: Oxford University Press

　1990c. "The Politics of Bureaucratic Structure," in John E. Chubb and Paul E. Peterson (eds.), *Can the Government Govern?* Washington, DC: Brookings Institution

Moon, Marilyn. 1993. *Medicare Now and in the Future*. Washington, DC: Urban Institute

　1997. "No Medicare 'Gimmick'" *The Washington Post*, February 10

Moon, Marilyn and Mulvey, Janemarie. 1996. *Entitlements and the Elderly*. Washington, DC: The Urban Institute

Moore, John L. 1970. "Senate Approval Moves Airport-Airways Expansion Plan Closer To Enactment," *National Journal*, March 7

Mowbray, A.Q. 1969. "Magical Highway Trust Fund," *Road to Ruin*. Philadelphia and New York: J.B. Lippincott Company

Moynihan, Daniel Patrick. 1988. "Conspirators, Trillions, Limos in the Night," *The New York Times*, May 23, A19

Munnell, Alicia. 1988. "Social Security and National Saving," in John R. Gist (ed.), *Social Security and Economic Well-Being Across Generations*. Washington, DC: American Association of Retired Persons

Munnell, Alicia H. and Ernsberger, C. Nicole. 1990. "Foreign Experience With Public Pension Surpluses and National Savings," in Carolyn Weaver (ed.), *Social Security's Looming Surpluses*. Washington, DC: American Enterprise Institute

　1991. "Will Social Security Be There When the Baby Boomers Retire?" *The 1991 E. J. Faulkner Lecture Series*. College of Business Administration, University of Nebraska, Lincoln

Murray, Mark. 1999. "Another Year, Another Trust Fund Fracas," *National Journal*, 27, February

Myers, Robert J. 1961. "Old Age Survivors, and Disability Insurance:

Financing Basis And Policy Under the 1961 Amendments," *Social Security Bulletin*, September

1975. *Social Security*. Bryn Mawr, Pennsylvania: McCahan Foundation.

1981. "Old-Age, Survivors, and Disability Insurance: Financing Basis and Policy Under the 1961 Amendments," *Social Security Bulletin*. September

1993. *Social Security*. Fourth Edition. Philadelphia: University of Pennsylvania Press

1994. "How Bad Were the Original Actuarial Estimates for Medicare's Hospital Insurance Program?" *The Actuary*, February

1997. "Will Social Security Be There For Me?" in Eric R. Kingson and James H. Schultz (eds.), *Social Security in the 21st Century*. New York: Oxford University Press

National Bipartisan Commission on the Future of Medicare. 1999. "Final Breaux-Thomas Medicare Reform Proposal," Washington, DC: Government Printing Office

National Economic Commission Report. 1989. Washington, DC: Government Printing Office

National Highway Users Conference. 1958. "The Highway Trust Fund: Its Origin and Administration and First Two Years of Operation," November, Washington, DC

National Journal. 1970. "Congress Moves Toward Enactment of 10–Year Airport Airways Plan," November 15

New York Times. 1955a. "Highway Program Attacked by Byrd," 16 June
1955b. "U.S. Road Program is Backed by Moses," 10 May
1955c. US Highway Plan Assailed by Byrd." June 16, 56

Nicola, Thomas J. and Rosenberg, Morton. 1995. "Authority to Tap Trust Funds and Establish Payment Priorities if the Debt Limit is Not Increased," *Congressional Research Service Report for Congress*, November 9

Niskanen, William. 1971. *Bureaucracy and Representative Government*. Chicago: Aldine Atherton

Nivola, Pietro and Crandall, Robert W. 1995. *The Extra Mile: Rethinking Energy Policy for Automotive Transportation*. Washington, DC: Brookings Institution

Noah, Timothy. 1995. "Superfund Plan Is Revised By GOP for Senate Action," *The Wall Street Journal*, March 25

Noto, Nonna A. and Talley, Louis Alan. 1993. "Excise Tax Financing of Federal Trust Funds," Congressional Research Service Report for Congress, Washington, DC: Government Printing Office. 5 January. 95–11109 A

North, Douglass C. 1990. "A Transaction Cost Theory of Politics," *Journal of Theoretical Politics*, 2
1996. "Epilogue: Economic Performance Through Time," in Lee J. Alston,

Thrainn Eggertsson, and Douglass C. North (eds.), *Empirical Studies in Institutional Change*. New York: Cambridge University Press

North, Douglass C. and Weingast, Barry R. 1996. "Constitutions and Commitment: The Evolution of Institutions Governing Public Choice In Seventeenth-Century England," in Lee J. Alston, Thrainn Eggertsson, and Douglass C. North (eds.), *Empirical Studies in Institutional Change*. New York: Cambridge University Press

Oberlander, Jonathan B. 1995. "Medicare and the American State: The Politics of Federal Health Insurance, 1965–1995," Doctoral Dissertation. Yale University

1998. "Medicare: The End of Consensus." Paper Delivered at the American Political Science Association Convention, September 3–6, Boston, MA

Office of Management and Budget (OMB). 1994. *Budget of the United States Government, Historical Tables, Fiscal Year 1995*. Washington, DC

1996. *Budget of the United States Government, Fiscal Year 1997 – Analytic Perspectives*. Washington, DC

1999. *Budget of the US Government FY 1999--Historical Tables*. Washington, DC

Office of Technology Assessment. 1985. *Superfund Strategy*. Washington, DC: Office of Technology Assessment

Omang, Joanne. 1980. "House Approves Fund to Cleanup Chemical Waste," September 24, A1

Orren, Karen and Skowronek, Steven. 1994. "Beyond the Iconography of Order, "in Lawrence C. Dodd and Calvin Jillson (eds,), *The Dynamics of Social Policy*. Boulder, CO: Westview Press

Palmer, John L. and Torrey, Barbara Boyle. 1982. "Health Care Financing and Pension Programs," in Gregory B. Mills and John L. Palmer (eds.), *Federal Budget Policy in the 1980s*. Washington, DC: The Urban Institute Press

Patashnik, Eric M. 1996. "The Contractual Nature of Budgeting: A Transaction Cost Perspective on the Design of Budgeting Institutions," *Policy Sciences*, 29

1997. "Unfolding Promises: Trust Funds and the Politics of Precommitment," *Political Science Quarterly*, 112

1997. "Divided Government, Partisan Politics, and Tax Policy Outcomes – Does Structure Matter?" Paper presented at the Meeting of the Midwest Political Science Association, Chicago, Illinois, April 10–12

Patashnik, Eric M. and Zelizer, Julian E. 1999. "Paying For Medicare: Benefits, Budgets, And Wilbur Mills's Policy Legacy," Paper Presented At the Policy History Conference.

Pechman, Joseph A. 1983. *Federal Tax Policy*. Fourth Edition. Washington, DC: Brookings Institution

Pechman, Joseph A., Aaron, Henry J., and Taussig, Michael K.1968. *Social Security: Perspectives for Reform*. Washington, DC: Brookings Institution

Pelham, Ann. 1979a. "Carter Pledges Oil Decontrol, Wants Windfall Profits Tax," *Congressional Quarterly Weekly Report*, April 7

    1979b. "House is About to Approve a Windfall Profits Tax, But Question is on the Rule," *Congressional Quarterly Weekly Report*, June 23

    1980. "Congress Clears Landmark Oil Profits Tax," *Congressional Quarterly Weekly Report*, March 29

Peters, B. Guy. 1991. *The Politics of Taxation: A Comparative Perspective*. Oxford: Blackwell

Peterson, Mark A. 1998. "The Politics of Health Care Policy: Overreaching in an Age of Polarization," in Margaret Weir (ed.), *The Social Divide*. Washington, DC: Brookings Institution

Peterson, Paul. E. 1985. "The New Politics of Deficits," in John E. Chubb and Paul E. Peterson (eds.), *The New Directions in American Politics*. Washington, DC: Brookings Institution

Pianin, Eric and Brossard, Mario. 1997. "Americans Oppose Cutting Entitlements to Fix Budget: Poll Finds Pessimism on Medicare, Social Security," *The Washington Post*, March 29

Pierce, Bert. 1955a. "All of US Called a Big Traffic Jam," *The New York Times*, January 14

    1955b. "Auto Association Condemns Tolls," *The New York Times*, January 15

Pierson, Paul. 1994. *Dismantling the Welfare State? Reagan, Thatcher, and the Politics Of Retrenchment*. Cambridge: Cambridge University Press

    1997. "Increasing Returns, Path Dependence, and the Study of Politics." Paper Presented to the American Political Science Association Convention

Pogue, Thomas F. and Sgontz, L.G. 1978. *Government and Economic Choice: An Introduction to Public Finance*. Boston: Houghton Mifflin Company

Pomper, Gerald M. 1980. *Elections in America: Control and Influence in Democratic Politics*. New York: Longman

Poterba, James M. 1994. "Budget Policy," in Alberto Alesina and Geoffrey Carliner (eds.), *American Economic Policy in the 1980s*. Chicago: University of Chicago Press

Probst, Katherine N., Fullerton, Don, Litan, Robert E., and Portney, Paul R. 1995. *Footing the Bill for Superfund Cleanups*. Washington, DC: Brookings Institution and Resources for the Future, 12

Przewroski, Adam and Limongi, Fernano. 1993. "Political Regimes and Economic Growth," *Journal of Economic Perspectives*, 7

Quadagno, Jill. 1996. "Social Security and the Myth of the Entitlement 'Crisis'," *Gerontoligist*, 36

Quinn, Dennis P. and Shapiro, Robert Y. 1991. "Business Political Power: The Case of Taxation," *American Political Science Review*, 85

Reisch, Mark. 1998. "Superfund Reauthorization Issues in the 105th Congress," *Congressional Research Service Report for Congress*. Washington, DC: Congressional Research Service

Reischauer, Robert D. 1997. "The Unfulfillable Promise: Cutting Nondefense Discretionary Spending," in Robert D. Reischauer (ed.), *Setting National Priorities: Budget Choices for the Next Century*. Washington, DC: Brookings Institution

Reno, Virginia P. and Friedland, Robert B. 1997. "Strong Support but Low Confidence," in Eric R. Kingson and James H. Schultz (eds.), *Social Security in the 21st Century*. New York: Oxford University Press

Report of the President's Commission on Budget Concepts. 1967. Washington, DC: Government Printing Office, October

Reports of the Quadrennial Advisory Council on Social Security. 1975. H. Doc 94–75, 94th Congress, 1st Session, Washington, DC: Government Printing Office

"Report on H. R. 3600." 1994. Subcommittee on Health of the Committee on Ways and Means, US Congress, House of Representatives, Washington, DC, April 15

Rich, Spencer. 1997. "Clinton's Medicare Proposal Draws Bipartisan Criticism At Senate Hearings," *The Washington Post*, January 24

Richey, Warren. 1985. "Superfund Tax Would Urge Recycling, Not Dumping," *The Christian Science Monitor*, April 26

Rivlin, Alice, Bryant, Ralph C., Schultze, Charles, White, Joseph, and Wildavsky, Aaron. 1990. "Four Reasons Not to Cut Social Security Taxes," *The Brookings Review*, Spring

Rivlin, Alice M. 1989. "The Continuing Search for a Popular Tax," *American Economic Review*, 79

Rose, Mark H. 1990. *Interstate: Express Highway Politics, 1939–1989*. Revised Edition. Lawrence: University Press of Kansas

Rose, Richard and Davies, Philip L. 1994. *Inheritance in Public Policy: Change Without Choice in Britain*. New Haven: Yale University Press

Rosenbaum, David C. 1985. "The Medicare Brawl: Finger-Pointing, Hyperbole and the Facts Behind Them," *The New York Times*, October 1
  1996. "Gloomy Forecast Touches Off Feud on Medicare Fund," *The New York Times*, June 6

Ross, Stanford. 1997. "Institutional and Administrative Issues," in Eric R. Kingson and James H. Schultz (eds.), *Social Security in the 21st Century*. New York: Oxford University Press

Rovner, Julie. 1995. "Congress's 'Catastrophic' Attempt to Fix Medicare," in Thomas E. Mann and Norman J. Ornstein (eds.), *Intensive Care: How Congress Shapes Health Policy*. Washington, DC: Brookings Institution

Rubin, Alissa J. 1994. "Clinton's Main Tenents Drive New Movement on
     Health," *Congressional Quarterly Weekly Report*, March 26
   1995. "Medicare's Woes, While Nothing New Are Politically Charged This
     Year," *Congressional Quarterly Weekly Report*, May 6
Rubin, Debrah. 1990. "Superfund Gets New, Lease on Life," *Engineering
     News-Record*, 225 (19), November 8
Rubin, Irene S. 1990. *The Politics of Public Budgeting*. Chatham, NJ: Chatham
     House Publishers
Sarasohn, Judy. 1979. "Proposed Energy Trust Fund: Will It Work?"
     Congressional Quarterly Weekly Report, August 18
Savage, James. 1988. *Balanced Budgets and American Politics*. Ithaca: Cornell
     University Press
Schelling, Thomas C. 1960. *The Strategy of Conflict*. Cambridge, MA:
     Harvard University Press
Schick, Allen. 1980. *Congress and Money*. Washington, DC: The Urban
     Institute
   1987. "Controlling the 'Uncontrollable': Budgeting for Health Care in an
     Age of Megadeficits," in Jack A. Meyer and Marion Ein Lewin (eds.),
     Charting the Future of Health Care. Washington, DC: American
     Enterprise Press
   1990. *The Capacity to Budget*. Washington, DC: The Urban Institute
   1995. *The Federal Budget: Politics, Policy, Process*. Washington, DC:
     Brookings Institution
Schneider, Anne and Ingram, Helen. June 1993. "Social Construction of
     Target Populations: Implications for Politics and Policy," *American
     Political Science Review*, 87
Schwartz, Gary T. 1976. "Urban Freeways and the Interstate System,"
     Southern California Law Review, 49
Semple, Jr. Robert B. 1969. "President Asks New User Taxes to Aid Airport,"
     The New York Times, June 17
Seniors Coalition. 1992. *What Everyone Should Know About Social Security*.
     McLean, VA
Shell, Ellen Ruppel. 1995. "An Element of Doubt," *The Atlantic*, December
Shepsle, Kenneth A. 1992. "Discretion, Institutions, and the Problem of
     Government Commitment," in Pierre Bourdieu and James S. Coleman
     (eds.), *Social Theory For a Changing Society*. Boulder, CO: Westview
     Press
Skocpol, Theda. 1994. "The Origins of Social Policy in the United States: A
     Polity Centered Analysis," in Lawrence C. Dodd and Calvin Jillson
     (eds.), *The Dynamics of Social Policy*. Boulder, CO: Westview Press
   1995. "Targeting Within Universalism: Politically Viable Policies to
     Combat Poverty in the United States," in Theda Skocpol (ed.), *Social
     Policy in the United States*. Princeton: Princeton University Press

Skowronek, Steven. 1982. *Building A New American State*. Cambridge: Cambridge University Press

Smith, David G. 1992. *Paying For Medicare: The Politics of Reform*. New York: Aldine

Social Security Bulletin. 1955. "Fifteenth Trustees Report on OASI Trust Fund," May

　　1965. "Report of the Advisory Council on Social Security: The Status of the Social Security Program and Recommendations for Its Improvement," March

　　1997. *Annual Statistical Supplement*

Stanfield, Rochelle L. 1983. "Mass Transit Lobby Wins a Big One, But Its Battles Not Over Yet," *National Journal*, January 29

　　1986. "Hill Stalemate Imperils the Superfund," *National Journal*, February 8

　　1992. "Why Indian Trust Funds Are In Disarray," *National Journal*, May 2

Starobin, Paul. 1989. "Obscure Trigger-Tax Provision Imperils Aviation Budget," *Congressional Quarterly Weekly Report*, April 8

Starr, Paul. 1988. "Social Security and the American Public Household," in Theodore R. Marmor and Jerry L. Mashaw (eds.), *Social Security: Beyond the Rhetoric of Crisis*. Princeton: Princeton University Press

Steuerle, Eugene. 1998. "Discretion to Do the Right Things," *The Washington Post*, May 18

　　1996. "Financing the American State at the Turn of the Century," in W. Elliot Brownlee (eds.), *Funding the Modern American State, 1941–1995: The Rise and Fall of the Era of Easy Finance*. Cambridge and Washington, DC: Cambridge University Press and Woodrow Wilson Center Press

Steuerle, C. Eugene and Kawai, Masahiro. 1996. "The New World Fiscal Order: Introduction," in C. Eugene Steuerle and Masahiro Kawai, (eds.), *The New World Fiscal Order: Implications for Industrialised Nations*. Washington, DC: The Urban Institute.

Stevenson, Richard W. and Clymer, Adam. 1999. "Clinton to Unveil Plan to Shore Up Social Security," *The New York Times*, June 29

Stewart III, Charles. 1989. *Budget Reform Politics: The Design of the Appropriations Process in the House of Representatives*. Cambridge: Cambridge University Press

Stockman, David A. 1986. *The Triumph of Politics*. New York: Harper & Row

Strahan, Randall. 1990. *New Ways and Means: Reform and Change in a Congressional Committee*. Chapel Hill: University of North Carolina Press

Surface Transportation Policy Project. 1997. *A Blueprint for ISTEA Reauthorization*. Washington, DC: Surface Transportation Policy Project

Tax Foundation. 1970. "Federal Trust Funds: Budgetary and Other
    Implications," New York
Taylor, Andrew. 1995. "Rubin's Footwork Frustrates GOP," *Congressional
    Quarterly Weekly Report*, December 16
    1999. "Clinton, GOP Bet the Farm on More and Bigger Surpluses,"
    Congressional Quarterly Weekly Report, November 20, 2767
Teja, Ranjit S. and Bracewell-Milnes, Barry. 1991. *The Case for Earmarked
    Taxes: Government Spending and Public Choice.* London: Institute of
    Economic Affairs
Twight, Charlotte W. 1994. "Political Transaction Cost Manipulation,"
    Journal of Theoretical Politics, 6
    1997. "Medicare's Origins: The Economics and Politics of Dependency,"
    The Cato Journal, 16
    1998. "Book Review of Dixit, The Making of Economic Policy," *The
    Independent Review: A Journal of Political Economy*, 111
US Congress. House of Representatives. *1998 Greenbook*. Committee on
    Ways and Means. 1998.
    1939. "Social Security," Hearings Relative to the Social Security Act
    Amendments of 1939 Before the Committee on Ways and Means. 66th
    Congress. 2nd Session
    1949. "Social Security Act Amendments of 1949," Hearings Before the
    Committee on Ways and Means. 81st Congress. 1st Session
    1956. "Highway Revenue Act of 1956," Hearings Before the Committee on
    Ways and Means. 84th Congress. 2nd Session
    1958. "Social Security Legislation," Hearings Before the Committee on
    Ways and Means. 85th Congress. 2nd Session
    1961. "Social Security Amendments of 1949," Executive Hearings Before
    the Committee on Ways and Means. 87th Congress. 1st Session
    1965. "Medical Care for the Aged," Hearing Before the House Committee
    on Ways and Means. Congress. 1st Session
    1968. "Aviation Facilities Maintenance and Development," Hearings
    Before the Committee on Interstate and Foreign Commerce. 92nd
    Congress. 2nd Session
    1969. "Aviation Facilities Maintenance and Development," Hearings
    Before the Committee on Interstate and Foreign Commerce. 91st
    Congress. 1st Session
    1971. "Airport and Airway Trust Fund," Hearings Before the
    Subcommittee on Transportation and Aeronautics of the Committee on
    Interstate and Foreign Commerce Committee. 92nd Congress. 1st Session
    1975. Hearings Before the Subcommittee on Social Security of the
    Committee on Ways and Means. 94th Congress. 1st Session
    1976. "Status of the Airport and Airway Trust Fund," Hearings Before the
    Committee on Ways and Means. 94th Congress. 2nd Session

1979. "Superfund," Hearings Before the Subcommittee on Transportation and Commerce of the Committee on Interstate and Foreign Commerce. 96th Congress. 1st Session.

1979. "Windfall Profits Tax and Energy Trust Fund," Hearings Before the Committee on Ways and Means. 96th Congress. 1st Session

1980. "Status of the Airport and Airway Trust Fund," Hearing Before the Committee on Ways and Means. 96th Congress. 2nd Session

1992. "Lead-Based Paint Hazard Abatement Act," Hearing Before the Subcommittee on Select Revenue Measures of the Committee on Ways and Means. 102nd Congress. 2nd Session

US Congress. Senate. 1972. "Proposed 1972 Highway Legislation," Hearings Before the Subcommittee on Roads, Committee on Public Works. 92nd Congress. 2nd Session

1969. "Airport/Airways Development," Hearings Before the Subcommittee on Aviation of the Committee on Commerce. 91st Congress. 1st Session

1971. "Airport and Airway Development and Revenue Act Amendments of 1971," Hearings Before the Subcommittee on Aviation of the Committee on Commerce. 92nd Congress. 2nd Session

1979. "Hazardous Waste Disposal," Joint Hearings Before the Subcommittees on Environmental Pollution and Resource Protection of the Committee on Environment and Public Works. 96th Congress. 1st Session

1981. "Airport and Airway System Development Act of 1981," Hearing Before the Subcommittee on Aviation of the Committee on Commerce, Science, and Transportation. 97th Congress. 2nd Session

US Congress. Senate Budget Committee. 1998. "Budget Bulletin." 105th Congress. 2nd Session. 30 March

United States Department of Transportation. 1971. "Fourth Annual Report, Fiscal Year 1970," Washington, DC: Department of Transportation

1973. "Airport and Airway Cost Allocation Study Part I Report: Determination, Allocation and Recovery of System Costs." Washington, DC: Department of Transportation

Victor, Kirk. 1995. "Trust Me," *National Journal*, March 11

Vivano, Frank. 1991. "How Superfund Became A Mess," *The San Francisco Chronicle*, May 20

Wall Street Journal. 1993. "Trust Them," May 14

Wallin, Bruce A. 1998. *From Revenue Sharing to Deficit Sharing: General Revenue Sharing and Cities*. Washington, DC: Georgetown University Press

Walters, Jonathan. 1995. "The Highway Revolution That Wasn't," *Governing*, May 1995, 33–7

Warford, Jeremy J. 1971. *Public Policy Toward General Aviation*. Washington, DC: Brookings Institution.

Washington Post. 1987. "Close Calls in the Air," April 24

 1995. "Excerpts From Speaker Gingrich's Opening Remarks," January 5

 1997. "Trust, but Verify," December 1

 1999. "The Aviation Money Grab," March 24

Weaver, Carolyn. 1982. *The Crisis in Social Security*. Durham, North Carolina: Duke University Press

 1990. *Social Security's Looming Surpluses*. Washington, DC: American Enterprise Institute

Weaver, R. Kent. 1985. "Controlling Entitlements," in John E. Chubb and Paul E. Peterson (eds.), *The New Direction in American Politics*. Washington, DC: Brookings Institution

 1986. "The Politics of Blame Avoidance," *Journal of Public Policy*, 6, October–December

 1988. *Automatic Government: The Politics of Indexation*. Washington, DC: Brookings Institution

Weingast, Barry R. 1990. "The Role of Credible Commitments in State Finance," *Public Choice*, 66

Weir, Margaret. 1998. *The Social Divide*. Washington, DC: Brookings Institution

Weisskopf, Michael. 1986. "White House Backs Off Superfund Veto Threat," *The Washington Post*, October 17

White, Joseph. 1996. "'Saving' Medicare – From What?" Paper Delivered At The American Political Science Association Convention, September 3–6, Boston, Massachusetts

 1998. "Entitlement Budgeting vs. Bureau Budgeting," *Public Administration Review*, 58(6) November/December

White, Joseph and Wildavsky, Aaron. 1989. *The Deficit and the Public Interest*. Berkeley: University of California Press

White, Lawrence J. 1981. *Reforming Regulation*. Englewood Cliffs: Prentice Hall

Wildavsky, Aaron. 1964. *The Politics of the Budgetary Process*. Boston: Little Brown

 1979. *Speaking Truth to Power*. New Brunswick, New Jersey: Transaction

Williamson, Oliver E. 1985. *The Economic Institutions of Capitalism*. New York: Free Press

 1999. "Public and Private Bureaucracies: A Transaction Cost Economics Perspective," *Journal of Law, Economics, and Organization*, 15

Wilson, James Q. 1973. *Political Organizations*. New York: Basic Books

 1980. *The Politics of Regulation*. New York: Basic Books.

Wines, Michael. 1996. "With Budget Bills in Limbo, A Lapsed Airline Tax Fuels a Growing Deficit," *The New York Times*, April 24

Winston, Donald C. 1969. "Trust Fund Plan Hits Opposition," *Aviation Week and Space Technology*, April 7

1969. "Nixon User Tax Plan Drops Trust Fund," *Aviation Week and Space Technology*, May 19

Witkin, Richard. 1986. "Aviation Leaders Eye Fund As Cushion for FAA Cuts," *The New York Times*, January 20

Wlezien, Christopher. 1996. "The President, Congress and Appropriations, 1951–1985," *American Politics Quarterly*, 24

Yager, Joseph A. 1981. "The Energy Crisis of 1979," in Craufurd D. Goodwin (ed.), *Energy Policy In Perspective*. Washington, DC: Brookings Institution

Yorty, Samuel W. 1953. "Your Stake in the Social Security Trust Fund." *Congressional Record*, August 1, A5020

Zelizer, Julian E. 1998. *Taxing America: Wilbur D. Mills, Congress, and the State, 1945–1975*. Cambridge: Cambridge University Press

Zorn, Kurt C. 1990. "The Airport and Airway Trust Fund: A Continuing Controversy," *Public Budgeting and Finance*, 10

Index